For the Love of It

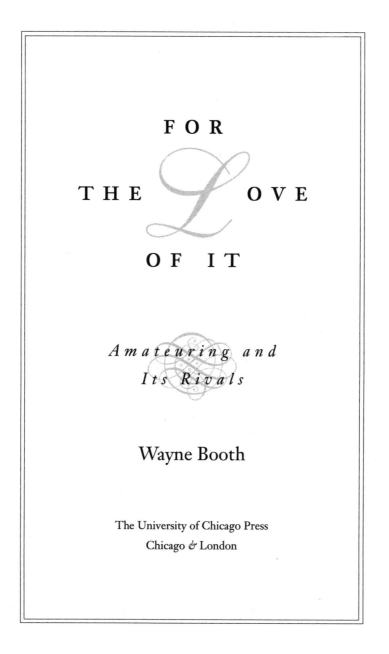

FOR THE LOVE OF IT

Amateuring and Its Rivals

Wayne Booth

The University of Chicago Press
Chicago & London

The University of Chicago Press, Chicago 60637
The University of Chicago Press, Ltd., London
©1999 by The University of Chicago
All rights reserved. Published 1999
Paperback edition 2000
09 08 07 06 05 04 03 02 01 00   3 4 5
ISBN: 0-226-06585-5 (cloth)
ISBN: 0-226-06586-3 (paperback)

Library of Congress Cataloging-in-Publication Data
Booth, Wayne C.
    For the love of it : amateuring and its rivals / Wayne Booth.
      p. cm.
    Includes bibliographical references and index.
    ISBN 0-226-06585-5 (cloth : alk. paper)
      1. Booth, Wayne C.   2. Violoncellists—United States—Biography.
I. Title.
ML418.B49A3   1999
787.4'092—dc21
    [b]   98-42920
                                                                   CIP
                                                                   MN

To Phyllis, who taught me the way to go,
And to the other four teachers who have done it right,
And to all the other amateurs we've played with,
And to all the other amateurs, including non-musicians,
And to the "pro-amateurs" who have been willing
to lift us up by "playing down."

A man and his Hobby-Horse, tho' I cannot say that they act and re-act exactly after the same manner in which the soul and body do upon each other: Yet doubtless there is a communication between them of some kind; and my opinion rather is, that there is something in it more of the manner of electrified bodies,—and that, by means of the heated parts of the rider, which come immediately into contact with the back of the Hobby-Horse,—by long journeys and much friction, it so happens, that the body of the rider is at length filled as full of Hobby-Horsical matter as it can hold;——so that if you are able to give but a clear description of the nature of the one, you may form a pretty exact notion of the genius and character of the other. . . .

In good truth, my uncle Toby mounted him with so much pleasure, and he carried my uncle Toby so well,——that he troubled his head very little with what the world either said or thought about it. LAURENCE STERNE, *Tristram Shandy*

❧

Cello Teacher William Turner:
"There's nothing wrong with being a good amateur."

His pupil, Mark Salzman:
"Amateur! How I hated that word!"

AS REPORTED IN SALZMAN'S *Lost in Place*

❧

Amateur, *n*. A public nuisance who mistakes taste for skill, and confounds his ambition with his ability.
AMBROSE BIERCE, *The Devil's Dictionary*

Contents

Acknowledgments

A British critic recently wrote a witty attack on the American practice of loading prefaces with prolonged thank-you notes. He may be right that we do too much thanking, some of it hypocritical. But for a book like this, in effect constructed by an entire community, I cannot do enough: to list all those who have made this book possible would confirm the critic's mockery.

Here is a selection.

Thanks first to all those we have played with in regularly scheduled sessions: Warren and Patricia Staebler and Larry Apgar, who along with Phyllis generously endured my starting and kept me at it; Joe and Allen Bein, Harold Kupper, and Jane Knourek, who kept us moving with regularly scheduled sessions; David and Peggy Bevington, who play with us often now. Then on to the "irregulars" we'd love to play with daily or weekly but can't: Marcia Alban, George Alvary, Gerda Bielitz, Ben Blackman, Morton Block, Beverly Bloom, Jane Bunster, Ginny Burd, Edith Cooper, Marcia Cozzi, Kay DeLuca, Susan Dubin, Alison Edwards, Ernst Eichwald, Becky Elliott, Alan Garber, Jean Henderson, Deon Hilger, Cecile Holvik, Elizabeth and John Horder, Charles Kligerman, Karen Kramer, Don Levine, Gretel Lowinsky, Jenny Hay-Macdonald, Ellen McGrew, Tom Morgan, Siegfried Moysich, Jean Radford, Tamara Schoenbaum, Paula and Frank Tachau, Caryl Thompson, Diana Tyson, Norma van der Meullen, and Fred Wellisch—and so on to scores of splendid one-timers. I have probably now wounded some overlooked amateurs who brought musical love into the room. Sorry.

Thanks to all of you, named and unnamed, for making it possible.

Thanks to all of the organizers of "weekends" and "coaching weeks." Patricia Badger and the Manhattan String Quartet grant us each year the gift of a full week of playing and coaching. Sam and Paula Golden and Zita Cogan organized, more than twenty-five years ago, the "Sleepy Hollow" weekends, introducing us for the first time into the full excitement of playing not just for an evening or morning session but morning, noon, and night for several days, with unpredictable groups. From Thursday night to Sunday noon, three or four times a year, these devoted amateurs have received and organized a mixed bag of players—sometimes as many as sixty. Sam, with his incredible mastery of the range of available compositions, grabs hold of whatever list turns up—the accidental mixture of cellos, violas, violins, pianos, and even clarinets and flutes and bassoons—and whips 'em together, day by day, into combinations that work. Somebody ought to do a book on that achievement alone: *Chambering at Sleepy Hollow? The Golden Years?*

Special thanks to Alan Thomas, editor and amateur photographer, who first suggested exploding my "cello-reach" into the world of other amateurs; and to Carol Saller, one of those rare "copy-editors" who goes beyond the call of duty, making helpful substantive suggestions throughout. And thanks to those readers who, along with Phyllis, have helped revise various drafts: Aaron Adams, Ajay Bhatt, Jeffrey Carlson, David Haglund, Adam Kissel, Jessica Madore, Dina Mannino, Geoffrey Pingree, Peter Rabinowitz, Alan Thomas, David Thompson, Frederick Whiting, Shannon Young—and my granddaughter, Emily Izakowitz.

For the Love of It

But yield who will to their separation,
My object in living is to unite
My avocation and my vocation
As my two eyes make one in sight.
Only where love and need are one,
And the work is play for mortal stakes,
Is the deed ever really done
For Heaven and the future's sakes.

ROBERT FROST, "TWO TRAMPS IN MUD TIME"

❧

With a hobby a man is reasonably secure against the whips and
arrows of the most outrageous fortune.   SIR WILLIAM OSLER

❧

Hell is full of musical amateurs: music is the brandy of the
damned.   GEORGE BERNARD SHAW

❧

There exists no real definition of an amateur.

BARON DE COUBERTIN

Overture

What Is an Amateur
and Why Amateuring Matters

"STOP! STOP! We've lost Zimmie! Let's go back to 'D.' And take it a touch slower and . . ."

"For crying out loud, Mink, there's no point in stopping us just because somebody gets lost for a few measures . . ."

"Dammit, let's go back to the fermata and work it over a couple of times, half as fast, so that . . ."

"I hate all this 'going back.' What're we here for if not to just get on with it, feeling it as a whole and moving on . . . ?"

"I don't agree at all; we're having trouble with it and we ought to try to *perfect* it. That's the whole point. From now on we ought to . . ."

"The fact is, the three of you *were* rushing. After all, Beethoven's marking was 84 per dotted quarter, and . . ."

"The trouble isn't *our* rushing, Zimmie. It's *your* counting it in threes; it'll feel a lot better if you do it just one to a measure. Dance it, for God's sake . . ."

Yes, though we may in some sense be doing it for God's sake, I'm afraid our evenings sometimes sound a bit like that. Fortunately, more of our talk goes like this:

"That solo was terrific, Sal. Even though we all were a bit ragged, you kept it moving . . ." Or:

"That was just wonderful; I don't think we've ever done it that good before."

(Grammarians, please relax. Grammar is the least of our worries, as it
   ought to be.) Or:
"Man alive, the way you two did that duet of sixteenths—that was thrilling.
   How do you do it?" Or:
"Hey, that was grand, you guys! Isn't that minuet about the best ever writ-
   ten? The way that viola part just . . ." She stops, in tears.

Sometimes the talk wanders pretty far away and has to be called back:

"That final section reminds me of the time when Solti was rehearsing the
   London Philharmonic, and he shouted out . . ."
"Oh, come on, Harold, we don't have time for another story. Let's get on
   with the Adagio . . ."

And once in a great while one of our companions gets her courage up
and says something like this:

"By the way, Wayne, you do rush things every time you have a rapid solo.
   Why not just relax and enjoy it?"

To which I'm likely to reply:

"You know, I don't think I'll ever be able to do that solo right, high up there
   in thumb position. I keep working at it, and . . ."

Fortunately, we do always turn back to *playing* together, in *almost* every
sense of the word.[1]

"OK, ready? Tricky opening here. A measure and three quarters for nothing. One, two, three, four; one, two, three . . ."

And we're off, into the heavens. Well, we would have been last night, but
just as we raised our bows, Deborah, who had arrived late, looked across at
Zita, playing first, and burst out, "Oh, Zita, I love what you've done to your
hair." And Zita answered in kind: "I think yours looks lovely, too."
   Even if you've never played a note of chamber music but are devoted to
some other amateur pursuit, you can guess that it took a few moments

---

1. This is by no means the only moment when I'm tempted to ride Sterne's Hobby Horse,
playing a bit with *double entendre*. Talk of loving play, of ecstasy, of musical climaxes—well,
Madame, as Sterne would say, the interpretations are in your hands.

to get our bows, to say nothing of our spirits, back into a different kind of love.

We amateurs never play without a lot of talk; we are living together in more ways than as amateur musicians. Unlike the Guarneri Quartet members who claim to avoid one another except when rehearsing or performing, we usually want more of one another. We dine together, even travel together. My wife Phyllis and I have played with very few aggressively silent, aloof amateurs, seemingly determined to have no friendship. With most there is lots of talk, and most of it, praise God, is friendly talk, even loving talk: about the joy-filled music, about the notes on the stands before us and how to realize them, about the fate of amateur chamber music and other amateur pursuits. Sometimes we even move on to talk about the wonders of "nature" or "God's creation": what makes all this blissfulness possible. "Have you ever read Boethius on what music *means?*" "I just read a wonderful complaint about the neglect of Sullivan's book on Beethoven . . ." We range, in short, over most of the questions I'll address here, just as amateurs pursuing other loves find themselves doing.

When everything goes as it should, we don't talk much, just play. Sometimes, as after the Adagio of Haydn's Opus 77, No. 1, last week, we sit stunned, silent, wiping tears, blowing noses. Sometimes, after a successful presto, always for us non troppo (which translates as "to hell with Beethoven's metronome commands!") we will all be smiling, or even laughing, or murmuring our "wow's."

Why Do It, When Some Version of Failure Is Certain?

As you'd expect, since most of us are not playing as well as we wish we could, we talk a lot about failure—sometimes too much. Phyllis has echoed others in asking me to give up my apologizing. "Your laments are much worse than your playing. They just distract us."

She's right. So why do many of us waste time apologizing? Is it nothing more than petty ego? Or is it because we have been longing for perfection—have felt it hovering closer and closer—and then have fallen into the sea, like Icarus when his wings melted? Perfection always flees, destroyed by some amateur*ish* oversight: a failure to observe a ritardando, a descending scale without a necessary F-sharp, a loud outburst where Beethoven has called for a subito pianissimo—perhaps most often a simple failure by one of us to listen intently to the others. (If you feel you *need* to, have a look at my glossary at the end.)

Just what is the purpose of amateuring, then, if full success, in the sense of winning, is always out of sight? That's the question driving this book—most often using the narrow territory of my hopeless cello struggles, my "cello-reach," as a metaphor for the whole range of amateuring. Why go on taking lessons and practicing daily when every playing session demonstrates that you will always play worse than every cellist, even the worst, in the youth orchestra you heard last week?

Well, the answer is obviously nothing like a hope for perfection. Though we amateurs are often driven, and even plagued, by the desire to do it better, the real drive is the sheer love of the playing itself—not just the music but the *playing* of, with, through, *in* the music. It is our conviction that if anything is worth doing at all, it is worth doing badly.[2] We usually manage to rise above the distractions and just play, for the sake of the playing. While the world is negotiating costs and benefits of a different kind, we are negotiating spirited interpretations. When everything goes well, the rewards are . . .

But as this book will demonstrate again and again, the rewards—joyful friendship, spiritual ecstasy, gratitude for life's mysterious unearned gifts—are as impossible to portray in words as is music itself.

Why a Book Rather Than a Catchy Ten-page Article?

The project began as an attempt at a spoofy article about the many hurdles that cellists stumble over. About fifteen years ago I was trying, in my early sixties, to conquer thumb position down toward the bridge of the cello (need I remind you that on this instrument physically down means musically up?)—the territory where you see Yo-Yo Ma and Rostropovich and Starker and a bunch of twelve-year-old prodigies looking so comfortable in TV close-ups. Phyllis and I had been playing chamber music ever since I took up the cello at age thirty-one. I thought I could amuse the world with a brief essay to be called something like "Why Bother to Learn Thumb Position When Moving into Your Seventh Decade?" Wouldn't it be fun to play with the perpetual mixture of bliss and bane, exaggerating your age with that "seventh"?

The trouble was that every time I tried to write briefly about my persistence as bumbling cellist I was quickly pushed into thoughts about other

---

2. This slogan, quoted widely, was used as the epigraph by Barry Targan in his story "Harry Belten and the Mendelssohn Violin Concerto." Actually I'm quite sure that it was spoken by Moses in Exodus, just after he dropped the plates and decided to keep working at the problem.

amateurs. The questions I faced were precisely those that everyone might well ask about ways of spending time—or wasting it, or salvaging it.

As I look at it now, the emerging book had begun long before I'd dreamed of writing about such matters, far back in 1952. That was when I bought that first cheap cello and bow and began to face the weird problems all cellists face in getting those two defiant creatures to work together. Having begun with boyish confidence, I quickly learned that I could never even approach the minor leagues. I was always going to sound like the "mere amateur" that Daniel Gregory Mason sneers at: the "hack in some scratch group, capable of producing no more than tones as unrelated [to one another] as the words of the schoolboy reciting 'The boy stood on the burning deck.'" Since I had never as schoolboy drilled the exercises into my muscles and bones and dendrites, I soon had to admit that I'd never play as well as Phyllis already played the violin. If Mason ever heard me even at my best, he'd hoot.

So the question of why I should keep on scratching at it became more and more intriguing. Why attempt the impossible? While actually playing I seldom had any doubts: this is the way to go. But when I tried to think about it, the questions became more puzzling. Why bother at any stage of life to work for some new skill or know-how instead of dwelling comfortably with skills already mastered? If you can be certain that you'll never even come close to professional competence, what's the point? Isn't anything worth doing worth doing *really* well—better than you'll ever paint or photograph or golf or play chess or surf or row a boat or perform the role of King Lear in an amateur production? And meanwhile, what about all those rival ways of spending what everybody these days calls leisure time?

Even when feeling hopeless about articulating an answer, I never consciously thought of escaping the commitment—though some of my nighttime dreams of disaster seemed to advise it. As the ratio of joyful to painful moments slowly rose, the rightness of my choice—what I am now tempted even to call the wisdom of it—became clearer and clearer. But simultaneously this quite different amateur pursuit, the mental probing of the why question, occupied more and more of my hours. The attempt to reduce the possible answers to essay length proved even more hopeless than the attempt to play Bach's unaccompanied suites the way they sounded on the Casals recording. Notebook and journal entries and drafts of possible chapters multiplied, as broader and broader questions flooded in, sometimes even intruding on my hour-a-day practice time.

Thus the inevitable connection of amateuring to every corner of life has turned the original drafts of a light essay into a project that has often felt simply unmanageable: many different voices calling for quite different books: "Keep it a playful autobiography!" "No, no, make it philosophical, even religious!" "Absurd: just confine it to a celebration of music." "Ridiculous: it should be a polemic about what our professionalized, expert-ridden world is doing to our leisure time; we don't even have any real carnivals any more!" If you are annoyed by books that are in any way polyphonic or contrapuntal, perhaps you should just stop reading now and go write a history of Occam's razor and the law of parsimony.

"Amateuring" Defined

What I hope finally harmonizes most of these basses and tenors and sopranos and contraltos is a celebration of what it means to do something worth doing for the sheer love of it, with no thought of future payoff—in a world where you can't even survive unless you do *some* thinking about payoff. As a first move toward that final harmony I must rescue that corrupted word "amateur." It relates in troublesome ways to other nouns applied to people like us: avocationists, connoisseurs, would-be or pre-professionals, leisure-timers, recreationists, hobbyists or hobby-horse riders, dabblers, dilettantes, novices, freaks, nuts.

"Amateur" has experienced bad luck in English. As long ago as 1904, in a book designed to celebrate "the amateur spirit," Bliss Perry was already playing with the rising negative connotations of the word: "If the connoisseur is the one who knows, and the dilettante the one who only thinks he knows, the amateur is often the one who would like to know, but is too lazy to learn." In some European languages the word still manages to maintain a bit of its original inheritance from the Latin love words, *amo, amas, amat.* But in English it's increasingly used to suggest merely incompetent dallying, as in Bierce's definition in my opening epigraph. Recently a father complained about the death of his soldier son in Somalia: "It's going to be hard to convince me that my son's death was not caused by an amateur [his officer]." And one full-length book by Donald Spencer claims that Jimmy Carter failed as president because he was an amateur, the opposite of an expert who has learned the professional arts of governing.

German and Russian seem to have done somewhat better in preserving it to mean simply "lover" in the non-erotic sense. The word's relatively high standing in France can be seen in the titles of two fairly recent books, one, *L'Amateur du poeme,* celebrating poetry for the sake of poetry, the other honoring the donor of a huge art collection to the National Museum of Modern Art at the Pompidou Center: *Donations Daniel Cordier: Le regard d'un amateur*. But in America it is on the defensive. The association of Amateur Chamber Music Players not long ago polled us members about whether we shouldn't drop the word "Amateur" from our name. Too many people, some were saying, see only the dismissive definition in the word. Many of us fought to retain it, and by now we who love the love word seem to have won our battle to keep it in the title. But who knows what will come?

Here is how the dictionaries define the word these days:

Am-a-teur (am'a-choor, -toor, am'a-tur') [F. fr. L. *amator* lover, fr. *amatus*, pp. of *amare* to love]. *n.* 1. One who practices an art or science or sport for his own pleasure, rather than as a profession. 2. One who does something without professional skill or ease.

Occasionally Phyllis and I play with other amateurs who would be annoyed by the second definition. Usually, though, we are all amateurs in both definitions: we play for the love of the playing, yet we often reveal signs that we lack professional skill or ease. We are especially vulnerable to that word "without" in the second definition.

I do quite literally love to play the cello—especially when others are playing with me: duets with Phyllis, piano trios and quartets and quintets, string quartets, and on through the Schubert and Brahms and Mozart and Dvořák viola and cello quintets to Mendelssohn's miraculous octet. Over the years all that playing has come to feel less and less like a mere addendum to life, a pastime, a hobby, and more and more like something beyond even an added luxury: it's now a necessity.

But though I fit the first definition, practicing the art lovingly, for my own pleasure, I still often practice it, after forty-six years of trying, with little skill or ease remotely resembling "professional." Throw me suddenly a few measures of rapid thirty-second notes, as Brahms did last night with his first sextet (Opus 18, B-flat Major; see figure, p. 10), when I had been playing along fairly comfortably on second cello, and I may well panic and flub it noisily. Or I may take the wiser path, just lower the bow and listen to how the passage, intended to be played in grumbling unison by both cellists, is handled by the better player on first. The fact is that if you present me with anything even close to that level of difficulty, I'm in trouble. Give me a high passage in thumb position and I may, after all these years of practice, produce sounds that would make any listener, amateur or professional, wince.

Obviously any effort to deal with troubles like that calls for some wrestling not just with what the word "amateur" is to mean but with the lack of adequate nouns and verbs to cover the neglected subject. For some

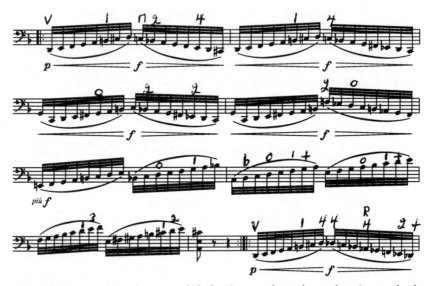

If you didn't have any music lessons as a kid, if you've never learned to read music at any level even though you like to listen or perhaps sing along, you may be baffled by such an illustration. You'll meet only a few similar difficulties as we move along—precisely at the points where a professional might complain about my dwelling on the obvious. But actually you won't have much trouble if you just skip freely. Better yet, you could get hold of some good introduction to musical know-how, like Imogen Holst's *An ABC of Music*, and read in it for a few hours. Wherever you have trouble with a musical term, see the Glossary—and ignore my jests.

reason the word "amateur" has never developed beyond the simple actor: I am an *amateur*. Do I like to—*amateur*? I think we need that verb, as we need the gerund in my title: I'm fully alive when *amateuring*. So far so good. But what do I call what I have chosen to do? Should it be one of the terms I've listed already, or perhaps my craft? my forte? my proficiency art? my field? my line? my shtick? my bag? my secondary field of expertise? my knack? my frolic? my thing?—the thing I do when I'm doing my thing? Should I follow Robert Stebbins and call it just "serious leisure"? Or should I follow a famous amateur gardener, Harold Epstein, who insisted on labeling his "hobby" as a "garden insanity": I'm writing about my cello insanity? My crazy passion?

Through several drafts I settled on a neologism, and even invented a dictionary entry for it.

> **Am-a-choice** (am′a-chois′) [F. L. *amator, -oris* lover; *amare* to love; *choice*, O.F. *chois choisir* to choose]. *n.* Any vigorous, demanding human pursuit *practiced* for love of the pursuit itself rather than for any practical use or payoff.

Unfortunately almost every reader bridled at this coinage, one actually calling it—pedantically and mistakenly, I believe—"barbarous." I backed down only when a medievalist said that to her it sounded like what a desperate CEO would cook up as a logo. And that left me with calling our ama-choices, throughout the book, by as many different names as we have for love itself. The generalized cello-reach remains unnamed.

Amateuring and Other Kinds of Loving Play

The dictionaries should follow me and put their word "practice" in italics, or add words like "vigorous" or "demanding." Although most true amateurs will never entirely escape being amateurish, they don't just dabble at something that they sort of enjoy doing occasionally. Instead, like any serious professional, they work at learning to do it better. Those of us who are lucky also love doing much of what we do. To talk only of doing things for the love of it, for the fun of it, thus opens up a huge domain of every conceivable disinterested pleasure—the massive world of "play" brilliantly celebrated by Johan Huizinga in his once famous but recently neglected book, *Homo Ludens*. "Why," I can imagine some reader of that book asking, "why on earth take up any laborious task (except to make a living), when you could use your leisure time just having plain carefree fun winning an occasional jackpot on a slot machine? Why downgrade joyful, loving though passive moments of the kind Huizinga celebrates just because they impose no requirements on the receiver? Aren't you simply expressing a moralistic bias?"

I do indeed imply throughout that some pastimes are in an inferior class, what I'll call "ice-cream pleasures"—received, not in any sense produced. (Some recreations are even more questionable, being harmful to others; but I will not discuss them much). Some deserve the playful mockery that Laurence Sterne applies, in *Tristram Shandy*, to many a "Hobby Horse." Like him I see some steeds as offering a worse ride than others, and some readers here may very well feel that I have downgraded theirs to an ass. In contrast, amateuring not only entails practice, even what might be called laboring: it lands us in aspirations that can produce a sense of failure.

MAY 9, 1994 [JOURNAL][4]—Here I am, not just 73 but 73-plus-almost-three-months-toward-74, and still not even a first draft of the book on

---

4. Since so many memoirists cheat these days by faking memories and records, perhaps I should hold up my right hand with three fingers erect and thumb crossed, and offer my Boy Scout oath that the journals I quote are honest, accurate recordings. They *are*—except, of course, for a bit of stylistic cleaning up here and there, and some altering of names and circumstances when my account might hurt someone.

amateuring completed—and still practicing "impossible" stuff, the sounds ranging from lovely to the kind of screeching that tortures not just neighbors but animals. Last night I felt really discouraged after a few minutes tackling for the first time Popper's Etude #25, assigned for the next lesson by my new teacher, Judy Stone. Am I really getting any better?

At our three-day chamber music weekend in Sleepy Hollow, Michigan, Ingrid, a not-bad violist, reported at breakfast on the second morning that she had dreamed she had a B-flat bicycle tire: she saw it as a comment on how she had played the night before. I thought of that dream as I felt really deflated last night about how badly my practice was going.

Even when amateuring does not produce minor disasters, it always reveals this one major difference from all the other kinds of loving play: the amateur *works* at it, or at least has done so in the past, aspiring to some level of competence or mastery or know-how or expertise. The amateur wants more of it not just because more brings more pleasure. More ice-cream will *almost* always give me more pleasure, but loving to gorge on ice-cream does not make me an amateur; working hard to earn more money to buy more ice-cream or a bigger yacht does not entitle the lover to membership in our unsecret society.

I dabble a few hours each year at the piano, improvising highly unmusical stuff that I enjoy. That's fun, but it doesn't earn me the title of "amateur pianist." I love to watch my favorite athletes, the Bulls, especially when they win, and in a sense I never get enough of them. I sometimes watch Wimbledon, unless I'm obsessed with a writing task. But such watching doesn't make me an amateur at either sport. Only getting out there and trying to serve an ace or sink at least one shot or receive one pass, and then laboring to learn how to do it better and better—only that would turn me into an amateur. As a boy I did that, in a way—with basketball for a time, and baseball for a time, and chess, and Monopoly, and juggling for even longer, and whatnot. As children we're likely to try out everything that comes our way, everything that seems lovable. But as soon as we face failure, we turn to something else. The true amateur, in contrast, goes on trying.

℞

My definition raises many intellectual and moral problems, some of which I'll address—briefly in chapter 1, more fully in chapters 10 and 11. But one

big issue—the challenge of celebrating amateuring's sheer "uselessness"—
cannot be postponed.

Uselessness and Responsibility

In a world faced with innumerable practical problems that any responsible
person ought to care about, how can anyone defend a "useless" task like
practicing the cello? Wherever I turn I see social ills that I really ought to
spend my time working on. Isn't my kind of amateuring, then, sheer social
waste, even cruel neglect? Wouldn't pursuing the pleasure of doing actual
good in the world—honorable politicking, philanthropy, working for a favorite social cure—be superior to fiddling? And isn't fiddling itself justified
mainly by how it restores the fiddler for more important tasks?

Winston Churchill seems to answer with a "yes," in his lively little book,
Painting as a Pastime, as he dwells almost entirely on the practical benefits of
amateuring. Like me, he made his choice in his middle years—at forty. His
very title hints at his downplaying the true feelings that he must have had
when sitting at the easel. Amateuring as a "pastime"? Already I feel offended.

He states the problem with characteristic force, beginning as if he might
join my claim that it's for the love of it, not for payoff:

> Broadly speaking, human beings may be divided into three classes: those
> who are toiled to death, those who are worried to death, and those who
> are bored to death. . . . Rational, industrious, useful human beings [that
> is, those who are not bored and not worked to death] are divided into
> two classes: first, those whose work is work [only] and whose pleasure is
> pleasure; and secondly, those whose work and pleasure are one. Of these
> the former are the majority . . . But Fortune's favoured children belong
> to the second class. Their life is a natural harmony. For them the work-
> ing hours are never long enough. Each day is a holiday, and ordinary hol-
> idays when they come are grudged as enforced interruptions in an ab-
> sorbing vocation.

But having moved toward celebration of doing-for-the-love-of-doing,
Churchill turns back to utility: work for the love of the work is a wonderful blessing, but even the happy worker needs a break: "Yet to both classes
the need of an alternative outlook, of a change of atmosphere, of a diver-
sion of effort, is essential." As a statesman performing really important
labors, presumably loving almost every moment, he still needs a break and
seeks "a change of atmosphere," to be found in painting.

As his choice of the word "pastime" suggests, and as his text later makes clear, Churchill thus has decided to talk of his newfound love as primarily useful in providing his overworked brain with a distraction from his more important political work: the painter serves the statesman. Though I suspect that in the hours of actual painting he often became a genuine amateur, he talks about it as in the service of something more important: it gives a holiday to the really useful part of the statesman's brain.

The same emphasis now comes from brain researchers who urge everyone to postpone senility by leading the brain into new territory—especially the kind of amateuring that makes intense demands. The July 1994 issue of *Life* magazine urges us not only to "do puzzles" or "fix something" but to take up dancing, or watercoloring, or—best of all—chamber playing. They quote the suggestion of Arnold Schneibel, of UCLA's Brain Research Institute.

> Try a musical instrument. As soon as you take up the violin, your brain has a whole new group of muscle-control problems to solve. But that's nothing compared with what the brain has to do before the violinist can begin to read notes on a page and correlate them with his or her fingers to create tones.

Obviously there must be such physiological benefits from chamber playing, but should we turn that into the main point? G. K. Chesterton provides my answer, responding to those who reduce the value of music to its service to healthy digestion: "They do not see that digestion exists for health, and health exists for life, and life exists for the love of music or beautiful things."

Can I be so fanatical about amateuring as to suggest that the time Churchill spent painting was as important, perhaps more important, than many of the hours he spent deciding on war strategies and election moves? Yes—but I don't want to go too far: if some foreign nation were about to nuke London, and the prime minister spent his time practicing the violin or playing jazz with a combo, I'd say he had his priorities confused. But would I have been committing the same fault if, on the morning in 1962 when I really believed that the Cuban missile crisis was leading to our total annihilation, I had invited my wife and kids to play some chamber music with me until the bomb fell?[5]

5. An example of this playing-to-the-bitter-end can be found in both the recent movie and the actual history of the *Titanic*. The ship's string quartet attempts to calm the panicked passengers by playing, first, bright and cheery music, and then more somber pieces. Even though no one listens, the quartet continues to play, not for any effect on the passengers, but for the beauty of the music itself. Finally, just moments before the ship is pulled under the sea,

And Who Are You?

The voices I hear addressing such questions—readers who have managed to get this far—are so radically diverse as to seem beyond harmonizing into a chorus: amateur chamber music players currently active; amateurs of every other kind of music, instrumental and vocal; amateurs of non-musical kinds; professionals who see love of music as their center; *lapsed* amateurs—those who formerly played or sang or did photography or wrote poems or pursued a historical passion and then sadly drifted away; devoted listeners who have never played but would like to; and, finally, philosophical types who speculate about the point of doing anything, whether for love or not: what makes life itself meaningful?

Though I naturally want to capture all of you, I'll feel especially disappointed if I lose those professional musicians who think of themselves as above amateuring. Listen to what that other kind of professional, Daniel Barenboim, has to say about the loss of "playing for the love of it":

> The idea of chamber music as the essence of music-making is gradually disappearing for a variety of reasons. First of all, it was very much linked to playing music in private homes—not only by amateurs, but by professionals, too. Now people have less time, and a greater interest in passive musical appreciation and listening. Today there are so many more millions of people listening to music, but far fewer playing chamber music just *for the pleasure of it*. It is a tradition that has been lost . . .
>
> I grew up in an environment where it was usual to play chamber music at home once a week. Even as late as the early 1960s we were playing regularly *for our own pleasure* in our London home.[6] [my italics]

Barenboim goes on to show just how a professional can behave as a true amateur—what I'll call a pro-amateur. When he met, for the first time, violinist Arnold Steinhardt, violist Abraham Skernik, and cellist Jules Eskin,

---

the leader ends the performance by celebrating, "Gentlemen, it has been an honor to play with you this evening."

6. So far as I can discover, that tradition of professionals playing music together regularly as amateurs has never been fully explored. Kerman reports that Beethoven, famous pianist and composer, "attended quartet parties that took place twice a week at the home of an older composer"—presumably playing viola with amateurs since his playing wasn't good enough to compete with top-flight professionals like his friend Schuppanzigh (see Winter and Martin). I hear many reports of professional jazz players who are easily seduced into jam sessions without pay. I offer some examples later of professional string players who have lifted us up by being willing to play down.

they rehearsed for a symphony concert, suddenly discovered musical rapport, and then

> went to Abraham Skernik's house afterwards, had something to eat, and then played chamber music all night. I did not return to the hotel, and when we finished playing the next morning, we had breakfast and went to the next rehearsal.

When Daniel Barenboim and I play chamber music it will never be in the same chamber, alas. Still, we are together in three essential respects: we are both *making* music, not just listening to it; we are both often playing the very same music, joining the same composers; and we are both eager to do it as well as we possibly can, with or without reward. We are not killing time; we are living it, making something of it. We have worked at it, we work as we play, and we keep on working. Whether or not your choice is in music, I hope I can provoke you to proclaim the value of amateuring of your own kind; maybe we can together talk more people into finding a love worth pursuing for the sake of the pursuit—even if they have, like us, good reason to fear some kind of jilting at the end.

I also hope you'll agree with my claim, addressed more fully in chapter 3, that the joys of amateuring deserve celebration of a kind undeserved by many leisure-time rivals. Amateuring is totally different from enjoying a time-killer or mere escape from boredom. It may be in a sense an "insanity," but, like very few other human pursuits, it carries us out of this world, into what I can only call the timeless.

❧

"Does your book have a plot?"

"How could it have a plot, when I don't know how it will turn out? I'm taking lessons and practicing daily as I write, getting either better or worse by the hour. Maybe by next month or year I'll be so good that all this talk about fear of failure will look absurd. More probably, some internal pipe, mental or physical, will have burst and I won't be able to play at all . . ."

"But a book, even if it's not primarily a story, has to have some kind of a plot!"

"Well, my plot will be realized 'out there,' in you—if anywhere. The plot will be a curious kind of divine comedy, provided that you know the right answer to give St. Peter, at the Pearly Gates, when he says:

I happen to know that a week ago your doctor informed you, in melancholy tones, that you had only a week to live. Like most of your kind, you had thought you had a long way to go. What we need to know, before accepting you, is, 'Did you cancel your final session with amateuring friends?' If you committed that sin, the only saving argument would be that you needed the time to spend on some other loving choice—would it be that serious yet joyful meditation that some people call prayer?"

FIRST
MOVEMENT

*The
Courtship*

The music in my heart I bore
Long after it was heard no more.
WORDSWORTH

❧

Musical training is a more potent instrument than any other, because rhythm and harmony find their way into the inward places
of the soul. . . . Gymnastics as well as music should begin in early
years.   PLATO

❧

If I were to begin life again, I would devote it to music. It is the
only cheap and unpunished rapture on earth.   SIDNEY SMITH,
IN A LETTER TO THE COUNTESS OF CARLISLE, 1844

❧

Often a single experience will open the young soul to music for
a whole lifetime. This experience cannot be left to chance, it is
the duty of the school to provide it.   KODALY

Chapter One

Getting It into My Bones

THE QUESTION RAISED in the Overture—why do it at all, when some kind of failure is unavoidable?—can move us in two contrary directions, autobiographical and conceptual or even theoretical. My own particular choice—the "cello-reach" and chamber music—can on the one side be explained, though not fully defended, by showing how my life from childhood on to marriage with a fine violinist determined that choice: my heritage and marriage taught me the way to go. This chapter and the next will trace that path.

But the larger question—why should *anyone* take on *any* tough cello-reach?—will land us later, as the Overture hinted, into some speculation about various loves and recreations, and thoughts about the meaning of life itself. For now, I'm relieved to be able to dodge that, take a deep breath, and simply probe early musical memories.

❦

No one in midlife is likely to take up any instrument, let alone the cello, without having fallen in love with music long before. Actually, most people do fall in love with music of one kind or another; all the cultures I know anything about are so steeped in music that their children never escape listening, singing, and dancing. And most of the children go on loving it, except when later experiences—often it's the wrong kind of music lessons, or the sheer pressure to survive—kill the love. What is sad is that too few go on producing it themselves.

As school boards these days cut music programs, in the service of what they consider more substantial subjects, and as parents in effect fund computer games and rock concerts rather than music lessons, we seem to be bringing up more and more kids with music only at most in their ears, not *in their bones*. I recently saw a TV show advising parents on the ten "experiences" children most need. There was not a word about music. Even in the one musical shot, of a nursery school teacher using singing as a teaching tool, they were singing the alphabet; the point was, "teach 'em to read."

In this chapter I'll do my best to avoid nostalgic lamentation. The point of the memories will be to explore how amateuring in our early years can lead to a lifetime of amateuring.

&

Musical memories are among my earliest—the only rivals are of physical pains and parental punishment for sexual exploring. Judging from the way my family lived, it's obvious that music must have filled my ears and soul even in the womb. My mother, a competent amateur pianist and choral singer, charmed me into marching and dancing around the living room, humming as she played "The Stars and Stripes Forever" or a Strauss waltz or an improvised set of chords that invited me to tromp like an elephant. Most of my eleven aunts and uncles played some instrument; all sang proudly in church choirs and the Mormon congregations' weekly hymn practice. I can remember at least three of them praising me for keeping time so well, when I was only five.

Although living barely above the poverty line, my Grandpa Clayson, with whom we lived for five years, somehow managed to afford music lessons for all eight of his children, and most of his grandchildren learned to play. He would often say, "You're eating me out of house and home: I'll end up in the poorhouse," or "The wolf is at the door." But then in the next breath he would ask, "How are your piano lessons going?"

Long before our move into his home when I was seven, we were singing all the time, happy songs, sad songs, patriotic songs. At five I followed a bunch of older kids up to the stage of our chapel, where we sang together a celebration of George Washington's birthday, which happened to be my own. The melody rings in my ears now, as vividly as the Beethoven sonata I worked on a bit last night.

Chop, chop, chop the chips do fly;
All around the ground they lie . . .

I can still feel the swings of my little hatchet chopping into the imagined cherry tree: the rhythm was getting into my bones. I was absolutely in time and tune—surely I *must* have been, as I was when singing all those other ditties we learned at home and in Mormon Sunday school and "Primary."

Little purple pansies, touched with yellow gold,
Growing in one corner of the garden old,
We are very tiny, but must try try try,
Just one spot to glaa-aa-aden, you and I.

I can remember being puzzled by that song's "you and I" ending on "mi" rather than "do"—a mournful three-note descent when the words seemed to call for a triumphant landing on the fundamental. All the other songs I knew ended either on "do"—the happy ones—or on "la"—the ones I loved best; they emphasized the relative minor with a dying fall, and they were sad. In fact, most of the songs I remember from those post–World War I years are mournful, calling for endless repetition, in the strange way that sad music manages to do. One favorite was sung in first person by an unsuspecting young mother, a soldier's wife, "seated by my window yester-morning," happy in the sunshine, actually singing in the major mode, but with mournful promises. Then the postman arrives:

But he little knew the sorrow that he brought me [dying fall]
When he handed me that letter edged in black.

Remember, this was 1925, when the griefs of the war and the flu epidemic were still filling our lives. Though most of the deaths in songs were not of soldiers, almost everybody in the songs died: orphans, mamas, siblings. No doubt my father's death, only two years after those memories begin, and my grandmother's death a year later, built in a conviction that the saddest songs are the truest, and that songs are the prime carriers of memory:

Oh, don't you remember,
A long time ago,
Two babes in the woods,
Their names I don't know.
They were . . . dumpty, dump dump dump,
They sighed and they cried,
And the poor little babes,
They lay down and died.

———

> Hello, Central, give me heaven,
> For my mother's there.
>
> ———
>
> If I only had a home sweet home,
> Someone to call my own [three dying falls in a row!]
> Like all the other boys and girls
> Who never are alone . . .

They all seemed to be, like that one, full of sad minor thirds and minor sixths and dying falls on a semitone (minor seconds), the kind exploited marvelously in much of the greatest music—for example, in the first movement of Brahms's Piano Quartet in C minor, Opus 60, or Desdemona's "Willow" song in Verdi's *Otello*, or the sighing, sighing, sighing in Tchaikovsky's tone poem, "Romeo and Juliet." Death and loss and fear were in the family, day and night, my grieving mother and aunts and uncles singing about orphans and widows—and also about other troubles:

> 'Tis the song, the song of the weary,
> Hard times, hard times, come again no more.
> Many times I have heard thee,
> Around my cabin door,
> Oh, hard times, come again no more!

❦

From at least the time of Plato, philosophers have argued that some musical modes move us naturally; my deep-felt response to minor-third and minor-second dying falls would for them not depend on cultural indoctrination. Deryck Cooke rightly insists that our emotional responses to particular intervals and harmonies are partly cultural inventions and partly natural. Consider the half-dying falls Mendelssohn exploits so wonderfully in the quartet Opus 44, No. 2 (E minor). If you worry about not being good at reading music, just look at how many notes, close together, go *down*. Roughly half of the changes are small-interval "sinkings."

Music like that brings me to tears not only because Western culture taught me to hear it as mournful but because the sad dying falls of those childhood songs reinforced something already in our nature—something that as we sang was discovering itself as already in our bones. With no radio until I was ten, no phonograph until I was eighteen, the music I had was mostly what we made. We were amateurs without—I suspect—even knowing the word.

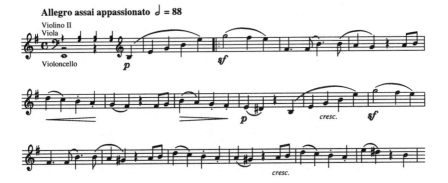

Our homemade music became slightly sophisticated by the purchase of a player piano when I was about eight: the technological age burst into our lives, and we were deflected a bit from our own music-making. The time spent pumping a player piano (or these days listening to a CD in the background while doing homework) is not time spent getting music into your own body. On the other hand, that weird pre-radio gadget brought into the house piano performances of a quality we could never have heard otherwise. I suppose it was one cause of my wanting to play music myself, and even of my dreaming of becoming a composer.

✤

In 1994 Shulamit Ran, composer in residence of the Chicago Symphony and professor of music at the University of Chicago, had a world premiere of her "Legends": a splendid, daring piece both "accessible" and deeply moving. In an interview before the concert, a man asked whether there was some one episode that had been a turning point in her becoming a composer. Her reply (as recorded in my journal) could be described as explaining how composing got into her bones:

> Yes, there was one that might qualify. When I was about eight I was making up songs, and I sang some of them to my mother, asking her to write down the words. She explained that the notes themselves would have to be written down—and she did take them down, without telling me, and sent them to a children's radio program. Then I heard them sung by a children's choir—and I can remember the thrill of hearing *my* songs *communicated back to me.*

I suddenly remembered my own experience as a "composer" when I was about four and a half. I was always making up songs, lovely songs. One day

I looked up from the floor where I was singing to myself and said: "Mama, why doesn't anybody ever sing *my* songs when all the time I just sing theirs?"

Unlike Shulamit Ran, I can't remember how my mother responded, except to tell the story over the years to friends. She certainly didn't transcribe my wonderful melodies and send them to any radio station: there was none. She did, though, go on filling my life with music and I went on making up tunes of my own, which I still do almost hourly; yesterday I caught myself whistling a jazz improvisation on Fauré's poignant "Elegy" for cello—I had played it through, three nights before, in my practice session, loving it, and here I was, from his point of view mutilating it unforgivably—but having my fun.

❧

By the time I was six, my proud mama had me singing in public—doing the harmony in two-part pop songs with beloved seven-year-old Virginia Shelley on the melody. There I was, just a few months before my father's death saddened everything, straw boater at a dashing angle and cane twirling, singing two-part harmony before an audience I saw as vast and enraptured, at the county fair fourteen miles from home:

WAYNE C. (as I was called): "Um-um-um, would you like to take a walk?"
VIRGINIA: "Um-um-um, do you think it's gonna rain?"
WAYNE C.: "Um-um-um, would you like a sars'parella?"
VIRGINIA: "Gee, the moon is yella!"
BOTH TOGETHER (Wayne C. doing delicious major and minor thirds as harmony, winking lubriciously at simpering, swaying Virginia): "*Sumpin' good will come from that!*"

When I was eight, my mother paid for piano lessons with Alice Parker, whom I had earlier loved as my teacher in first grade: she had us sing! On the whole I liked the lessons, enjoyed working up "Für Elise" and "Hearts and Flowers," and played them both finally in church. What changed everything was hearing, when I was ten, a competent clarinetist doing a Weber concertino with the Brigham Young University concert band. The sheer sound of that instrument convinced me at once that I had to learn to play it. But, my Mother would say, if you take up the clarinet you'll stop practicing the piano. No I won't. Honestly, mama, I promise. . . . But clarinets, she would insist, are very expensive, and we already have this fine piano.

I kept up the nagging, promised to continue with the piano, and finally she dipped into her tiny savings account and bought me, for $82.50 (almost a month's salary), a Boehm clarinet: shiny, silver, beautiful. I began to learn how marvelous it feels when a note vibrates in your head.

At almost the same time as my successful campaign for a clarinet, I had a stroke of good fortune that I didn't appreciate for decades. In our little school there in rural Utah we had a teacher of the fifth and sixth grades who obviously loved teaching music. Though he was hired, we were told, to teach penmanship and history, he actually spent a great deal of time teaching us sight-reading: how to count the rhythms with our index finger going up and down, and how to calculate intervals using what he never called anything like sol-fa or solfeggio. "Remember now, when it's flats, you call the next to the last flat 'do.' And when it's sharps, you count the last sharp as 'ti' and count up one to 'do.'"

He insisted that we learn the fun of not just singing but sight-reading our parts in three-part harmony. Whenever we faced a new piece, we'd do a little exercise with the arpeggio, whether major (do-mi-sol-mi-do-sol-do) or minor (la-do-mi-do-la-mi-la), looking at the spaces and lines on the page as we sang. By the end of the second year, most of us could pick up a new piece and sing it in three-part harmony, by sight. How many sixth graders get that today?

Think about it, fond parent, harried teacher. There we were, in an impoverished school district, with equipment that would probably make the worst-equipped school of today look luxurious by comparison. Almost all of us were poor, as measured by today's standards of the poverty line. Some were from families with little or no educational background. And we sight-read (and then sometimes performed for the school) three-part renditions of song after song.

🎵

Coaxing out a tone sounding even remotely like music turned out to be considerably harder on the clarinet than on the piano. But with the help of the only teacher in our town, I was soon in the school band and orchestra. I entered regional contests: playing Weber's Concertino No. 26; singing, as a would-be bass, somebody's version of Shakespeare's "Blow, blow thou winter wind." I always failed to win anything better than a second ranking and often a third, for reasons I can now fully understand.

What I did get from the clarinet years, including the marching bands, was the gripping experience of playing with other lively players: John

Philip Sousa's marches (with the gratifying result that even today I can set our tempo at 120 per minute without using the metronome); Schubert's "Unfinished Symphony"; selections from "Tannhäuser"; and "The Bartered Bride" (which we called "The Battered Bride").

We also sang a lot in the Glee Club and in Gilbert and Sullivan operettas. It was never high quality and it was always, as I see it now, tainted a bit with questionable motives. K. J. Bird, our director, had sold me my role as the pirate king: if I would take singing lessons from him, he'd give me a key part, the pirate king! Did he sell other parts in his annual operas? I know he had a full lesson schedule, afternoons and Saturdays. Whether he loved music or not I'll never know, but he clearly lacked any sense of satire, producing *Pirates of Penzance* as a kind of romance with a tiny number of inexplicable moments of comedy. To keep from being bored, we kids would make up our own versions of the (to us, mysterious) lyrics—not "A paradox, a paradox, a most ingenious paradox," but:

A pair of sox, a pair of sox
An interwoven pair of sox,
Ha, ha, ha, ha, ha, ha, ha, ha
A pair of sox!

Though none of us could truly appreciate the wit and satire of *Penzance*, all of us were absorbing Sullivan's melodies and harmonies into our—I can't quite say "souls" here—call it guts. That singing impregnated us with clever musical clichés that I'm sure paid off in later listening and playing. Though "Birdie" could be venal, he at least insisted that we sing in tune, and he talked the high school into supporting one good opera a year. How many high schools have all that today?

*

By the time we did that opera, I had heard almost no classical music except for a few serenades sung by amateurs in church. Utah had no symphony orchestra, and if Salt Lake City, about fifty miles away, was on the national circuit for professionals, I never heard about it. . . .

Except for one glorious time. My closest friend, just a year before he died on the operating table at fourteen, invited me to go with his family north to the big city to hear Leopold Stokowski and the Philadelphia Orchestra in the Mormon Tabernacle.

Today it's hard to imagine the experience of a boy who had never before heard any professionally competent music, little if any really good jazz, no symphony orchestra. Even the most impoverished street kid today probably hears more competent performances in a week—of rap, of rock, of performers on commercials—than I had heard in my whole life.

I can even now picture where we sat, under that impressive, sacred dome. I can see that silver-haired old man, conducting without a baton, that orchestra, those clarinetists![1]

What did they play? I remember only the Tchaikovsky Fourth. That was enough, a turning point. From then on, I listened fairly regularly to the Sunday broadcasts of the New York Philharmonic. I tried even harder to listen to the Saturday afternoon broadcasts from the Metropolitan Opera, but that just didn't work: the voices grated on my ears.

The symphonies seldom grated, but they often felt remote, unintelligible. Though I was president of the Beethovan Club (as I spelled it in my boastful journal entry), and though we listened to stories of the operas at our club meetings, I never heard any recording of classical music except a few Caruso selections that our neighbor played on an old wind-up machine.

❧

In college everything changed again. I saved up and bought my first radio-phonograph, an electric portable. I really listened to Brahms's first symphony on a New York Philharmonic broadcast, fell in love with it, bought it, played it until practically memorized. And I heard my first string quartet, a group who came annually to the Brigham Young University lyceum series.

JUNE 19, 1940 [END OF MY SOPHOMORE YEAR]—This week the Roth Quartet is playing five concerts in the [Provo] Tabernacle. Under the direction of Feri Roth, 1st violinist, the group has become one of the best string quartets in the world, possibly the best . . . Free entry, with Mother's faculty card; $2.00 for the week for everybody else . . .

It's the finest thing that ever comes to Provo. Although hard to describe adequately, the music is the most divinely inspiring, the most thrilling, exquisite of any I have ever heard. Haydn, Brahms, Tchai-Tsychowsky (Sp?), Beethoven Opus 95, Bach, and a few lesser names, all

1. One reader has claimed that my memory is obviously faulty here: Stokowski wasn't old enough to have silver hair in 1934—or was it '35? If this were a different kind of book, I'd check it out. But memory is absolutely clear.

sounding as the masters themselves would have had them sound . . .
Such listening is all the heaven I ever want.

The tone here amuses me: the boy pretends to know what "the masters"
would have wanted and how the Roth group outmatched others in the world,
none of whom he'd heard. It reminds me of earlier pretensions: once when
he was sixteen he recorded in his diary, "I have been accepted for membership in the Book-of-the-Month club!"

JUNE 20, 1940—With E. Robert Schmitz as guest pianist, the Roth played
a quintet by Cezar [sic] Franck. Last night, without Schmitz (I like the
quartet sans pianoforte better than with) three quartets, Bach, Borodin,
and Chadwick . . . All in all the week has been one of the best I've ever
spent.

Again I wonder what my musical life would have been like a few decades
earlier, when there was no radio and no phonograph. Though "the age of
mechanical reproduction" did some of the bad things to us that Walter
Benjamin has written about, it was absolutely essential for my developing
love of music. Until I was twenty I could never have heard more than those
three or four concerts a year without mechanical reproduction.

I didn't just listen to my few records; I tried to capture every classical
broadcast. I even tried to record them, on the hopelessly inadequate equipment that came with my phonograph. One night a midnight broadcast had
been promised by the newspaper—a performance of Beethoven's C-sharp
minor quartet, by the Budapest. For about an hour I struggled there, listening intently through the static, fumbling with the machinery—doing
my best to follow that overwhelmingly complex music.

I still own the totally unlistenable recording. And when I hear the C-sharp
minor played today, I find myself reconstructing some of what I felt then.

❦

Reading over my journals, I'm struck by how often I tried to describe the
indescribable spiritual effects of music. In October 1942, for example, as a
Mormon missionary "making friends for the Church" by performing in a
male quartet, I worked hard to convince myself that in singing Mormon
hymns and "Mood Indigo" and "The Lord's Prayer" for schools and Ki-
wanis Clubs, and in mouthing my little introductory disguised sermons, I

was providing, as my journal puts it, a "spiritual encounter with genuine Christianity." But behind those public scenes, I was trying even harder to relate my fumbling religious views to what I felt when I heard great music performed.

OCTOBER 29, 1942 [COLUMBUS, OHIO]—Heard Bach's concerto in A minor for violin, played and discussed on a [radio] program from Ohio State University. It left me feeling breathless and almost tearful . . . Though I confess that Bach sometimes leaves me cold, this concerto lifted me higher than I have been in—well, in several weeks . . . I was cross and disgusted before listening, as Maugham [my missionary companion, baritone in the quartet] had been bemoaning my turning on "that symphony stuff again: Is that pretty, Booth? Do you like that, Booth?" I didn't trouble to reply, and suddenly, illogically, miraculously, Bach came to my rescue with his divine call to peace and serenity, tremendous, mysterious, ineffable.

And then the lonely twenty-one-year-old launches another probe into that "ineffability" that permeates this book. He is aware as he goes on that he is parroting various mystics he's been reading—he lists Ernest Hocking, Reinhold Niebuhr, Kant, Spinoza ("mystical in part, anyway"), Plato, and Rudolf Otto with his "mysterium tremendum"—and he is aware that no words can say what he wants to say. That doesn't prevent his going on, obviously thinking it worth the try.

One reason for unfailing optimism about life is the vast reservoir of unheard or unheeded Bach to be listened to and enjoyed. After having been with him for an hour I am unable to understand why I allow myself to become discouraged and moodily pessimistic about life and its meaning. One such experience, as of that concerto grosso, if there were no other value to all of existence and creation, would be worth all the "trouble." If man is doomed to eventual extinction—a possibility which I doubt more and more [he goes back and forth on that one over the years]—his existence would be justified by the ineffable communion Bach and I have just experienced. Multiply this experience by the hundreds and perhaps thousands of times I can hope to have it in my life and again by the millions of men who have enjoyed in the past and will enjoy in the future similar experiences with Bach and other composers, add the similar experiences with great literature and painting and sculpture and architecture, calculate as materialistically as you please the totals, and you have reasons infinite in number for creation; and they are reasons totally beyond, wholly other than, any material judgment of life.

Though that bit of theodicy is clumsy, I'm still moved by it, even a bit impressed by it. I'll be unable to resist pursuing its subject later on.

❧

In the fall of 1944, as a belated draftee, a "clerk-typist," I was being shipped toward the European theater. On our last day in boot camp, the temporary sergeant lined us up and shouted, "Ya better get it outa your fuckin' heads you're gonna be clerk-typists, see? You're gonna be fuckin' riflemen. Get it?"

As I sat in the slow train from Camp Roberts in California to Fort Meade in Maryland, I was beginning to believe that I would die in this war, a war in which I saw our role as necessary and *perhaps* noble. I had no idea of how the war was progressing, but it was clear that even if we won in Europe, we still had years, maybe decades, of war with Japan. So I was doomed, and I might as well adjust to the tragic early death of the "promising young man" that on the good days I thought I was. I would die like the young Schubert, with music alive in me.

At Fort Meade we found ourselves waiting from day to day for orders. There was nothing to do but wait: no drilling, no "policing the area" for cigarette butts, nothing but killing time from day to day. I was in a sense trapped, but I had never before had so much free time: nothing to do but "shit, shave, and shower" and then decide what to do with about fourteen or fifteen hours. Day after day.

My bored buddies and I did manage some interesting talk. But even if we had been the best conversationalists of all time, even if we had been clones of Samuel Coleridge, we couldn't have redeemed those fifteen hours just talking. So I would write a few letters and maybe a journal entry, play a little Ping-Pong, chat a while, play a bit of poker, and then wander off to the Red Cross Center, which had a few books and a phonograph.

As an aspiring high-culturalist, I naturally turned to the collection of classical records, foolishly ignoring the much larger section of jazz. That October I wrote Phyllis, my eighteen-year-old beloved and *almost* betrothed:

Dearest, yourself,
. . . I spent all afternoon listening to records (part of this evening, too), and that's what I want to talk about tomorrow. No, I'll do it tonight. . . .

In the future, if anyone wants to evoke in me all the flavor of my stay here at Meade, it will be easy: make a simple line drawing of a solitary soldier, G.I. haircut, in olive drab, sitting in an old mauve armchair, leg flung over the arm, eyes closed, listening to a tiny phonograph. . . . Yesterday the library got some more records, and wonder of wonders, among them were Beethoven, Stravinsky, and Mozart. This afternoon I started with Die Grosse Fuge (originally the movement of the B-flat major quartet, but now handled as a separate work, opus 133), played by the Busch Chamber Orchestra. I may have heard it before but don't remember ever "getting" it. I've never been so completely taken out of myself by any music. The mood was just right, the performance superb, and I was quite literally put out of this world. All my loneliness, all my aspirations, all my questions and answers, were somehow there. I listened over and over again, for three hours and another hour tonight. Each time new subtleties and wonders appeared. I prayed, I silently shouted and openly wept and longed for you, and exulted; I was *not* sentimentalizing, either, though this sounds like it. It was pure, the feeling I had of rightness, of power, of unearthly beauty. . . .

I was worn out when I finished—I'm sorry to confess that B. had as much effect on my heart-beat and respiration as you have, partly, I'll admit, because you were associated in the enjoyment. You were there; I had just read your letter . . . and it was such a good one. I loved you so much that the music was you. It's true. The beauty he creates is very close to your loveliness. That's impossible to explain, but very nice to feel. . . .

That letter, twice as long as my quotation, understates—indeed does not even mention—the accidental blessing of the sense of total leisure, that precious freedom to listen until "worn out," utterly drained, totally possessed: that freedom to be an amateur listener without qualification. How rarely in life do we stumble into anything like that. The soldier could not have guessed—poised for shipment not to death but to boring months ahead— just how few are our chances for such totally free, fully active listening.

A professor of music I know, who directs a student choir, says that most of his listening these days is slightly deflected into thinking about how to teach it, or whether to have the choir learn it. Everything is turned into questions about use. There's nothing really wrong in that: we couldn't survive without professionals thinking such thoughts. I am flooded with them as I read any book preparing to teach it. But we should also never forget the blessing of total freedom from *use:* though I was entrapped in my private's uniform, I've never been freer than in those hours with that great fugue.

❦

Once something like that has happened, you of course carry your "possession" with you wherever you go. Shoved into the hold of the troop-converted *Île de France*, lying in the bottom bed of a four-tiered bunk—that is, unable to find, anywhere on that ship, any place to sit down except on the deck—I played the "Grosse Fuge" in my head. We played poker, too, naturally. And we talked and talked, sometimes arguing through the night about whether the war was justified. Behind it all, what I remember most strongly is playing that fugue.

And I went on playing it as I was shipped from Glasgow down through London and on to Le Havre and then, on a cattle car, for thirty-six hours down past Paris and on up to Givet. That fugue somehow promised to be my ultimate, final possession before my immanent and uniquely heroic death.

Reminded more and more often that we were to be fuckin' riflemen, not fuckin' clerks, hearing finally the bombardments going on up beyond us, we saw even more clearly that we were doomed. I remember consciously deciding that one good way to go, fighting those satanic Germans, would be singing in my head the greatest composition ever created—and that by a German!

SCENE: Cold, wet morning; men lined up. As each name is called the man
    shouts "here" and climbs into a truck, to be shipped to the front lines.
Booth!
Here!
You're not goin'. You're goin' back to Paris to be a fuckin' typist!

My eighty-word typing speed had saved me! Yet somehow I felt more lost, and far less fugue-haunted, than when I had been heading for doom. Riding back to Paris in a rough, cold army truck, I thought long and hard about the unfairness of my rescue. Many of my buddies had wives and children back home, while I . . . well, all I had was a fiancée who could easily find another man. Gradually as we rolled along I came to an absolute decision about God, for the first time since my childhood orthodoxy. It was not now just a strong suspicion but a firm rejection: any God who could play an unfair trick like this on those miserable buddies was no God at all. He had died, and along with Him somehow the music faded. I had been singing it as my sacred death dirge; now it had no special place. The sacred had fled, while I was being "saved."

❧

The music came back, blessedly, though my original God never did return. The sacred continued to hover in the wings—especially when listening to music in Paris—and various Gods, in various hazy definitions, have later returned to preoccupy my life and thought—as in the final chapter here. It was music, though, not religious inquiry, that was at the center.

Even in that cold winter of 1944–45, with no heat in the concert halls, I could attend the complete series of Beethoven quartets, played by the Loewenguth (spelled "Lowengüt" in my letter to Phyllis). And suddenly, there it was!—the "Grosse Fuge," at the end of Opus 130, where Beethoven had wanted it to be. The music had changed, astonishingly. The fugue I knew, from the Busch version, was not at all what Beethoven had in mind: in some ways the quartet performance was inevitably weaker, less grand, much more plaintive—and even greater.

What it did have came closer to my theme in this book: it accommodated the sheer physical struggle of it, the struggle performed with love but without hope of total success. Those complex phrasings and fingerings were often slightly beyond those committed players in that freezing hall, and as I play at them now, realizing that those four players must all now be long since dead, I honor them for the life they brought back to me.

BOSWELL: I should have liked to hear you play on the violoncello. *That* would have been *your* instrument.

JOHNSON: Sir, I might as well have played on the violoncello as another; but I should have done nothing else. No, Sir; a man would never undertake great things, could he be amused with small. I once tried knotting . . . BOSWELL'S *Life*

❧

The violoncello, in unison with his own frame of mind, glided melodiously into "The Harmonious Blacksmith," which he played over and over again, until his ruddy and serene face gleamed. . . . In fine, the violoncello and the empty chair were the companions of his bachelorhood until nearly midnight; and when he took his supper, the violoncello, set up on end in the sofa corner, big with the latent harmony of a whole foundry full of harmonious blacksmiths, seemed to ogle the empty chair out of its crooked eyes, with unutterable intelligence. DICKENS, *Dombey and Son*

❧

That friend of friends, that choice ally that had never deserted him, that eloquent companion that would always, when asked, discourse such pleasant music, that violoncello of his—ah, how happy he had been! THE WARDEN, IN ANTHONY TROLLOPE'S *The Warden*

Seduced by the Cello

THE REAL CAUSES of any successful seduction can never be fully traced. What could lead an "over-thirty" man who loves to *listen* to music to the kind of assignment I gave myself last night: a half hour of practice on one thumb-position passage in Dvořák's Opus 105 (A-flat minor)? The loving I described in chapter 1 could have led in many different directions. The complex path from there to here, from listening to playing, from hours with near perfection to hours of radical and sometimes painful imperfection—that path winds into mysterious and perhaps impenetrable forests. More to the point, why the cello-path rather than dozens of other musical and non-musical possibilities?

Could it be that my choice began with my enjoying, in adolescence, the new macho power yielded by the bass line—I often called it, incorrectly, the *basso profundo* line—in hymns and in barbershop quartets? That line was underlined when my Mormon Missionary Quartet won a prize one year at a convention of the Society for the Preservation and Encouragement of Barber Shop Quartet Singing in America![1]

The first hint of my cello choice I find quite late in my letters to Phyllis, reporting about the music scene in Paris in the early spring of '45: those ice-cold halls, the electric heaters aimed over the hands of the pianists, the overcoated and behatted and begloved auditors. The orchestras were often

---

1. I'm surprised, and pleased, to discover that Robert Stebbins has now written a whole book on barbershop singing.

badly rehearsed—and freezing: *they* had no electric heaters. For some reason the string quartets managed to be better, and the lonely GI went to every possible concert. He also did a lot of listening on the Red Cross phonograph.

Dearest Phyllis:

Before studying French this afternoon I played [a recording of] the A-minor Beethoven, opus 132.[2] Just thought you'd like to know that I wish I could play the cello so that I could play the cello part of that quartet, especially the fantastic opening of the last movement. It seems a little improbable, but if I were to devote the next ten years of my life to the job, and finally succeed, I'd be more sure of having spent my time profitably than most men are after ten years in *anything*.

Memory tells me nothing of that blind fantasy of success, expressed seven years before I ever grasped a cello. What memory does call up now is the image I treasured then of the lovely seventeen-year-old Phyllis, more than a year before, playing a solo at the church service held for my Missionary Homecoming. A few days later she played the viola part in a public performance of the Mozart Flute Quartet—and the fusion of two forms of loveliness, the music and the girl, captured me.

I may never have had the fantasy that I might someday play the cello part with *her* on violin or viola, but I have reams of proof that throughout my army years my two loves, of Phyllis and music, seemed inseparable. Does an hour spent each day writing to an eighteen-year-old who one hopes will turn out to have been one's fiancée count as amateuring? I felt engaged but we were not engaged, and many of my buddies were receiving "Dear John" rejection letters from actual fiancées back home.

❧

We married just two weeks after my return, and we then moved to four years of graduate work that pretty much drowned any impulse toward amateuring. Then, with the Ph.D. finally in hand, I thought about the choices. Why not the clarinet? After all, I had actually played the third part of a Beethoven trio arranged for clarinets, on the radio! Why not choral music? I had sung the bass line in public performances of the Bach B-minor Mass

2. Unlike many of the opus numbers I had mentioned in earlier letters, when the war was still on, this one did not get clipped out by the censor!

and Beethoven's Ninth. I had enjoyed singing in something like three hundred barbershop quartet performances (another story). I had loved singing the bass parts in Renaissance madrigals, on the rare occasions when we graduate students, overworked, managed to squeeze out a bit of time. I had even been paid—a professional!—for weekly performances in the Unitarian Church choir; that fifteen bucks a week made quite a difference in our monthly budget. Or why not the piano, next to the guitar the most useful of all instruments in producing music with others? After all, I had fiddled around on the piano for more than two decades.

Why oh why then the totally foreign cello?

Well, at first it was not the cello. Once the dissertation was accepted, I bought a far better clarinet than my first one, and tried it again—nine years after having dropped it cold. Within an hour or so of laboring with my feeble embouchure, I knew that I had no desire to have a renewed affair with that hostile, squeaking, spit-dripping beast, though my fingerings were coming back fast. So I turned to what seemed a more amiable friend from the past, the piano. I was already a lot further along on it than Noah Adams was when, as he tells the story in *Piano Lessons*, he bought his piano and started lessons, at fifty-one. I could already perform, amateurishly, the slower parts of "the Moonlight Sonata," and I could sort of accompany Phyllis in simple adagio movements of violin sonatas. So I looked around for a teacher and heard everyone recommending Margot Varro, former associate of Bartók, specialist in teaching counterpoint, famously patient with adult learners.

Madame Varro accepted me after an audition and started me off on a wonderful experience with the Bach Two-Part Inventions: singing one line while playing the other one, first the top line with right hand, then the bottom line with left. It was genuine music making from the beginning; I had found what I had longed for.

But then, only three months later, we left my job at Chicago for Haverford College and I lost forever—without realizing it—not only that teacher but all hopes for serious piano playing. What was not lost, as we moved away, was my rising suspicion that playing music in groups would be even better than playing by myself. That suspicion, that seductive invitation, had sprung mainly from two strokes of fortune.

The first lovely moment came in our second year in Chicago, when I was teaching full time and desperately struggling with the dissertation while trying not to be too unfair to Phyllis in apportioning care time with our new daughter, Katherine. My mind was centered on becoming a professional teacher and scholar.

In early 1947, Phyllis was invited to an evening of chamber playing with a group of Europeans, mostly Jewish refugees, at the home of a psychoanalyst. Tagging along as mate, I found it the most glorious evening I had known since the night in early 1946 in Bremen, Germany, when, in a partly bombed-out house, I had heard Beethoven's "An die ferne Geliebte" sung and played by first-class musicians, half-starved but pulling themselves together in the ruins. A year later, then, here were Phyllis and another amateur violinist playing a Bach two-violin concerto, with a fine amateur pianist. We then heard some well-sung *Lieder*. And finally there was a wrenching first hearing of the Schubert four-hand Fantasia in F minor—performed by exhilarated amateurs.

As I listened I wondered whether, if I'd kept up on the clarinet, I could have talked any of those threateningly cultivated players into playing anything written for *it*. Probably not. Anyway, I knew that my coarse way of playing Sousa could never enter that world. (I hadn't then even heard of Brahms's fabulous trio and quintet for my formerly beloved clarinet. But if I'd known them, I would also have known how far they were beyond me.) What the gathering had actually needed that night, what they had said they badly needed, was a cellist; even an average player would have expanded the repertoire.

That point didn't sink in until later. The main effect came from seeing, in the faces and bodies of those totally absorbed players, a kind of physical joy that no mere listener could ever duplicate. And since the four-hand Fantasia had been the high point of the evening, I left determined to build on Varro's lessons and work the piano up—someday—to the point of playing chamber music.

The second piece of fortune overlaps here in ways I can't fully sort out. For all I know, it may have provided a stronger motive than the "purer" ones I'm always tempted to dwell on. It was my envy of Phyllis's amateuring. She had played in the Collegium Musicum of the University—a near-professional group I had applied to, as bass, and been rejected by. What's more, her fine playing had been noticed there by a group of young male chamber players, all medical residents, and they had invited her to join them in their evenings. You can see where that left me: back home, listening, not playing—and strongly envious of her evenings with those guys. The trouble was that I never got to hear them—only to hear her accounts of how those doctors, having done a good day's work, as Benjamin Franklin put it, "spent the evening jollily."

So again I thought of the piano, speculating that if I could find at Haverford, when we moved from Chicago, a piano teacher as stimulating as Varro, I might—well, who knows? As I look at it now, that was an even more foolish ambition than hoping to become a first-class cellist. To try to work up the piano to the level of those players, while pursuing a career as an English teacher, would have been a pathetic dream. As the pianist Russell Sherman puts it in *Piano Pieces*, "The appropriate coordination for playing the piano might seem baffling if one began in one's thirties." "Might" is not the right word; Sherman should have said "would certainly." It might be true that if one had the talent of a Sherman, of a Gould, of a Goode, of a Brendel, one could have . . . But if I'd had that, I wouldn't have waited until twenty-nine to work it up.[3]

Nor did I realize just how edgy good string players are about even good amateur pianists: "They play too loud, seeing themselves as soloists, they don't listen to us, they always insist on playing their favorites that they've worked up for years . . . "

❧

As we moved to my first full-time academic job, taking with me my envy of Phyllis's playing and leaving the piano behind, I was entering blindly a professionalized scene that could easily have killed the amateur in me. Haverford College had many fine traditions, including Quakerly contempt for superficial forms of ambition and success. (The tradition has its mockers: "When they drive Cadillacs, they drive *gray* Cadillacs." "They came to America to do good, and did very well!") But the Haverford English Department I met had long since been invaded by the twentieth century. I found myself surrounded by young male colleagues whose sole purpose in life seemed to be to come as close to Harvard as possible—or at least to get tenure at Haverford, "the best men's college in the country." No doubt many of the faculty members had hobbies, but I can't remember any hint about them, except for tennis. Nobody I met was playing chamber music: in fact the Haverford brand of Quakerism had traditionally seen music as sinful; memory says that to practice an instrument students still had to retreat to a small cottage at the edge of campus.

What saved me from complete surrender to the rat race was that Phyllis went on playing chamber music with new friends outside the college. Most important were Catherine Drinker Bowen (see Bibliography) and her brother Henry Drinker. Catherine was a passionate chamber player, and she invited Phyllis for some quartet sessions. That led to her brother's inviting Phyllis to join his monthly musical gatherings. Drinker had built a home

3. There are now some persuasive accounts of how taking up any instrument is, as John Holt writes of taking up the cello, "never too late." See Wilson; Charles Cooke; Adams. But none of them pretends that it's not too late to achieve top quality.

with a huge music room, and once a month he invited fifty or so players and singers to come for supper and a performance, or "reading," of choral works. The strings would arrive in the afternoon and rehearse whatever was on the evening's program. Then the singers would come and eat and then sight-read what the strings had worked on.

Phyllis somehow managed to get me invited to join the basses, and we had some glorious evenings amateuring from scores (mostly of Bach and Brahms) that Drinker himself had edited. What we performed cannot quite be called chamber music, though his grand hall could well be called a chamber. What was impressive was the amateur spirit filling the room. Lawyer Drinker's approach to music was in many ways like that of the best string amateurs: he was devoting his fortune and time to making music with no thought of any external reward. In those amateur evenings my musical dreams were kept alive, in spite of the mounting professional anxieties about being an uncouth assistant professor from what was contemptuously referred to as "the West," competing for tenure in the eastern establishment scene. The evenings also taught me that the amateur world needed amateur cellists much more than it needed amateur basses, violinists, pianists, or clarinetists. Drinker never had enough cellists.

After two years at Haverford, we left the competitive scene for a year's leave—miraculously funded by the Ford Foundation—as my application put it, "to read ethical philosophy on my own." And suddenly it occurred to me that I could exploit the fellowship a bit and let the Ford gurus finance, without knowing it, some hours not on reading philosophy but on beginning cello lessons. Just how unethical was that? It all depends on how you see the relation of music and philosophy. Wasn't I doing a kind of ethical philosophy? If, as many a philosopher has claimed, music *is* philosophy, and highly ethical philosophy at that, why worry?

Anyhow, what the Forders did, willy-nilly, was perhaps the noblest act of their entire ambivalent career. Needless to say, my report to them never confessed that throughout that year I was never reading ethical philosophy all day long; I was taking an hour or so off, each day, to learn not thumb position (my first teacher, Herr Wetzels, never even got around to mentioning that threat) but finger positions numbers 1, 2, 3, and 4. And bowing. And vibrato.

❧

None of this answers fully the question of why it was the cello. If Phyllis had been a cellist an obvious choice would have been either the violin or viola. My strongest motive was wanting to join her in playing chamber music. I knew that the piano was out, because on it I could never come close to the skill needed for even the simplest chamber music parts, providing real musical pleasure to others. On the other hand, if I took up a string instrument, it seemed obvious that I could soon be doing a not-bad job of playing some of the easier chamber music, depending on Phyllis and other better players to do the harder stuff on the other parts.

But which string instrument? I here offer as evidence for the rightness of my choice a meticulous, unprecedented calculation of the Ratio of the Disparity of Instrumental Difficulties, or RDID. Take as an example the finale of Haydn's Opus 64, No. 5, D Major. The violin plays, according to my quick, indeed impatient count, 857 notes, most of them sixteenths, most of them entailing a change not just of bowing but of fingering from the preceding note. The viola plays 368 notes, many of them sixteenths, and most of them requiring finger changes. Meanwhile the cello is asked to play only 122 notes, with only 72 rapid sixteenths, and with 32 of those sixteenths resting comfortably either on the tonic or dominant. Many of them are followed by a lovely rest period providing time to seek out the next note. Now there we have a clear measure of why it was wiser for me to take up the cello than the violin or even the viola: an RDID of viola to cello of precisely 3 to 1 and of violin to cello of about 7 to 1.

The fact is that there are many wonderful moments with RDIDs even better than that, when the only challenge to the cellist is to produce a single tolerable note sustained for measure after measure. At one point in the Haydn I am offered a comfortable low A while the first violin plays 63 notes! Timeless moments like that rightly tempted me—the chance to dwell lovingly on a single note while feeling as if I were playing all the parts.

Of course I am not saying that anything even remotely like that RDID holds for all chamber music. I'm glad it doesn't. But if I were to count piano and cello notes for an early piano trio by Beethoven, say, the RDID would be even more striking. In more modern works a greater democratic balance is sought and sometimes achieved, but the cello still has far more occasions to rest easy while one or more of the others capers.

Even without counting the RDID I already had a strong enough hunch to guide my choice. Though I loved listening to some of the "display" cello concertos that at many points actually reverse the RDID fraction, I fortunately knew that a lot of chamber literature issued me a simple invitation: not "come and play me, as a star, as a leader" but "come and play me as a deeply feeling accompanist for the stars."

I hope it's clear that I'm not mocking the choice of other string instruments; if you're already good at one of them, get better. Both my playing and my listening depends on them. But I can't resist a warning to lovers of other instruments—one that may mistakenly sound like mockery: you flute or clarinet lovers, you would-be pianists. Unless you are already highly skilful on your instrument, and unless what you want in life is to do most of your playing alone or in a third-rate orchestra, you should not take up now, in your mature years, any instrument for which the literature provides no easy parts in first-class compositions for more than one player.

The painful truth is that if you are no better at the piano or violin than I am at the cello, other amateurs who are quite willing to play with *me* are not likely to want to play with *you.* Your parts in the standard repertory will be just too hard. There is really no chamber music for piano trios or quartets or quintets that a fully amateur*ish* pianist can play well enough to give the fiddlers and cellists a rewarding experience. The pianist, the first fiddle—these are the leaders. Though the cellists and violists must be steady—and in the more modern compositions they must be as good in their way as the others—the fact remains that so long as they count, keep up, really hear what the others are doing and accommodate to it, the rewards will come. Within a year or two you can begin to hold your own, more or less, in a lot of Baroque combos and many a quartet or piano trio by Mozart and Haydn—to say nothing of a host of other competent but less famous composers.

❧

I still love it when a composer throws me into a bit of totally relaxed accompaniment while the others make tough parts sound better than I could. Though in some moderns the RDID can often approach 1/1, or even, as in the first thirty-four measures of the third movement of Bartók's fourth quartet, reverse itself to about 1/100, there are some great modern works that let me think I'm making the music when actually I'm doing not much more than humming along.

Consider the Shostakovich No. 8 (Opus 110, C minor), one of the most emotionally wrenching works ever composed—one that you'll meet again toward the end. After a very slow, easily played beginning, I suddenly find myself able to dwell for seventeen measures on a low C, left hand not even needed, then for four measures on a low G, left hand still dangling, then for another eight measures on a low C again, left hand feeling blessed.

Just think of how that contrasts with what that hand faced in my illustration in the Overture.

It's true that the other players are also here playing extremely slowly and meditatively, each of them with some prolonged single notes. But the

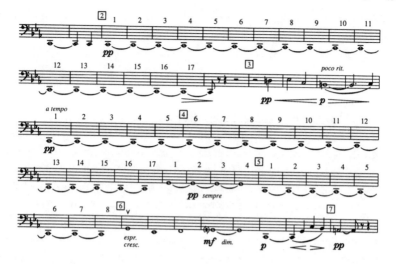

RDID between me and the first fiddle is lower than 1/9. Don't misunderstand: I'm not in any sense musically out of it. I have to pay absolute attention to intonation and dynamics and the progression of feeling. If I ignore those dynamic markings,

I ruin it. The blessing is that in such passages the lack of childhood drill no longer makes any difference. It can be a glorious liberation to settle into a note like that, carefully in tune, with calm vibrato, blissfully listening to the music emerge from the others' parts. It's almost as if it were all coming from my cello and not from the combination of my easy note with their loving skill.

❧

All of this presupposes that you have available other players who are better than you are (and what if they are worse? See chapter 6). It also assumes that you have no insatiable need to shine. Many professional cellists and violists don't enjoy playing pieces that give them little to do beyond do-sol sol-do (I-V, V-I) or um-pah-pah um-pah-pah. We don't need any testimony from them—the absence of compositions like that from most professionals' programs tells it all. When was the last time you heard a first-class group doing the early Haydn piano trios? The cellists have just backed off.

But there are exceptions—professionals who teach us how much bliss can be found in an easy part.

JANUARY 18, 1994

Last week I heard the wonderful Tschaikovsky Trio, all originally from Moscow, now scattered over Europe except when touring together. They began their program with a Mozart Divertimento (K. 254)—a lovely work that gives the cellist mainly "accompaniment" that some would call boring. I admit that I wondered, hearing Anatole Leibermann, even though his comforting RDID-ratio um-pahs were lovely, whether he was as good a performer as the other marvelous two: he was required to play relatively few notes, and no passages beyond even my level of competence. In other words, though their total performance of the trio was first class, he was mostly background. Only when they turned to the later works did he turn out to be more than a master of the most difficult passages, especially in the Shostakovich trio—the one with the high opening melody in harmonics, much of it in thumb position!

What was clear, looking back on what he'd done in the Mozart, was that he had played the easy trio lovingly: he was *listening* to the others, turning his simple single notes into musical proof that he *was* playing his subordinate role with love.

❦

Not the shadow of doubt then: I was right not to pursue the violin or piano or clarinet. I'm not suggesting—to repeat—that every music-loving would-be amateur should follow my choice. If you've already got some other instrument in your bones, carry on. If you push at it, you can find people to play with. Consult the directory of the Amateur Chamber Players of America or subscribe to *Music for the Love of It*. What's more, you can always have fun just playing melodies by yourself, or playing with the recordings that deliberately leave one part out: yours.

In our summer place in the Utah mountains we are sometimes waked early by a trumpeter who climbs a couple of hundred yards up the mountain above us and serenades the dawn, himself—and us. That's no doubt a delight for him, and though it's not much fun for us, I'd scorn any neighbor who called the International Cultural Police Office, asking them to come and force him to change over to the cello.

❦

There is one strong reason for approaching even the most beautiful string instrument with caution. Though most of my reasons for choosing the cello seem to me as good as they did at the time of the choice, there was another one that looks just plain stupid now. I had the notion that it would be easier on the cello than on the clarinet to avoid annoying fellow players with bad intonation. A few years earlier I had learned just how badly out of tune I played: my clarinet teachers hadn't even bothered about precise pitch, seeming always to stress speed and rhythm. My two closest college friends, Max Dalby and Ralph Laycock, fine clarinetists who became professional music teachers and performers, taught me that my intonation was lousy—to say nothing of my blatty timbre: "You simply have got to learn to humor the notes—not just that B-flat that even you know is always sharp, but actually most of them. Your instrument does not, by itself, play in tune. The pipes are not made that way."

Remembering all the struggles that fact had caused, it struck me as obvious that when playing a string instrument it should be easy to humor any note on it: all you'd have to do is raise or lower your finger a bit, and you'd be in tune.

I said as much when I first talked with Herr Wetzels. He must have wondered what in the name of the Muse I was thinking of, though he didn't say a critical word. After all, my point was an attractive half-truth: if you want to play just one or two slow notes for awhile, in tune with somebody else's slow notes, as in the Shostakovich, and you notice that the first try is slightly sharp or flat, you can indeed correct the problem much more easily on the cello than on any non-string instrument except, obviously, the trombone. Not long ago I heard Rostropovich doing just that more than once. It is also true that all winds, even the best professionals, have to work harder at correcting their instruments' inclinations in this one respect than do professional cellists. Cellos have no intonational inclinations of their own; clarinets, flutes, recorders, French horns, oboes are obstinate. A pro-amateur bagpipe player told me that the slightest change in temperature or humidity "throws me into deep doo-doo, intonation-wise."

What I overlooked was that down here in the middle range of ability, when you are faced with any kind of demand for rapid playing, without years of muscular habituation, it's a lot easier on the clarinet to reach an approximation to what is wanted than it is on the cello. The clarinet does a lot of the work on its own, if also too much of it; the cello does absolutely nothing about placing notes.

In other words, instead of moving as I hoped into more comfortable terrain I was headed for a variety of troublesome discoveries, like what happens in the fourth movement of that Shostakovich: after the haunting but relaxed sixty-one measures demanding only four finger changes—one of the most reassuring RDIDs ever—*suddenly* I have to leap from the low, mournful C sharp up three octaves to another C sharp for a solo on the A string, in thumb position! Oh dear—will it be sharp or flat or maybe for once right on? And will my bow arm remember how to manage a decent tone up in that squeaky territory—up toward that high E?

In my practice hour this afternoon I'll repeat that particular shift ten or twelve times, knowing that when I play it with the others tomorrow I'll still have trouble with it. Many more troubles lie in wait for us in the next chapter. Like amateurs in every practice, I play while the sword of Damocles, labeled "failure," hangs over my head.

But as I play about with my laboring, please remember that even in the worst struggling hours, I usually experience some soaring. When practicing the easier parts I can actually "sing it," or even "dance it," as I anticipate where all four of us will be as we join Shostakovich in his mournful offering.

The ruling passion *et les egarements du coeur* are the very things which mark, and distinguish a man's character; I would as soon leave out a man's head as his hobby-horse. LAURENCE STERNE, ON THE "HOBBY" OF WRITING *Tristram Shandy*

❀

I know that I play guitar and write songs not because I want to see my picture someday flashed up on the television screen, but because I need to feel some of that magic of creating. If I didn't have my six-string friend beside me, I think I might go a little nuts. Maybe I should scrawl on my guitar, "This machine keeps me sane." ZANE ZIELINSKI

❀

The true amateur athlete . . . is one who takes up sport for the fun of it and the love of it, and to whom success or defeat is a secondary matter so long as the play is good. . . . it is from doing the thing well, doing the thing handsomely, doing the thing intelligently that one derives the *pleasure* which is the essence of sport. WILLIAM JAMES

C h a p t e r   T h r e e

Amateuring and Rival Pleasures

REVELING IN THE good fortune of being seduced into the cello-reach can provide only hints about how to answer that why question raised in the Overture. The half-baked answer I gave there might be summarized like this:

Since all other motives—fame, money, power, even honor—are thrown out the window the moment I pick up that cello bow, the only plausible reason for doing it is that overworked word "love," the irresistible motive that leads in mystifying ways to both intense pleasures and intense pains. I do it because I love doing it, even when the results are disappointing. I do it to do it. It is not just a way to stave off the despair or boredom or anxiety that threatens every life, however blessed or lucky. I do it not just as one might eat, drink, and feign to be merry because tomorrow one may (must) die. It's not simply another pastime to make life tolerable and postpone death. I do it not only because it feels good but because when considered from any angle, including tough critical probing, it stands up as *the way to go.*

Some versions of hedonism may be close cousins of that summary; their pursuers do pursue "for the fun of the pursuit." But "for the love of it" is not quite the same as "because I want to." My key phrase can take on many meanings, depending on conflicting definitions of "love" and "it." "Love" is almost as ambiguous a term as "God" or "religion"; nobody, not even Plato, has ever been able to pin it down. And "it," the practice, though relatively clear at any moment when I'm "doing it," collects thousands of references when we think of the entire amateuring world. And that becomes millions when we think of all the loving pleasures available to us. Your mailbox, like mine, must be flooded with catalogues offering those millions.

What, after all, distinguishes any of them from genuine amateuring? (The two best recent attempts to address that question are by Jarmila Horna and Robert Stebbins.)

To approach an answer, it helps to narrow it all down to a particular case: mine. Why does Booth work at his particular "it"? Facing that question has sometimes tempted me into a full-length "Autobiography of an Amateur," extending the memoirs offered in chapters 1 and 2. Short of that rejected project, let's see what happens if we put Booth on the witness stand and grill him.

Since you now know with absolute certainty that you will never play the cello "with professional skill or ease," why go on doing it? After more than four decades of learning, true excellence is still further away than it would be for a gifted twelve-year-old who has studied with a good teacher for one or two years. You know that the world offers lovers a multitude of easier, less frustrating pleasures than you experience wrestling with that instrument. Why not turn to these?

If you had worked an hour a day studying trilobites, say, you could be holding an international conference with the three other world-class trilobite experts—all of you "at the top." Though that wouldn't yield quite the hype you'd get if you landed a Rover on Mars, it would feel like the kind of triumph that will never be yours as an amateur cellist. How much better even your feeble performance as a literary critic would have been if, instead of starting up with the cello in 1952 you had devoted a systematic, hour-a-day study to Aristotle, to Samuel Johnson, to Shakespeare, to George Eliot, to Yeats. You could have written at least a respectable study of—well, the list is endless: an hour a day on almost anything will make you more of an expert on it than you'll ever be on the cello.

Here you are, moving at an astonishing rate toward either being eighty or dying, almost half a century since the day you bought that cheap cello and bow and phoned Herr Wetzels to ask if he would be willing to take you on as an "older student." Four and a half decades at it and still not very good! Shouldn't you have known better?

There is one tempting autobiographical answer that I'll mostly dodge: it all sprang from a puritanical upbringing that celebrated aspiration. If you are brought up as a Mormon, taught daily to see the goal of life as getting better all the time, in as many dimensions as possible, you cannot escape that daily betterment command. The same point can of course be made for many religions, but my hunch is that it would be hard to match Mormonism in its doctrine of eternal "bettering."

Another kind of answer can be found in the journal entries written as the pleasures increased, and as the immensity of the challenges became clearer.

FEBRUARY 4, 1953 [ABOUT SIX MONTHS AFTER STARTING]—Cello lessons going well. Had fun with some simple duets with Phyllis. By the end of the year I'll be able to play fairly decently in larger groups, which was my goal when I first took it up. A great prospect . . .

FEBRUARY 6, 1954—. . . What redeems all that [I had reported feeling overwhelmed by teaching and administration at Earlham College] is that at last I am actually playing string quartets, after a year and a half of learning—only about eight months of it taking lessons and managing daily practice. I'm no good yet, but good enough to play easy Mozart with Phyllis and the Staeblers [Warren and Patricia, who became our weekly playing companions for another six years], and excited enough about it to flip my lid (as the students are saying these days) whenever we get together, which is not often enough. . . .

Over the following years I find mounting gratitude for my choice and the player-friends it brought into my life. I also find myself saying, in various ways, that if I had even dimly suspected, in 1952, how resistant a cello can be, and how much harder it is to play chamber music well than it had been fifteen years earlier to play marching band music on my clarinet, I would never have tackled it. I'd have returned to improving some other defensible but less demanding choice: playing at the piano by myself or singing the bass line occasionally in a madrigal or barbershop quartet, or perhaps taking up the guitar to accompany folk singing. Yet I always conclude such what-ifs with: that would have been a serious loss, even though I would never have consciously realized it.

Why am I so unequivocal about that? That is the form of the why question that forces us now out of autobiography into some semi-philosophical probing of the very notion of love, of pleasure, of leisure, and of play. Thinking about distinctions may save us from making either too strong or too weak a case for amateuring.

Pleasures: The Harmful vs. the Harmless

I'll resist spending any time on what to most but not all of us is blatantly obvious: that to hurt others for the fun of it is ultimately indefensible. For those who find the hurting of others fun, no arguments against it can fully succeed, and the history of efforts to explain why "human nature" includes such impulses and what we might do to combat them could fill a library: books on the history of Satan and the Fall, on the cosmogonies of other cultures, on our genetic inheritance, including recently the structure of our brains, on sadism and why it is terrible or defensible. And so on. I'll just hope that here we can all agree that to hurt or harm for the fun of it is self-evidently not a loving choice.[1]

One embarrassing qualification: we amateurish amateurs do often inflict pain on others. We just don't do it on purpose.

Work and Play, Work as Play

To celebrate playing for the love of it risks downgrading the work we do that we love. In fact we amateurs are often tempted to talk snobbishly about those who cannot claim that what they do they do for the love of it. As Bliss Perry put the danger: "[T]he prejudice which the amateur feels toward the professional, the more or less veiled hostility between the man who does something for love which another man does for money, is one of those instinctive reactions—like the vague alarm of some wild creature in the woods—which give a hint of danger."

The words "professional" and "work" are almost as ambiguous as the word "love." Some work is fun, some gruesome. Churchill loved his work—but needed to escape it regularly. I hated most of the farm work I did as an adolescent, and escaped it as soon as possible. I hated having to dig ditches eight hours a day for twenty-five cents an hour. Yet working as teacher and a scholar, I have loved most of my duties—even the drudgery parts. A member of the Chicago Symphony Orchestra told me that he hates his work—his playing—and is eager for retirement. Politicians celebrate work as what will save welfare recipients from degradation; for them, to require people to work, even if they're underpaid and even if the job is awful, is a virtuous act.

Such a mishmash of implied definitions makes it impossible to place work in any simple opposition to play or pleasure. In *Homo Ludens* Huizinga occasionally writes as if the whole point of life were to have fun by *escaping*

1. A fine discussion of the dangers threatened by "doing things for the love of the doing" is given by Roger Shattuck in *Forbidden Knowledge*. Shattuck argues that the art-for-art's-sake movement, with its many echoes of Pater's celebration of "burning" with a "hard, gemlike flame" and living for the "highest quality" of a given moment, risks moving us toward "worship of pure experience without restraint of any kind." The temptations of sadistic ecstasies lurk in the wings. As I shall insist again and again, to make sense out of a title like *For the Love of It* requires careful distinction among diverse "loves," many of them potentially harmful.

work. I think he was right to celebrate "man the playing animal"—a creature who deserves to be rescued from all forms of oppressive work. Joyful,
carefree play is, as he argues, one of the greatest gifts of creation. But the
word "carefree" has its own ambiguities. Every real amateur feels responsible to some notion of doing the loving well, and that entails a kind of caring, both practice and intensity of effort, that could be called work. On the
other hand, many of those who say, "Sorry, I've got to get to work now,"
are really moving toward the tasks they most love to perform: they qualify
as pro-amateurs.

Thus one subpoint of this book could be an exhortation to all workers
to recover ways of loving their work. The media are full of unproved claims
that loved work is on a steep decline. The Sunday papers could almost be
summarized like this:

> These days in America too many people, whether in business or sports
> or entertainment, work only for money or fame or power or, at a mini-
> mum, some kind of success. Instead of playing, or discovering work that
> is itself playing, they labor—and then when they escape the detested la-
> bor, they passively watch others play—the Olympics, Wimbledon, NBA
> championships, Court TV—and ask themselves, "Are we having fun
> yet?" Instead of pursuing joyful conversations with friends, they watch
> other people's destructive conversations on talk shows. Instead of play-
> ing music, they buy a more expensive CD player. Instead of having their
> kids take piano lessons and then playing music with them, they buy them
> laptops that teach them how to play solitaire and computerized contests
> in "virtual worlds," and CDs and VCRs that keep them entertained.
> Professional athletes lament that "the fun has gone out of it." Football
> quarterbacks are being injured deliberately by their enemies. Kids no
> longer really *play* in the sandlot: they compete for prizes in the Little
> League. Olympic "amateurs" have become laboring professionals, con-
> fessing anger about the fortunes other amateurs are making from adver-
> tising: "her perks are higher than my perks!" Baseball and basketball
> players and managers sacrifice whatever pleasure the contests might yield
> by competing for larger fortunes. Piano sales are going down fast, and
> the only thing that's saving the dealers is the number of player pianos
> being sold—the new kind that use CDs to produce an excellent imita-
> tion of Glenn Gould right in your home: you not only don't have to learn
> to play a note, you no longer even have to learn how to pump steadily.

Regardless of whether there is a provable general decline of this sort—
I return to that question in chapter 10—there are plenty of convincing

anecdotes about particular losses. A couple of years ago I happened on a television interview with Martina Navratilova, who complained that the young tennis competitors she meets are so intent on winning that they have no other life of their own: they have no time or energy or interest, she said, for reading, or walking in the woods, or doing anything but training to win. (Am I inventing the memory that she said something like, "Nobody is an amateur any more"?)

My actual experience outside media reports includes enough genuine amateurs (including those who love their work) to make such laments seem excessive. My point is not to claim that things are getting worse—who knows?—but to argue that there are no clear battle lines between work and play, and that many a worker could salvage life by turning the work into a practice that proves rewarding.

Unconditional Loves vs. the Give-upable

Some of our loves, when life goes as it should, lead to total, irreversible, unconditional commitments that cannot be thought of simply as choices. The most obvious is having children. Whether or not to spend time at parenting is not a choice for any half-decent parent, at least not after the child is born. It's true that lots of people have children accidentally, and some do not love the unsought result of "making love" when it thrusts itself into their busy lives. For most of us parents, however, having a child is obviously so central that words like "choice" and "amateur" no longer make sense, though we may often feel amateur*ish* in raising the child.

How is such full human loving different from the chamber playing that I have sometimes thought of as a necessity? Well, to give up the cello is to me at least in some sense thinkable. As I've already confessed, at times I've actually thought it. It's a choice. Indeed the time will certainly come when I'll choose to give it up, perhaps weeping, because my playing has become so bad. But to give up my children or grandchildren—that's simply *un*thinkable.

No doubt some parents debate whether or not to have a child in roughly the same way that some might ponder the choice between learning to golf and learning to play the piano: pleasant rival ways of using future leisure time. After the child arrives, though, that way of thinking no longer works for most parents: the child becomes immeasurably more important than anything else in the world. Most of us feel the same unconditional love for our parents and closest friends, and even with the rising divorce rate it's still true that a majority do not give up our spouses: they are in the non-choice class—irreplaceable, simply not subject to any act of choice about how to spend leisure time.

Almost everyone can name some love less provisional than amateuring. For some it would be religion, or justice, or patriotism, or sex. Almost all of us could add "life itself," whatever the suicide rates. The amateur chooses, day by day, hour by hour, to pursue what life does not require.

Earned Pleasures and the Purchasable

Here we touch again on "sensations" of amateur playing as they compare with a host of ice-cream pleasures, some of them, such as drugs and cigarettes and fat-rich cuisines and bungee jumping, so lovable that they put life itself at risk.

What is it that distinguishes amateuring from seeking your favorite coq au vin or sushi at the best restaurant in town? You certainly go to the restaurant for the sake of the going: you could claim that you do it for the love of it. So the borderline is never clear, but it is obvious that many "leisure pursuits" of the kind tried out by Stephen Jarvis, in preparing his *Bizarre Leisure Book*, are about as important, in measuring the value of time spent, as ordering a dish of ice-cream: competitive pipe-smoking, toe-wrestling, collecting barbed wire or straitjackets. Others—those "crazy" hobby horses that require some practice—might claim to be moving toward the right to join my loving community: conker matches, conversational Anglo-Saxon, tiddlywink tournaments.

Almost any easy love can be elevated when the lover discovers the need for action rather than passive purchase. The gourmand seeks the closest restaurant and then gourmandizes, guzzles. The gourmet rises toward the badge of amateur by acquiring experience, paying attention, learning thoughtful discriminations. As Ted Cohen argues, no one attending baseball games is a full amateur until all the intricacies of rules and plays have been mastered. A wine lover is no amateur of wines, is at best a connoisseur or aficionado, until the mere craving rises to demand increased knowledge and loving attention to subtle distinctions: *then* we have an oenologist, an amateur perhaps on the way to becoming a professional. Someone seeking risky thrills can take up bungee jumping: absolutely no practice or skill required. The thrill seeker becomes an amateur only when he chooses to *practice* something like hang gliding—as I sometimes think I would do if I were twenty: the thrills are earned, not just bought.

The amateur can always say, "Even if I were a billionaire, I could never buy this from anybody."

Future Payoff vs. Love Now

Though amateur loves are less nearly absolute than family loves, the two are surprisingly alike in one crucial respect: they are pursued in and for the present, with little thought of future reward. Though it's warming to believe that the future will include our maturing children and grandchildren, we don't—or at least shouldn't—spend our hours calculating how much fame or money or power or caretaking they will grant us in our declining years. Though we obviously think about the children's future, our love when genuine is never reduced to "I'm caring for this child now primarily because of what she will bring me in the future." (Those parents who destroy a child's happiness in the name of future stardom usually destroy the later star as well.) The reward, like the reward of playing music, is now, in the doing.

We don't need a scientific study to prove that far more amateurs than parents or lovers can be seduced or bribed into abandoning their loves. A subtler qualification however is that the very thought of practicing in order to *get better at it* involves the future: a different kind of payoff. My hours spent on Popper's Études are often more future-tainted than my hours spent playing full versions of Beethoven or Brahms. As I practice, too often my being is centered not on making music but on questions like, "What will my exacting teacher think next week when I still miss that leap to the high E?" "What will our fiddler friend Louise think when I fail to keep that long unison passage in perfect octaves with her?" I never quite go so far in this direction as to justify what Nietzsche has to say about it: "The striving for excellence is the striving to overwhelm one's neighbor, even if only very indirectly or only in one's own feelings." But that temptation to corruption is always in the background.

In my journal entries, many of them written long before I conceived of this book, I meet the frequent claim that I often quote here: *I'm getting better all the time.* Such glances backward while leaning forward are essential to learning any skill, and it is important to acknowledge how they can become an amusing corruption of the true game. A sadder version is what happens to some players, especially professionals, when they realize that they are not getting better but worse; I have met several musicians who, because they can no longer shine, refuse now to play at all.

So again we end in paradox: no one could survive by refusing ever to balance pleasures of the moment against future consequences; yet no trap is more destructive of life than consequentialist or utilitarian calculation—

the curse of "futurism." Some simple versions of cost-benefit analysis that the more extreme economists urge upon us can invade amateur territory and, if taken literally, would wipe out this book.

Love and Money

The most striking payoff is of course money—along with the fame and power that yield it. When amateur wine-tasters or cellists or lovers of literature pursue their skill with sufficient passion and hard work, they are likely to discover, suddenly, another pleasure: being paid for their skill. They can become professionals. And before they know it, they are not quite sure whether they are doing it for love or for money. Soon, they find themselves saying—there's lots of evidence for this—that the love has faded as the chance for more and more money has blossomed, or as the pressures of the job have mounted.

Again the borders separating amateurs, pro-amateurs, and other professionals are vague, and judgments are dangerous when they reject professional values. In our society you obviously cannot survive without money, and unless you inherit a fortune, you have to get a job—usually hoping to become a well-paid professional. It would be absurd to say that to be paid—as I have been paid for a lifetime of teaching literature and writing books—is necessarily a corruption of life, making my profession somehow less defensible than my cello playing. At the same time, I am flooded with memories of how my job—called a professional appointment—did sometimes poison the full pleasure of reading and writing and conversing. As I write here, fully intending to sell the book, am I being an amateur? (I return to "the profession of an amateur writer" in the Interlude.)

As professor, I never felt that what I was paid had any effect on what or why I taught, and I can't remember ever careening off the true path—teaching and writing—in search of extra cash. But thinking harder about it now dramatizes the fact that money did often influence matters. I confess that I did deflect many hours into doing three commercial textbooks, always defending the projects to my conscience as "in the service of education." But I must have known then and confess now that one text was largely motivated by the editor's barefaced promise: "This will make you rich." My friend Marshall Gregory and I then spent untold hours tiptoeing on the borderline toward—well, not corruption, exactly, but certainly something far different from working for the love of it. Fortunately, as I see it now, the publisher's promise proved to be silly: nothing would have been worse for us than becoming rich. Also fortunately, our book-construction did at times become sheer fun, because of Greg's spirited labors. Friendship can transform even poor choices.

It's also clear to me now that my salary at various moments affected both whom I taught and what. If some high school had offered me a salary equal to what the University of Chicago was paying (along with a decently small teaching load), believing as I did then and do now that high-school teaching is more important than college teaching, I'm fairly sure I would have accepted. But my university pay kept me happily located with students who needed me much less than did the sophomores in any neighboring high school.

Rewards of money, and the gold medals and fame that carry money with them, are obviously not in themselves necessarily contemptible. In fact Huizinga sees competitiveness for money and prizes as one of the most defensible forms of play. What would the history of games be without the incentives of payoff? What would our lives be if every professional player or businessman or politician gave it all up for full-time amateur playing? Or if every amateur suddenly became satisfied to remain amateurish, a mere dabbler? Or if professionals gave up all ambition to win in international competitions? Still, we should never forget how much is lost when the fun of winning eclipses the fun of doing something you love as well as you can do it, along with others who love the doing, regardless of pay.

The true distinction, then, is not between lovers paid and lovers unpaid, as if being paid is the same as being prostituted. Rather it's between those who do what they do for the love of it, whether paid or not, and those whose lives are poisoned, whether from choice or circumstance, by the money pressures. (We'll meet many of them in chapter 10.)

My heroes through all this are the professionals I call pro-amateurs— those who are willing to join amateurs, pursuing the love together.

FALL, 1955 [EARLHAM COLLEGE]—The Juilliard Quartet, the best we've ever heard, has given us three fantastic days of Bartók—public rehearsals in the daytime, recitals at night. After one performance, at about ten p.m., Robert Koff, their second violinist, learned through the Staeblers that the four of us were playing quartets as amateurs—and asked if he could join us for some playing! And he did. Even after playing quartets all day long, he still hadn't had enough, so he took on three of us for a kind of free coaching session. He was patient, attentive to our needs, un-domineering—and we played *better than we'd ever played before.* [Italics added, 1998]

SEPTEMBER 28, 1997 [ISLAND OF CORFU, FORTY-TWO YEARS LATER]—
Our week of splendid and poor chamber playing ended this morning
with two wonderful hours coached by Igor Polesitsky, principal violist
of the Maggio Orchestra in Florence. Because one fiddler and one violist had left, Phyllis and I wondered what Igor would do with just the two
of us. He immediately decided not just to coach but to play.

"What *trio* would you like to play?" Our hearts leapt up.

"Well, we have the Beethoven op. 3, and Bach's 'Art of the Fugue,'
with its two trio movements. We've worked on them some . . ."

"I love 'em both," he said. So we played—and played and played. His
advice was mostly his playing; only rarely did he stop to make suggestions. We both had the illusion of being elevated almost to his level of
playing, and we both were justly exhilarated by his praise: "You're real
players! This is more fun than playing with some of the pros I'm stuck
with."

We believed him, perhaps naively, and we played some more. A couple
of times I had to wipe tears.

At the end he said, "Oh, if only Russia, or Italy, had more amateurs
like you. When being trained in Russia, it was all 'Either make it as a pro
or quit.' Playing Bach and Beethoven with amateurs like you has really
purged my soul."

Obviously Igor deserves my praise-term—not pro, not amateur, but
pro-amateur. He has purged my soul.

How many such pro-amateurs are on the scene we'll never know.[2] When
you attend a symphony concert, you may well be looking down upon a majority of bored professionals or a majority of genuine lovers. And you'll usually not be able to distinguish them by how well they play. It all depends on
what's happening in their souls.

Our world is thus full of borderline cases. When Samuel Johnson said,
"No man but a blockhead ever wrote, except for money," he was obviously
kidding, but he provides a shrewd reminder that the relation of love and
money is even more complicated in amateuring than it is in sex.

Loves Shared vs. Loves Solitary

Some admirable amateurs play utterly alone. Whether or not they ignore
future payoff, they depend only on themselves and the nature of the task.

2. For a splendid, brief celebration of one such pro-am, see Helen Spielman's account of
the flutist Jeanne Baxtresser.

Solitary mountain climbing produces, as any watcher of TV documentaries has been told, indescribable thrills. An amateur perusing medieval manuscripts, alone in some rare book room, with no thought of publication, could be ranked among the purest of the pure. Some pianists play only for themselves, refusing invitations to play chamber music and never playing for an audience.

Obviously such private hours can be wonderful, but they rule out much that group playing provides: the multiplying of pleasure by sharing it. The player who never plays with others can certainly be said to be "saved," as an amateur. But to me it's a bit too close to a deathbed repentance without a priest or family member present.

Any solitude-loving pianist will want to answer this downgrading of solitude, perhaps like this:

> The truth is that private playing for the sake of the private playing is in fact the ultimate in amateuring. We pianists reach the peak of purified "uselessness." A better word for it, if it were not corrupted these days into meaning "bored," would be "disinterestedness." Doesn't the private player after all represent the very essence of what music itself really is? And besides, unlike you loners practicing an isolated part on the cello, when we pianists play a Bach fugue or a Chopin prelude, we are not alone: Bach or Chopin, in all his richness, is in the room. You have one lone line; we have the whole show.

Russell Sherman sounds a bit like that in his book, *Piano Pieces;* like most ardent lovers, he cannot resist placing his love on the same pinnacle as is occupied by mine after an especially good playing evening:

> To know the piano is to know the universe. To master the piano is to master the universe. The spectrum of piano sound acts as a prism through which all musical and non-musical sounds may be filtered. The grunts of sheep, the braying of mules [and on through a long list to] whistles, scrapes, bleatings, caresses, thuds, hoots, plus sweet and sour pluckings—fall within the sovereignty of this most bare and dissembling chameleon.

Well, as I do my pluckings that he feels sovereign over, I naturally reject his and other pianists' sense of dominance. I wonder why he never hints at the difference between the fun of playing alone and the fun of playing with some of us sweet and sour pluckers. And I wonder how he would respond to the late distinguished chamber music pianist Lamar Crowson. When asked why, as a virtuoso pianist, he had turned entirely to playing with others, Crowson said "because solo work is bare and lonely."

Loves Useful to Others vs. Those "Useful" Only to Myself

An overlapping point is raised by my Churchill example in the Overture: the distinction between amateuring that somehow serves the world and amateuring that is useless except in the sense of saving the lover's soul.

Some totally admirable choices, unlike mine, offer clear benefits to the world out there. Running a volunteer food kitchen, reading to the blind, fostering neglected children, taking one's piano or guitar skills into a group of children to help them sing. Such "social-amateurs" work to achieve some good even more important than the joy they sometimes feel when the working *works*.

No such hope can motivate any but the most gifted amateur cellist. Professional musicians can be said to be useful to all who hear them. When Janos Starker performs in public, he is "doing good" to his hearers. His recordings can be used by therapists to calm patients down or even hypnotize them. We have evidence that listening to Mozart can improve math test scores. Kings, presidents, and führers know that music is indispensably useful to inflame the troops. Businesses use it on their answering machines to reduce our frustration as we wait for a human voice.

My playing can claim none of these uses, good or bad. I may kid myself into thinking that I do some kind of "good" in the "world" just by helping to keep amateur chamber music "alive," but all three terms demand those scare quotes: any notion of practical usefulness or future reward for my playing is so trivial as to be ludicrous. If there is to be any reward for anyone, it is in the quality of the time spent, here and now. And that reward is for the amateurs—only rarely does any listener take any pleasure hearing us play.

Would I argue that passionate chamber playing is in any sense morally, philosophically, religiously, superior to running a soup kitchen without pay? Absolutely not. But am I admitting, then, that running the soup kitchen is superior to chamber playing? Absolutely not. We are thus dealing here, in contrast to some of the previous comparisons, with two conflicting but genuine values: the loving pursuit of what the eighteenth century called the "beautiful and the sublime" and the loving pursuit of others' welfare.

I have an absurdly incoherent image of the ideal human being: a man or woman serving both of these values with equal passion, in all waking hours. The impossibility of fully uniting such unquestionable values has led many philosophers this century to play with the term "incommensurable." The choice of either good is utterly defensible; neither is merely culturally determined, since in all societies both would be of value. Yet the full pursuit of each one entails some downgrading or interference with the other: they simply cannot be measured against each other. That is why, as I've already said and will say again, my highfalutin, purely loving pursuit of chamber music produces—in those moments when I think about it, not in the moments of playing—some guilt about the many other goods it shoves aside. But the truth is that when I miss a practice session because I'm spending two hours reading for the blind, I also can feel (mildly) guilty. Is it not wicked to avoid practicing?

Obviously the way to deal with such guilt (some but not all of it springing from my Mormon upbringing) is to take a closer look at the definition of what is useful. George Sand once found her devotion to art attacked by a fellow revolutionary, on the grounds that art could never face up to the question "What use is it?" He argued that Sand's picture of the French revolution should be honored by devoting all of her energies to building the New Jerusalem. Sand's brilliant defense of what might be called the higher usefulness of the arts might make a good retort to those members of Congress who argue that government funds should be cut from the NEA and thus reserved for what is defensible as useful (for many of them that would be lower taxes for the wealthy):

> [Y]ou tell me that whatever exists outside the rules of Utility can never become either truly great or truly good . . . [But] when the time comes to build the Great City of the Mind, you may be sure everyone will help build it according to his powers: Berlioz [whom her friend had attacked] with pick and shovel, I with my golden toothpick, the rest with their two arms and their will. But the New Jerusalem will, I trust, have days of rest and joy, and it will be permitted to some to go back to their pianos, and to others to cultivate their gardens—each innocently following his capacities and tastes.

Memorizing that passage, I find my guilt evaporating. As I sit down tonight to practice the Mozart viola quintet (C major), preparing for the upcoming Sunday session that will include the two Brahms quintets, my soul will feel pure as the driven snow: I'm innocent.

❦

It is said that Nero not only fiddled while Rome burned, he tried to turn himself into a professional by commanding his minions to sit through hours of his no doubt amateurish playing. When they failed to show enough enthusiasm for how he performed, he would have them tortured.

Wouldn't it have been better if, instead of arranging a command performance, Nero had just gone to his music stand and practiced? Or better yet, played a trio with slaves chosen from his plentiful supply? We could still blame him for not going out into the streets and taking up a fire hose, but at least we could then honor him with the title of amateur.

SECOND
MOVEMENT

*The
Marriage*

[Playing music] has a ceaseless knack of dishing out euphoric "highs" one moment and terrible "lows" the next. This happens with such startling regularity that it is often hard to know whether you are scaling a height, plumbing a depth or clutching vaguely at the limbo in between. JULIAN LLOYD WEBBER, *Travels With My Cello*

❦

It makes an immense difference with respect to pleasure to consider a thing one's own. ARISTOTLE, *Politics*

❦

There is nothing, I think, in which the power of art is shown so much as in playing the fiddle. In all other things we can do something at first. Any man will forge a bar of iron, if you give him a box, though a clumsy one; but give him a fiddle, and a fiddle-stick and he can do nothing. SAMUEL JOHNSON, IN BOSWELL'S *Life*

❦

I said, "It's certain there is no fine thing
Since Adam's fall but needs much labouring."
WILLIAM BUTLER YEATS

Chapter Four

The Zen of Thumb
Position Maintenance

PERHAPS THE BEST WAY to dramatize the bite of the "why bother" question, as faced by any genuine amateur, is to dwell on the looming hurdles and frequent setbacks. As I describe my cumbersome efforts, many *now* viewed as comic, some viewed *then* as pathetic, I again see my cello-reach as a metaphor for all difficult amateur choices. Every question I ask can be transposed into every amateur territory—or at least into those that seduce one into sheer physical training. But as I play with unpredicted threats and disasters, both here and in parts of chapter 7, they should never suggest that the pains of amateuring, comic or not, overshadow the bliss.

Not too long ago, an acquaintance who had heard about my celebration of amateuring said, "That's silly; I spent decades collecting coins, and I wish I hadn't thrown those hours away; I'd be a better professional if I'd stuck to what's important." He hadn't caught my hint that his hobby, his pastime was not full amateuring. Of all hobbies, collecting of any kind is about the hardest to turn into genuine amateuring. If you are a collector, perhaps you could show me how it can be realized.

I seldom have felt my hours of practice as hours thrown away, except for those that were demanded by poor teachers. The sometimes painful laboring is an essential part of the blossoming that any choice can yield; only those choices that require manual reshaping and training can yield the curious mixture of bane and bliss. As Charles Cooke says about learning to play the piano, "we are talking about work here . . . tiring work, refreshing work."

I recently read that Russian president Boris Yeltsin when on vacation has a passion for fishing. He has his staff arrange for workers to go to the lake in advance, dig worms, and plant 10,000 fish so that he'll be sure to catch a lot. What would be the proper word for that kind of labor-free hobby? How much practice does it take to catch one of 10,000 fish that have been planted in order to be caught? Can Yeltsin's pleasures even be mentioned in the same breath as the fly-casting pleasures celebrated in Norman Maclean's *A River Runs Through It*, depending as they do on years of disciplined casting practice?

❧

Why does the cello-reach so often fall short? My first two answers apply equally to all amateur choices; the third applies mainly to cellists, but with overtones that ring threateningly for all beginning string players.

Rising Physical Sluggishness

To any experienced musician, the most obvious absurdity in my picking up that bow at thirty-one is the sheer physical impossibility of mastery. Recent research is confirming what everybody already knew: the older the body (including the mind), the more reluctant it is to learn new skills. Even when the skill seems primarily mental—taking up Russian, say, as Edmund Wilson did in his middle years, in order to read Pushkin—the learning always goes more slowly than it would have done earlier.

If you have any doubts about the problem of picking up the bow belatedly, try brushing your teeth tonight with the other hand. Then ask any child you know to attempt the same. Record which of you makes the transfer more easily, and then note tomorrow which one can perform without hesitation the strokes she worked on today. Now add "brush your teeth with the wrong hand while simultaneously patting your head with your other hand." See what I mean? You're moving toward a small part of the problems a beginning cellist faces. Elaine Parhamovich, who took up the violin at thirty-nine, puts the problem like this: "To say I ran into a brick wall equates to referring to a napalm bomb as a firecracker. . . . Once my lessons began, I quickly realized what I had gotten myself into. . . . I practiced faithfully every night after my child went to sleep (I'll never know how she slept through that first year of screeching . . .)."

Even if, as was true with me, you already have some knowledge about the new territory, the task can turn out to be not just tough but scary. I knew, after all, how a high E or A-flat should sound when played by a fine cellist;

how to count ¼ and ⅝ and ¼; how to manage the three beats against two that Brahms exploits so grandly; how to keep track of the wild alternation of measure lengths that Shostakovich and Bartók revel in; how the parts of fiendish works like the "Grosse Fuge" interrelate. But though a part of my soul knew "music," my body/mind was dragging its feet all the way.

Whether you can teach an old dog new tricks depends both on the dog and on just how old is old. The aging body, whether twenty or eighty, frequently decides to quarrel with that part of the mind that remains perpetually young—call it the ego, the id, the soul. Anyway, the perpetually young psyche remains always about what it was at age six or sixteen, feeling young as ever, ready to take on new tasks or new friends, and always astonished as it looks in the mirror and sees, not the "sixty year old *smiling* public man," that Yeats describes in "Among School Children," or even the "tattered coat upon a stick" who haunts "Sailing to Byzantium," but a seventy-seven-year-old scowling, unpublic man. The youngster encounters an oldster whose muscles and brain ain't wot they useta be. Even if one rejects, as I do, the ancient strict dualism between body and soul, it often feels as if the body were cheating on the psyche.

When the mind feels young it likes to take charge, urging to action. It loves to chant "I think I can, I think I can," and it loves to hear the teacher say, "Of course you can; it'll take a bit longer than it would have at ten, but you can do it." But suddenly the non-brain part of the body starts complaining:

> No matter what you think, my neck aches, from the shoulder right up to just under my right ear, all caused by that excessively tense practicing you forced it to do last night; you forgot what your teacher said about relaxing and about lowering your right shoulder. And what about my arthritis? Look at those lumps on my left index finger, the most important finger any cello player ever had—except for the thumb. Wake up, man, you're just wasting your time on me. I'm sure to let you down, soon.

Before you know it the chant turns into advice to quit, with messages like Kenneth Grahame's warning: "Those who painfully and with bleeding feet have scaled the crags of mastery over musical instruments have yet their loss in this,—that the wild joy of strumming has become a vanished sense." [1]

---

1. When physical decline finally enforces the demand to quit, will that sacrifice produce more misery than the similar moment when I'll be forced to abandon my beloved bicycle? Of course it will, even though the skills of biking penetrated my bones and dendrites more deeply, as a kid, than the skills of celloing ever will.

For me it has not become a vanished sense. As I continue my twice-monthly lessons and my daily practice, I never think of the time as wasted. "What, never? Well, hardly ever." No matter how much my body complains, "I" will force it to continue my lessons, "down here" in the everyday world of time. And I'll continue to practice, dammit, an hour or two a day stolen from other—more obviously worthy?—pursuits.

The Delicate, Ambitious Ego

As you have long since recognized here, psychic blights have at least as much effect as physical decline. If you have an ego at all like mine, taught from birth to aim for perfection and thus to fear failures, you're headed for troubles if you aim for unattainable goals. My anxieties are often most clearly revealed in dreams.

JANUARY 31, 1994 [DREAM]—I am to do a chamber evening with a group, mainly relatives; Aunt Ann, generous-spirited fine violinist; Sam, another wonderful violinist, sure to think of me as clumsy; and Phyllis. I'm terrified. I turn out to be not just clumsy but comically so: a caricature of Victor Borge, dropping my music on the floor, unable to find my bow or mute, falling off my chair, unable to tune properly. Strings break. I try to make jokes to cover up: nobody laughs. Everything goes wrong. I'm a helpless old fart.

Why should my subconscious place all that in front of my favorite aunt—in the dream portrayed as a late teenager, in life now well beyond the age the dream portrays as mine? Obviously my cello bunglings represent my general guilt toward that Mormon family, my failure to live according to their expectations. I have let them down by becoming what I call a "peripheral Mormon," bungling my part, and spending too much of my time on hopeless irrelevancies. The least I could have done would be to choose something leading toward moral or religious progress, if not perfection or even salvation. Many of my amateur friends who were raised with religious demands have reported similar anxieties: they should be praying, not playing.

Threats to the ego are frequently more blatant than that. I have sometimes seen my fellow players, when I had felt myself lost in the joys of quartet playing, suddenly cringe slightly as I struggle with a bit of "thumbing."

Too often a favorite piano companion will stop us when I'm in the middle of a solo passage—in the slow movement of Beethoven's first trio, perhaps—and say, "Why can't you put in a little more feeling as you go from the F to the C? You know, *phrase* it? *Caress* it? Like this?" I then try it—but my embarrassment makes me play it even worse.

If she did that every time I fail to reach her standards, we'd never finish a movement. It would no doubt shock her if she discovered how the little boy in me cringes over those failures. It shocks me. So I usually try to conceal how much feeling of a non-musical kind has gone into my unimpressive phrasings: anxiety, tension, a sense of inadequacy.

At such moments I feel that I am committing at least four betrayals: of Phyllis, of the other players, of the composers who wrote this miraculous stuff and are writhing in their graves, and—most of all—of the true spirit of playing for the love of it and not just for credit.

That ego blight is clearest in my reluctance to perform for any audience. For some decades, in fact, the very presence of anyone but fellow players made me play worse. I didn't even want to be heard practicing, by anyone, musical or not.

JUNE 1, 1992 [LONDON]—An amusing ego blip this morning: There I am, practicing thumb position like a demon (should this one go into the work on "Thumb"?)—and I see the house painter just outside the window—in hearing distance! Since I can't endure the thought of his having to listen I go to the back room where he won't hear me. Then, ten minutes later, there he is outside of *that* window—and I retreat to the front room! Nobody should have to hear me when I have no other players to cover my sounds!

That kind of foolish worry does diminish a bit over the years, but it can grow even worse when the "audience" is a professional coach.

JUNE 21, 1996 [RACINE, WISCONSIN: OUR "MANHATTAN QUARTET WEEK"]—I enter the assigned playing room apprehensive; the coach, Chris Finkel, will be coming in soon, maybe even before we've warmed up.

What's my problem? Well, this time it's not *only* silly childish stage fright. We four total strangers have been assigned, long since, to work up Beethoven's tough quartet opus 127 (along with Bartók's second,

Mozart's K. 499, and Brahms's 2nd—a tough repertory for anybody) and this morning we're to be coached on its fiendishly difficult third movement, the Scherzando vivace.

This quartet, the first one Beethoven wrote after fourteen years of "quartet-silence," is actually the one that flummoxed his previously favorite professional group, led by Schuppanzigh. Beethoven knew the kind of trouble he had created for them; when he gave it to them to prepare he required each one to sign a pledge to "do his best." As Mason tells the story (1947), Linke, the worried cellist, signed his oath as "The Grand Master's accursed violoncello." "Poor Schuppanzigh," Mason reports, "protested that he could easily master the technical difficulties, but it was hard to arrive at the spirit of the work: the ensemble was faulty, because of this fact and too few rehearsals." And when they performed it in public they did it so disappointingly, with hostile audience response, that Beethoven dropped the whole group and found another one willing and able to work it up.

Unlike Linke when he signed the oath, I have long since learned, through listening, to love this quartet, and I've spent hours and hours working it up and playing it with others—often with great reward. But as I think of what happened to those professionals and what may well happen to me this morning, I am indeed an "accursed violoncellist."

As we tune up I'm tense and I can feel tensions in the other three. At the back of my mind I hear dozens of voices from the past: "Just relax; enjoy the music; let it flow." But the "front" of my mind joins my fingers in worrying about that opening cello solo that demands not just delicacy, not anything like sweet flow, but rather lively aggressive controlled *bounce*.

After a bit more shifting of chairs and squabbling about the right "A," we raise our bows, or rather I raise my bow, preparing to begin that solo "ta dum ti dum"—

And Chris walks in.

"All right," he beams, "are you ready?"

Of course we're not. The violist looks as sour as I can remember any player ever looking. The first violinist looks scared. The second violinist is smiling deferentially. How I look of course I don't know, but I feel the way any child feels when asked to recite a poem but is unable to remember which one he's expected to recite. Stage fright is not quite the word for it, because I'm not trembling. But my heart is pounding as I plunge into those dotted eighths and sixteenths.

I hit the notes close to right, in pitch and rhythm, but a bit scratchy and feeble and lumbering. Chris stops me.

"Why not bow that third note with a hook?"

"A what?" Is my confusion from poor hearing or from ignorance?

"A hook. Like this." And he sings as he moves his arm: "Ta dum ti *dum*, so you come *down* not up on the D!"

I feel my arm tightening. Though my mind knows exactly what he means—I've practiced a million "hooks" in the past—my arm has long worked on that other bowing:—down up, *down up*, not down up, *up down*. It has memorized a pattern and wants to continue following it. I feel the way you'd feel if a driving instructor suggested crossing your arms and driving with your right arm on the left side of the wheel.

As we go over the opening several times, I keep on playing the passage worse than I've played it in several months—sometimes in his pattern, sometimes falling back into the memorized one. When we move on to other passages, it sometimes feels as if I'd never seen them before. For what is perhaps twenty minutes but seems like hours, I'm miserable, full of self-contempt—combined with some irritation against Chris: Why did this wonderful coach start out by landing on my bowing?

When his allotted time is up he goes to the door, turns and says, "That was fine; I can tell that you all have been really working on it." Can he mean it?

We go on through another hour and a half, increasingly relaxed but never fully harmonious. It is clear to me that regardless of any of *their* difficulties, the whole session would have been far more rewarding if little-boy Booth could just grow up.

It comforts me, slightly, that professionals often confess to similar anxieties. Their playing changes, they say—sometimes for the better but often for the worse—when they're not alone. Here's how Julian Lloyd Webber describes his suffering in his earliest professional appearances:

My left hand fingers would start sweating profusely and I'd slide to all the wrong notes. My concentration would suddenly disappear and I'd forget all my hard-learned fingerings. I'd suddenly get cramp in my legs and have to twist around the chair like a demented snake and my right hand would start to shake, sending the bow shuddering and trembling along the strings . . . The more you try to stop the bow shaking, the more it shakes and in the end you find you've dropped the wretched thing altogether . . . I remember being very surprised when Sir Adrian Boult told me, toward the end of his active conducting days, that he could honestly say he was no longer nervous before concerts.

If pros suffer that kind of anxiety, why should I go on cursing myself for trembling a bit, when a professional coach enters the room?

Later on we'll meet some disastrous quarreling produced by amateur egos even more fragile than mine. Fortunately they are rare, partly because most amateurs know their own inadequacies and don't want to set off a bloody contest, but also because for them put-downs violate the whole point of it. In fact all of us are likely to be fairly busy not just with our own parts but relating those parts to a hearing of the music as intended, not as it's actually being played. What we hear is closer to the composer's intent than the actual sounds we produce. Our minds fill in the gaps that our fingers leave open. If the music is already familiar from records or concerts, and if none of us obtrudes false notes too aggressively, we hear *something like* the music that Brahms or Beethoven wrote.

As I write that sentence, suddenly I "hear" the opening of Brahms's viola quintet in G major, the one with an impossible cello solo. How do I hear it? Literally as we played it last Sunday night? Not at all. I hear it played perfectly—better than it ever gets.

Sometimes when everything feels totally friendly and the notes get too difficult, I may even sing a tough phrase rather than play it. Of course that spoils the ensemble sound, but though some players must feel quite unforgiving of that kind of distraction—it's worse than just going silent—they never say so. After all, it proves, surely, that I'm there for the music and not for ego-stroking, right?

If only that could be true all the time—if only I were always playing for the love of it.

The Physical Challenge of the Cello Itself

What are the technical hurdles that partially justify my childish anxieties? As I turn now to what I see as the comic/pathetic/exhilarating details of cello playing, some of you may want to get off the boat: why bother other "reachers"—a trumpeter, say, or gardener, or painter—with all that? They have plenty of problems of their own.

At the very least what follows should increase your admiration for Yo-Yo Ma next time you hear him cavorting around as if effortlessly. You might also use it to shatter the confidence of the next Artificial Intelligence nut you encounter: no machine, no robot, will ever play a string instrument successfully, even though recording machines will undoubtedly go on getting better and better at imitations of playing. Every mechanical complexity I describe is always accompanied by emotions that change the result. The cello player is not a machine.

How can I demonstrate Samuel Johnson's point that playing any string instrument is the hardest of all human learnings? (I could offer as a rival learning to write well; the goal of perfection there feels to me equally elusive, even when, draft after draft, I pretend to be a pro-amateur.) First, a polite demurrer: I'm not saying that other instruments are easy to play well. Nothing could be more miraculous than what a pianist does in covering all of the notes of a Brahms sonata, not just technically but with full emotional engagement.[2] I suspect that all instruments become equally challenging as the player inches toward "the top": the competition up there must force performers to work as hard on the flute as on a Steinway grand. No doubt an amateur trombonist could construct an almost equally daunting account of what the beginner faces.

Still, to get a passable note and even a melody out of most other instruments is easier: real music can emerge much more quickly than for any fiddler. Hit a single piano key and you can get a sound approaching that of a Brendel. Hit two keys in a row and, as any professional knows, you reveal yourself as a beginner. Even so, the sound is still tolerable: it won't cause your dog to howl. As a kid I learned that on every band instrument except the oboe and bassoon I could extract a recognizable tone after an hour or so of experimenting. But to get even a tolerable single note out of a cello is—well, I won't say the work of a lifetime, but it takes a while.

Why?

I've already mentioned that the two arms and hands of the player are in perpetual conflict. Contrasting motions from your two hands and arms are hard to learn. Here the right arm is moving left and right as it pulls the bow

---

2. If you want to read about that I suggest you might look again at Barenboim's *A Life In Music*. He's wonderful on just how much goes into genuinely musical playing. For more about how hard it all is to achieve, have a look at Frank R. Wilson's *Tone Deaf and All Thumbs* or Noah Adams's *Piano Lessons*.

back and forth, and the left arm is moving up and down along the finger board, in order to get the fingers in place for different notes. When playing the piano or clarinet both arms (or hands) move on the same plane.

The fingers of the right hand are holding the delicate stick that is asked to maintain infinitely varying pressure on the strings, locating itself at various distances from the bridge—not just for variations in loudness but for differences of tone quality. The fingers of the left hand are meanwhile executing elaborate drummings, in various arm positions and with various degrees of hand-stretching and vibrating.

A second threat is that the cello's playing surface—the length of the "neck" along which the strings are fingered—is several inches more than twice that of the violin. Except in half-sized cellos designed for kids, the distance your arm, hand, and fingers have to travel is more than twice the distance that those lucky fiddlers have to cover in moving from note to note. (Some proud fiddlers will interrupt to say that having the notes closer together makes it harder to play the violin, but don't listen to them— unless they have huge hands with thick fingers, in which case they should shift to the cello!) In playing most chamber music written before this century, a cellist's fingers cover only about 2 ⅝ octaves of notes: that's twelve to fifteen possible notes on the bottom two strings—the C and G—plus twenty-four possible notes on the higher two strings; in modern music the lower two also are dragged up into the empyrean, increasing the total, and the difficulty, but only rarely.

You can't understand the true challenge of landing on the right note over all that distance, though, until you understand that the fingerings are, unlike those on the piano or flute or trumpet, variably separated. The distance between a B-flat and a B in half position on the A string by fingers number 1 and 2, with the hand as close as it ever gets to the shoulder, has to be slightly larger than the distance between a C and a C-sharp, up about a half inch from first position (and played with fingers 2 and 3—or sometimes 1 and 2, or sometimes 3 and 4!). And so on up (down!) the string, each interval having to be slightly smaller.

An even tougher problem for one's muscles and dendrites is that the space between a D-sharp, say, and an E, when you're playing a tune in the key of E, is slightly different from the "same" space, when you're playing a tune in the key of C-sharp minor, say, even when the hand is in the same spot and the notes are in one sense "the same." This fact adds immensely to the difficulty of playing a cello really in tune, and especially to playing in thumb position, when at the top your fingers are squeezed together, turning you into a would-be violinist.

Do you understand by now the envy I feel for the amateur pianist who can move up three octaves, see just by *looking* precisely where the F-sharp is, and connect notes with fingers spaced exactly as they were down below—and never have to worry for a moment about intonation or changing the intervals slightly depending on the key signature? (If you don't happen to understand that last clause, you need to read up on the history of "the well-tempered clavichord, or clavier." It's so complicated that I dodge the full issue, even in my Glossary at the end.)

A Humble Acknowledgment to Other Instrumentalists Who May Be Angry by Now

Yes, yes, I know that you have faced many similar problems, none of which will be fully mastered by anyone starting late. We all join together as we listen to the top stars: all of them started when very young. If you can locate even one who started lessons after the age of eighteen, I hereby offer you a grand prize: I'll give you a free performance of Bach's unaccompanied suite No. 6, one that, if you win, will require of me more than a year of concentrated labor.

🦋

To get a sharper sense of how tough all this is for late-budding cellists, just imagine yourself now with your elbow bent sharply back so that your wrist is close to your chin, and you are asked to learn to toss a tiny pebble to land accurately on any one of seventy-five different unmarked spots from a half inch up to about twenty-five inches away—the distances between the spots varying all the way. You're expected to do it at the rate of—well, let's keep the tempo fairly easy here, say four notes per beat, a hundred and twenty beats per minute—that is, sixteenth notes with the tempo at 120 quarter notes per minute, two beats a second: the tempo that your high-school band marched to.

So now you're going to toss a pebble at one or another of those seventy-five possible spots 480 times a minute—with an error tolerance of what feels like about one-millionth of an inch for each landing. As pebble-tosser you have a great advantage over a cellist in that only one hand and arm are involved: the cellist has to be working both arms, both hands, all ten fingers, to say nothing of shoulders and bottom, together. And he has to be prepared to jiggle the wrist and arm when he lands, in order to produce a vibrato that makes the tone sound more friendly, even as the finger must stay firmly in place.

As I play here with the complexity of that playing, I'm probably understating the physiological complexities—about which I really know very little. The sheer physical richness entailed in all exercising of musical skills is stressed by Frank R. Wilson in his book about amateur piano playing, *Tone Deaf and All Thumbs*. Though his main point is that by practicing diligently you *can* triumph, his actual account is a bit daunting. Addressing the question of what the brain must coordinate, when it deals with the "full panoply of contractions and relaxations" that players face, he quotes an estimate made in 1873 of the number of "separate motor actions"—tosses of the pebble?—required of a pianist playing Schumann's C-Major Toccata, Opus 7. It comes out at "400 to 600 per second"—without counting what has to be done by wrist, forearm, shoulder, and trunk. That's also not counting the mind's effort to make the whole thing sound musical, and—for a cellist—the effort of the wrist and forearm to get that vibrato going a split second after the landing.[3]

I'm sure that a physiological count of a cellist's playing of a Schumann quartet would prove at least as daunting—and as insidious in tempting one to go back to an easier instrument like the clarinet. How professional strings do some of the things they do is beyond me.

What all cellists do have that the pebble-tosser would not have are richer muscular and tactile connections among the various "tosses": finger and wrist and thumb most often move to adjacent points, and the hand becomes familiar with the feel of the cello's neck and body; there are thus physical connections among the notes and between the notes and the ears. It's a lot easier to put down finger 3 close to finger 2, with the hand in the same place, than it would be to toss a pebble between the two points. But the analogy still dramatizes what I was up against when I began. Besides, as I just showed you, sometimes the "toss" is from an A or C down here to an F or G or A-flat a foot and a half away, with no physical ties whatever. Yet I'm required to produce a pitch that will be rejected by all hearers, even the least fussy, if it is as much as ¼ of an inch off.

Remember: all this time my right arm is trying to learn . . .

3. I have a violist friend who is now, in his sixties, trying to develop the vibrato "that I never much bothered about before." He's taking lessons on it. But because he didn't develop that quiver as a kid—he took up the viola in college—it's no surprise that he finds it to be "fiendishly difficult."

Enough! That's surely more than enough to demonstrate that it's all impossible. That is why one is expected to practice each precise leap thousands of times, sometimes landing first on the thumb, sometimes doing a little quick test with the third finger on the harmonic A or E and sliding up or down a bit before landing: *practice practice practice*—until your muscles say to themselves, when they see an E-flat approaching, "Oh, I know how to get to Carnegie Hall: it's right there." They also must learn how to follow Rostropovich and do an almost inaudible bit of sliding, after a slightly false landing, so that listeners get the illusion that the player has done it right. That takes more hours of practice: the adjustment should not be heard.

If you think I'm exaggerating, listen to this bit of testimony from Daniel Barenboim, who as a pianist ought surely to be trusted on how hard it is to play a cello:

Casals . . . was probably the first cellist who had an almost fanatical need to play well in tune. Until Casals came along I think people accepted the fact that the cello was such an impossibly difficult instrument that, when the music went in its higher register, it was the convention that cellists played out of tune.

Is it any wonder that I often feel like Carter Mackley, the rock climber who recently wrote like this about a moment of crisis?

"What am I doing here?" I muttered to myself in disgust. I was six hundred feet up Cannon Cliff in New Hampshire on the popular rock-climbing route, Moby Grape. We had two hundred feet to go, had been rained on twice, and it was starting to get late. This [climbing] had lost its appeal. And familiar feelings of guilt at engaging in risky recreation were resurfacing.

The grand difference between his doubts and mine is that as he writes he has survived the risk, he has reached the top, in triumph. The mountain I am climbing, in total contrast, has no top; it offers only other kinds of reward en route, including those rest camps when I can settle into slow notes as the others caper above me. What I always face is the strong likelihood that I'll never even get beyond the base camp.

The Age-Old Mind-Body Problem

When I was about eighteen, my mother assigned me the job of removing the old, dark varnish from our dining-room furniture so that it could be bleached and revarnished. Working away in the basement, day after day in the hot summer, scraping claw foot after claw foot, I felt increasing resentment at the demandingly delicate but repetitive task. One day, when Mother came downstairs to see how I was doing, I uttered what seems to me now one of the most absurdly arrogant lines ever committed by an adolescent.

"Mother, a man who can read and understand Plato should not be spending his time at chores like this." I can't remember whether she laughed or cried, but she did not excuse me from my ungentlemanly task.

I didn't know it at the time, but I was joining a long tradition of writers who considered mastery of manual techniques, or indeed physical tasks of any kind except sports and fighting, as beneath the elevated life of any true gentleman. Plutarch in several of his Lives echoes Aristotle by showing contempt for any aristocrat who would bother about learning to play the flute: it is an illiberal art required and enjoyed by liberal listeners as they pursue a purer leisure. Montaigne reports on Plutarch's reports—and on other similar scoffing at performers:

> [T]o appear so excellent in these less necessary qualities is to testify that one has misspent one's leisure and study, which should have been employed in more necessary and useful things. So that King Philip of Macedon, after hearing the great Alexander, his son, sing at a feast in an attempt to vie with the best musicians, said to him: "Aren't you ashamed to sing so well?" . . .
>
> A king should be able to reply as Iphicrates replied to the orator who was assailing him in his invective with these questions: "Well, what are you, to play so brave? Are you a man-at-arms? Are you an archer? Are you a pikesman?" "I am none of these, but I am the man who knows how to command them all."
>
> And Antisthenes took it as evidence of the little worth of Ismenias that he was praised for being an excellent flute player.

Montaigne dwells on this point as part of his plea that critics should judge him for his substance, his good sense, rather than for his polished style: to polish style is like practicing the flute—a petty art slightly beneath any true gentleman. He doesn't quite state, though he surely implies, that even to write his essays at all, let alone to polish them, is a labor a bit like learning thumb position: a true gentleman should have his mind on higher things.

Continuing with my thumb-position problem as a metaphor for the whole issue of bodily mastery and bodily threat, I'm tempted here to digress into the long tradition of relating bodily limits and mutilation to higher achievements. In the *Mahabharata*, for example, a master archer, Ekalavya, aspiring to discipleship with the guru Drona, "the master of human and celestial arms," agrees to demonstrate his sincerity by cutting off his own thumb and thus destroying his archery: spirit triumphs over mere bodily skill.[4]

There have indeed been times when I have wished that someone could have cut off my thumb, in one way or another, and thus forced me into absolutely unmitigated devotion to listening—a subject I return to in chapter 8. How impressive would be my mastery of the entire repertory by now! My stronger temptation goes in the other direction, downgrading those "gentlemen and ladies," "pure" listeners who join the hoity-toity classicists and scoff at those of us who grovel in such humiliating tasks.

To move in either direction would be to join that long and lamentable tradition of sharply separating mind and body and then putting one or the other down. The "soul" tradition downgraded not only musical performance; it deflected science from experimenting to unproductive reliance on "pure" theory. As Carl Sagan laments, in his *Cosmos*, manual experiment, for many ancients, was beneath the true thinker. As a result, we waited longer than we needed to for the explosion of laboratory-based discoveries that changed our world.

❧

None of this comes close to answering the big question: What sense can be made of my sitting down and requiring my aching shoulder and arthritic

---

4. For the *Mahabharata* example I'm indebted to Ajay Bhatt.

Montaigne does manage to devote one whole page to a sympathetic account of thumb mistreatment. In an essay "Of Thumbs," he recalls that "the thumbs are the master fingers of the hand," that "the Romans exempted from war those who were wounded in the thumb," that someone—he can't remember who—"having won a naval battle, had the thumbs of his vanquished enemies cut off," so they couldn't pull an oar, and that "in Lacedaemon the schoolmaster chastised children by biting their thumbs" (2.26, pp. 522–23). His account, and a few others I've run into, almost tempt me into narrowing down my topic again to thumb position, and doing a whole history of the kinds of thumb abuse I have inflicted on mine.

right thumb—the one I haven't even mentioned so far—to saw away for as long as I did last night, sweating in the summer heat, the cello a bit resistant in the excessive humidity? Is the fact that I was "out of this world"—that I actually lost track of time and thought as I quit that it was only nine o'clock when it was actually ten—is that sufficient justification for playing beneath the level of all those youngsters? Am I really leaving the quotidian world, escaping time more effectively, when we put it all together, than I would be if I had been listening to the Amadeus playing the same stuff well? In chapter 8, I address that question by celebrating what playing has done for my listening.

❧

Has this chapter of laboring pains led you to think that I dwell day by day more on pains than I do on the glorious births? For me, the comedy of struggle and failure is not just part of the fun but an essential element in all amateuring—precisely what distinguishes it from Yeltsin's fishing in a lake that his staff has stocked with 10,000 fish.

Yeats's way of relating dancing and laboring dramatizes the ambiguities we face:

Labour is blossoming or dancing where
The body is not bruised to pleasure soul,
Nor beauty born out of its own despair,
Nor blear-eyed wisdom out of midnight oil.

Is he telling me not to labor on the cello-reach, producing despair by bruising my body to please my soul? Or is he celebrating the very kind of labor that I'm praising?

Though sometimes the body does feel a bit bruised in the service of my love, the fact is that here in 1998, still *getting better all the time,* even the practicing is itself mainly a kind of dancing. Phyllis calls, "It's time to get ready to leave for dinner at the Browns'; you'll have to hurry," and I can't believe it. After all, I was, for the first time ever, getting that opening solo of the Shostakovich sonata into something like the shape, the style, the *feeling* it calls for—into the way a cello should sound. I feel like saying, "Let's call and cancel—we could stay here and play duets . . . "

So you see: the laboring, even when it's in solitude, has rewards that almost match the joys of joining other lovers. And when it yields the joining, the spirit of amateuring can look the philosophical skeptic in the eye and say, "Even if life provided nothing more than this, even if everything else were mere suffering and want and loss, to live even one of these timeless moments is to have been given a priceless gift."

No bubble is so iridescent or floats longer than that blown by the successful teacher. SIR WILLIAM OSLER

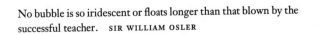

For most people, piano lessons were unpleasant experiences—sitting next to a stranger. DAVID SUDNOW, AS REPORTED BY NOAH ADAMS

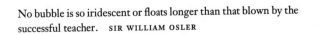

No nation can ever prosper if it does not honor its teachers. PLATO

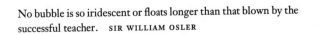

To be a teacher is quite obviously *not* a noble thing. . . . But it is at least one good way to combat the horrors. ANONYMOUS

C h a p t e r   F i v e

Teaching the Love

SINCE ONE OF the prime purposes of this book is to multiply amateurs in coming generations, we must think about how teachers enrich or destroy "the love of it." Beginners, even mature beginners, usually fail to recognize a bad teacher until they've experienced a good one. I labored for some decades with mostly poor teachers, never even suspecting how poor they were until I finally landed with a good one. Several of the early ones could easily have destroyed any young beginner, or even an older novice not as committed as I was.

Though they did sometimes dampen my enthusiasm, I possessed two shields against their arrows: my passion for music and Phyllis's persistent support. It was not just that she tolerated the screeches I hurled through our rooms. What really saved me was her invitation to start playing with her some of the easier chamber music, often labeled *Hausmusik*. Our shelves were soon full of violin/cello duets (including arrangements editors had stolen from Telemann or Vivaldi or Bach). We also played a lot of faked duets of our own: the violin and cello parts of early Haydn and Mozart quartets. Phyllis thus became my best teacher, and carried me on to our first encounter with other amateurs who were willing to endure a rank beginner. Thanks to them I was from the beginning engaged with music, not just with technique. If only all teachers, in whatever practice, in school or out, would work to provide something like that for their beginners!

Obviously teachers, like everybody else, can be classified in many different ways besides the musical versus the mere drillers: the knowing vs. the ignorant, the tolerant vs. the cruel, the attentive vs. the distracted, the up-to-date vs. the old-fashioned (for most cellists this means roughly pre-Casals vs. post-Casals), the suitable-for-beginners vs. the suitable-for-advanced, even the drunks vs. the sober. Oh, yes, I had one who would arrive at my house drunk, though not quite staggering; after I'd play a bit, hoping to have him recommend a better fingering or bowing, he'd mumble, "Well, just do it the easy way." I endured him for three lessons.

Whatever your choice as amateur, you shouldn't have too much trouble translating into your domain a rule like "Don't study with a drunkard."

Drills and Thrills

To me the most important distinction has been between the dry drillers and the loving polishers. Herr Wetzels had me spend my first weeks on bowing exercises, with never a melody heard or played. It was decades before I fell under the care of Karl Fruh, a teacher whose lessons implied that we should be having as much fun together as I had playing with friends. I'll never understand why the five between those two extremes failed to insist that I keep my ears and mind on the sound of the music *as music*, from tuning to practice to performance.

Daniel Barenboim, in his enviable account of how he was taught as a child, dwells on how learning technique can itself be musical.

> I studied with my father till I was about seventeen. . . .
>
> For me, learning to play the piano was as natural as learning to walk. My father had an obsession about wanting things to be natural. I was brought up on the fundamental principle that there is no division between musical and technical problems. This was an integral part of his philosophy. I was never made to practice scales or arpeggios. . . [only] the pieces themselves. A principle that was hammered into me early, and which I still adhere to, is never to play any note mechanically. My father's teaching was based on the belief that there are enough scales in Mozart's concertos.

Such advice would have infuriated some of my teachers. But those of you readers who started on an instrument while young, were pushed by loving parents, and then quit after being bored silly by enforced practice, will know why they'd be wrong. You probably met a teacher like Wetzels, étude-bound. My assigned exercise books by now make a pile at least a foot high, most of them largely unused: *Tägliche Übungen, Exercises Journalières, Etüden,* "High Schools" of Cello Playing. Would I be a better player if I'd used them more systematically? Possibly. But was their use sometimes destructive? Absolutely.

It's true that many of the exercises can be made to produce music, if taught and embraced lovingly. It's also true that even the worst drillers often reveal outside the lesson room that they love serious music. Shortly before his death, Wetzels played his part beautifully in a performance of the Schubert two-cello C major: he must have loved it. But that love never entered our lesson room. The point is that too many teachers too much of the time provide too few hints of what it's all about.

I've heard many a mature amateur complain about how years of joy were lost because of the wrong start.

JULY 28, 1994—Last night we played for the first time with Ben and Harry and began with the Haydn Opus 20, #5 (F minor). It went wonderfully.
WB: You know, Ben, you really played that whole quartet so . . . well, so *musically.* You really *sang* it, and made us want to sing it with you.
BEN: Oh, how I love to hear you say that! I often feel angry about my early teachers who stressed nothing but technical exercises; they were leading me, they hoped, to the conservatory, but they finally drove me away from playing anything at all, for decades. None of them ever said a word about the music *as music*—there was nothing about *doing it musically.* Oh, maybe they would say something like "play it with more feeling," but I never had any sense of what they meant. They never played along with me and never had me play with others.
PHYLLIS (feeling good because of how well she's just played the viola part, after not touching the viola for months): One of my early teachers used to say something like that. "Play it with more soul." I hadn't a clue about what "soul" might be, and I can't remember his making any effort to explain what he had in mind.
BEN: Right! Teachers ought to think about and work on how to get kids to *feel* the point of it. Now that I *do* see the point of it—well, it's just made all the difference, I mean everything is now more and more exciting. As you know, I'm playing quartets at least once a week, no matter how hard it is to find a group—you see why I called the three of you tonight, because my regular group couldn't come . . .

And then the rest of us plunge in with anecdotes about how teachers who only "worry about the notes" can spoil the "music," and with some footnotes on why *some* drill is required.

In all fairness to harried teachers, I should add that many music pupils, children and adults, suffer psychological pressures that may quash even the most sensitive efforts to instill love. Sometimes the destroyer is an ambitious parent; if the child were to ask the question I dwell on here, "Why am I doing this?" the answer could only be, " 'Cause Mom makes me."

Often the answer from the child's unconscious would be a bit like the one discovered by Mark Salzman in his late teens, after years of laboring on the cello. In *Lost in Place*, Salzman describes his younger self as undersized, unhonored by the world, and taking up the cello in the hope of impressing his parents. He had worked at it slavishly, though at intervals, through childhood into late adolescence. Then, just before lugging his cello to Yale, where he had been promised a music scholarship, feeling anxious about getting to the top, he asked his teacher about his chances. The teacher replied in the best possible way: "Well, you have gotten better, but let's face it, there's a lot of people out there who are still a lot better than you are. But whether or not you can make a career out of it isn't everything, Mark. The main thing is, you can get pleasure from it for the rest of your life." Mark was shattered: "Pleasure? I thought. Who said anything about *pleasure?* If I wanted pleasure, I would have done something *fun*, for God's sake, not play the cello."

Then he happened to hear Yo-Yo Ma at a concert, playing joyfully with a skill totally beyond Mark's reach. More shattering. He realized that in all his years of practice and orchestra playing, he had felt no love whatever for either the cello or classical music:

> Beginning with wanting to please my parents, continuing with wanting to please my parents . . . for me music was a means of acquiring an identity. . . . If I worked hard . . . it would be like studying for a contractor's license; eventually I'd pass the test, be allowed to work and make money, and people would have to take me seriously. It honestly had not occurred to me to worry that I never was turned on by the music itself.

Love vs. Money

Often the love-killing springs not so much from the assignment of boring or threatening exercises as from the teacher's projected inner feelings about

the very act of teaching. Of course no pupil, however mature, can make secure inferences about where the teacher's soul is at the moment. But even
the least attentive kid is likely to notice when the love of music leaves the
room. Whether pupils are seven or seventy, they breathe the air in the
room. And they quickly decide, usually unconsciously: "This is the kind of
person I'd like to become," or "God save me from ever behaving like this."

One amateur violinist we play with, who teaches violin several hours each
week, tells us that she usually comes away from her lessons exhilarated by
how well the pupils are doing. "Because my husband's income is higher now,
I could just quit giving lessons—but I really don't want to." Looking into
her eyes, remembering how beautifully she plays, I see the kind of teacher
everyone should pray for.

The truth is, though, that it's hard for any instrument teacher to be a
pro-amateur in the full loving sense, at least during the hour she spends
with somebody like me. Even if she loves teaching and wants to build love
for the music, she can't love much of what she hears coming from my efforts:
it just isn't musically blissful. Even when I'm at my best during the lesson,
my teacher must hear mainly the flaws—flaws according to her standards
and usually according to mine as well. No doubt that's why so many teachers, even the loving ones, dwell so long on drilling: to hear all those wrong
notes is painful, so let's get them out of the way first and worry about the
musicality later.

Is a given teacher doing it for the love of music and the teaching of it?
It's always hard to tell. A few of my teachers have taught, like my present
one, as if even winning a fortune would not stop their teaching; more of
them made it painfully clear that they were simply eking out a living. When
Signora X spent several minutes complaining because I'd bought my cello
without using her as paid go-between, I felt that music had long since left
the room. But when Kim Scholes moved over to the piano, began to play
the piano part of the cello sonata I had just dragged out, and shouted, "Come
on, *dance it with me!*" he was a passionately engaged teacher.

❦

The last thing I would want to suggest is that there is something inherently
immoral in charging for lessons or making a living from them. Paying a
teacher tells us nothing in itself about whether she teaches for the love of it;
it certainly tells us little about whether the teaching is any good or whether
the teacher would like to produce genuine amateurs and pro-amateurs. Was

Beethoven to be condemned for selling daily piano lessons, for twenty florins a month, as Leon Botstein reports? Indeed we probably wouldn't have the Razumovsky quartets if the count had not paid Beethoven a large commission for them. Should the students in my literature courses mistrust me because they know I am being paid?

As I write here about such matters, I live on retirement income, freed by that income to write for the love of it, to play for the love of it. I'm even able to resist (except for about once a week) wondering whether this book will make any money. Indeed, since I have in the remote past known what it feels like to long for and even scrounge for a bit of cash, and since I have in fact done some things for cash that I would never have done for love, I feel great sympathy for those teachers who are forced, week after week, year after year, to go through roughly the same scales and études with student after student, just for the fee that is always less than a doctor or lawyer or psychoanalyst would charge.

If I had an unlimited fortune, I would set up a fund to free all of the good teachers to teach only when and whom they wanted to teach. I've sometimes even said that if I had the power to re-create the world, I'd build in the provision that nobody would have to do any hated work: as Rabelais puts it in the motto to his utopian monastery: *Fay ce que vouldras*—"Do what you wanna do." A minor trouble with that wish is that it might very well turn away all teachers of amateurs like me. A major problem is that it might invite back into our room those who seek the kind of sadistic fun proclaimed by the Marquis de Sade and Georges Bataille.

❧

Having thus demonstrated so decisively that I am incapable of cheap moralizing or elitist sniping, I am now forced, by the very nature of amateuring, into laying down an elaborate classification of "paid-for-work" people, whether lawyers or car mechanics or teachers (including me during more than four decades of paid-for teaching). Moving outward from music to all teaching, consider five levels of being paid for work.

1. *Paid for doing something that not just your culture but you yourself consider dishonorable, harmful, unjust, beneath contempt:* preparing tobacco ads to appeal to children; defending a corporation you know has deliberately harmed clients. No cello teacher I have known or can imagine would fit this one: the pay would never be high enough.

2. *Paid for doing something you detest or think trivial, or beneath you, even though your culture considers it necessary or even honorable:* sewer cleaners, toll-road collectors, etc. Obviously some teachers would fit here—those having to teach skills they themselves detest.

3. *Paid for doing something that your culture requires and pays for, but that you would rather avoid because, though you respect it, you don't enjoy it.* On rare occasions I myself have fallen under this one: forced to work up a grammar lesson as an "English teacher," say, when I'd rather be working up Plato or George Eliot or Wallace Stevens. About half of my teachers, in all subjects including music, seemed at least much of the time to belong here. After all, as I've said, teaching music students, and especially string players, is for most teachers much of the time sheer drudgery. I'm only guessing, but it's been pretty clear as I've labored under fifteen private teachers on three instruments and one on voice. How could they resist, most of them, looking longingly at the careers of better players and better teachers who were making more money for fewer hours?

4. *Paid for doing something you would want to do even if not paid.* All teachers with a vocation fit here, as do social service workers (some of them); doctors (some of them); lawyers (only one-fourth of them, according to a recent *New York Times* study). It's not hard to think of hundreds of examples—but only four of my cello teachers have seemed unequivocally in this category.

5. *Paid for doing something you would do even if it cost you far more than you are paid.* Here we are thinking of a rare breed that may not even exist: heroes and saints who would not quit teaching if offered the world. "If I offer to give you twice your present income to stop teaching, will you stop?" "Of course not—how silly of you."

No music teacher is ever faced with such a clearly defined choice. For too many teachers the choice is infinitely simpler: teach or starve. For some of my relatives the choice was between giving lessons or losing the cash, sometimes called "egg-money," that their families needed to live decently. Some musical friends of mine say that giving lessons (worn-out after coming home from other full-time jobs) was what made college education possible for their children.

❧

Most pertinent here, obviously, are those who teach, regardless of pay, as if the real pay were the teaching itself. Some of the professionals who have coached us would join them. By all accounts, Yo-Yo Ma could never be bought out of playing, or teaching others to play better. Wherever he goes he volunteers to conduct master classes, and the descriptions I've seen of those classes make him sound almost unbelievably committed to teaching. After one long session teaching talented inner-city high-school students, he was reported as saying, "This, I hope, becomes a passion for these people— becomes an inner life. When you can dig down and find something stirring inside you that you never knew was there, you've just identified a little bit of you. The two [students he had just coached], they have that inner life." And the two high-schoolers who had been coached said, "We'll never be the same."

My "heroic four" teachers have often visibly joined level 4, obviously enjoying teaching for the sake of teaching. One actually phoned me once to offer a technical suggestion that she'd overlooked during the lesson. With that call she surely moved toward the saintly circle.

Though we're not constructing a modern Inferno here, we sink pretty far down the stairs when we come to Sally Climber, professional cellist, hoping to become a member of a major symphony. She spent much of my paid-for hour practicing études herself. That was not her way of describing it, not at all: she was "demonstrating how to play the études." She had me bring a tape recorder, and she would record her interpretation, for perhaps half or two-thirds of the hour, and I was then to take the tape home and imitate what I heard. She never mentioned what I later learned: that I could have bought much better recordings of those same études—by Janos Starker for example.

What shocks me now is that I didn't quit after the first time she used this ploy. I hung on for several months, while she played away, paying little attention to my real problems. It was sheer exploitation by a woman who would have much preferred to do her practicing without my bothersome presence.

It remains true that even such an exploiter touches on the amateur kingdom at the moment she takes on an unpromising amateur. When teaching gifted youngsters a teacher may hope for some future reward in the form of credit in program notes: "Studied early with X." But teaching those without stellar potential could never raise their reputations even half a notch. Such teaching, even at its worst, consciously or unconsciously moves at least slightly toward the world of music for the sake of music.

How Loving Teachers Do It

One of my honored four, Juliet Merz, I located in London with the help of Kim Scholes. (Did you know that to get my cello to London—to fly it *any-where*—I must pay full airfare for it?) Arriving in late August, I was soon writing like this about life with the cello:

SEPTEMBER 11, 1992—Finally settled in London for ten months, aware that my technique has been rapidly deteriorating during the summer, with no teacher cracking the whip or wincing at my wincing. Traveled one hour on the crowded Tube for my first lesson with Juliet Merz; it ain't easy lugging a cello at rush hour. Feel nervous about what she'll think of my playing. So what do I choose to play for her? Do I choose something I can play decently? Not on your life. I choose one of the most difficult string quartets in the literature—Beethoven's A minor, Opus 132, a work that even professional cellists approach with fear and trembling—the one with that wonderful fourth movement opening [which I mentioned in my letter from Paris to Phyllis on page 32.] To me it is in the running for title of Greatest Piece of Music Ever Written, but it is definitely not the one to take to a new teacher to show what you can do.

What was I doing to my soul when I decided to ask for her help on that last page, where the cello soars up and up into a difficult thumb passage: a rapid, wonderfully intense melody to be played mainly in unison with the first violin. At the moment I can't think of any passage composed before—well, let's say before about Bartók—more difficult to play *musically*.

My reason for bringing that to an unknown teacher for help is that we'll be playing that quartet with two new acquaintances here next Monday, and maybe, just maybe, she can help me hold my own through that thrilling climax.

Fortunately she and I don't get to that climax for a long while. My nervous, hurried playing of a couple of the easier pages gives her enough faults to work on to last an hour—or rather a year. She hits upon exactly what every good teacher has nagged me about: bowing as the key to making it sound musical. But my mind is, as too often, more on thumb position. After an hour of help on bowing, I feel I have to get my money's worth [1] by receiving some hints about how to play that thumb stuff.

---

1. 1998: Could that young seventy-one-year-old have guessed then how that phrase would sound, appearing in this section of this chapter?

And what does she do, in her effort to show me how to play that passage? Does she settle in on my left hand, my fingering, my way of using my thumb? Not at all. She says, "You know, when you hit a difficult spot like that you seem to tense and scrunch up a bit, like this?" And she makes herself look positively ugly.

"What you've got to do is feel as if you are on top of the job—just settle your bottom into the chair, relax your legs and your hold on the cello, sit back and let yourself sing *the music of it.*"

I naturally remember that as precisely the advice Karl Fruh and Kim Scholes had given about *all* of my playing. Scholes's metaphor was "Dance it!"—in effect the same advice as "Sing it!" Or almost the same. Thus they spot the same problem and give the same advice: stop tensing up about thumb position and start playing *music.* Start playing as a *lover,* not a competitor, fearer, show-off, ego-ridden idiot.

❧

My journal, unlike this chapter, is these days free of complaints about teachers, as I work with my new teacher, Judy Stone. In fact I'm beginning to wonder whether the faults have all been mine. As you saw in chapter 4, too often the competitive side of me infiltrates the amateur world, as if to say, "What do I have to do to get my 'A,' teacher? I'll do anything you ask." Sometimes when I play badly at a lesson I burst out with something like, "Oh, I'm so embarrassed about that. I really did it much much better yesterday." Instead of dancing it or singing it I've just tensed my jaw and made what Merz called a bloody mess of it. Such behavior provides the mechanistic teachers like Wetzels with their golden opportunity for corrupting: the relation of teacher and learner turns into a *folie à deux.*

Some Complications about "Love"

To think about my teachers as falling into various levels of amateur-love and selling out raises many questions that I touched on in the Overture and that will never be answered fully. The "selfless love" of my top category— is that always a good thing? Are not many of the world's worst disasters caused by "free spirits" who love without limit? Don't terrorists often act with little thought about personal gain or loss? What about "selfless" murders of doctors by "amateurs of abortion ban"? As I praise only teachers who teach because they love teaching am I not idealizing the world? Could any world of any kind allow us all at every stage of life to do what we most long to do, provided we don't do it for personal gain? Would it be good for the world if nobody had to do, unlovingly, what other people want or need? Shouldn't every amateur like me be forced to work for a full day at least once a year as a manual laborer in subzero or 100-degree weather? If any reader has satisfactory answers to such questions, please let me know.

How Amateur Companions Teach

Official teachers are not our only teachers. As you have detected long since, to me the least blessed amateurs are those who have no companions to play with and thus be taught by. In music, these are more often pianists than string players. What can save the pianists is the piano literature itself—they get to hear rich harmonies and counterpoints as they play alone. Sad to say, we've met a surprising number of string players who out of fear or laziness actually prefer to play or practice by themselves. They miss the best teaching of all—not the kind you pay for but the kind that fellow players give. There is a buzzing, blooming community of players all over the world, most of them free with their advice (some of them a bit threateningly). From this point of view, those conversational gambits with which I opened this book take on a new light.

—"Pianissimo!" one player will shout, when I have overlooked the *ppp* mark. "In Beethoven the contrasts are *everything*."
—"I think we should do that section over again, a bit slower," another will say; "it felt clunky."
—"When I was studying at the conservatory, we were taught to do that passage like this: . . . " and then follows a useful demonstration.
—"Well, you know I did my MA thesis on the Debussy"—this from Joe Bein, a lifetime pro-amateur viola teacher—"and we definitely must do that movement again and pay attention to . . . " with wonderful suggestions.

Once in a while such efforts to teach fall into quarreling, and the music is temporarily destroyed. More often we don't exactly quarrel but politely exchange views, attempting to teach one another, and then we come to a compromise. Sometimes the disagreements don't get expressed at all except in divergent interpretations: as if to say, "You play the solo your way, and when it's my turn I'll play it mine." (Nobody has ever openly *said* anything like that in my hearing.) The implicit advice given by their playing is often more helpful than the explicit criticism.

FEBRUARY 18, 1994—Last night David, with whom we play frequently, brought along a graduate student, Michael, to play second fiddle. He turned out to be unusually steady, not just competent but an experienced fiddler who was feeling with the music in ways that often don't occur in a first meeting, especially with technically proficient youngsters.

He kept claiming that he was *not* experienced in chamber music. I never know how to interpret such claims. Was he lying when he said that he had never played any of our three selections before? How could he have played them so well if he had never played them before?

We began with the Haydn "Kaiser," Opus 76 #3, the one with the "Deutschland über alles" theme for the second movement. David chose it; I felt mildly opposed. We've had some rather dreary times playing that theme-and-variations with various groups, and my Nazi associations with it don't go away. In fact after a boring session decades ago, I penciled at the top of my part: "Don't play again until at least 1992!" (I did not record the names of those who had helped me destroy it.)

But tonight, two years after my *dead*line, the first movement went surprisingly well. When the "Deutschland" loomed, somehow it all jelled and swelled—mainly I think because of what happened in the first variation. The second violin takes over the theme while Phyllis on first takes off into elaborate obligato. The viola and cello are silent for all twenty measures: just the kind of "playing" by me that I love when the others do their duty.

Michael rose to the occasion. He made the theme sound not like a Nazi hymn but like a *hymn*, almost as fine as Phyllis had played it in the first statement, and that lifted Phyllis to a level that she'd never reached on that obligato before: she soared.

Then I had my turn with the simple melody, and I found myself playing it almost as well as Michael and Phyllis had done—certainly *better than ever before*. Then David had his turn on the viola, and *he* played better than ever. And as Haydn worked his wondrous ways with slight but marvelous changes on throughout the movement, we all felt more and more moved: fully together.

At the end, David—the sixty-year-old world-famous Shakespearean —suddenly burst into sobs. We waited as he calmed down. Michael said nothing. I tried to comfort David a bit, with some chat about my many weepings over chamber music. He then pulled himself together, apologized unnecessarily, and on we went, through the next two movements, honoring Haydn all the way.

For me that is a clear example of how players can serve as the best of teachers. The movement that I had found boring had been demonstrated by young Michael as thrilling. That's what the chamber music community has been doing for us all along. If I'd depended only on my paid-for teachers, I'd have played mostly sonatas, perhaps even concertos, the Bach unaccompanied suites—all wonderful stuff but not the chamber music I most adore. Those others, the amateur teachers, our playing companions, have stretched us outward into the literature, and they have been our main instructors in how to make the works glow.

At our best we teach one another in songs without words. Though the Everest of faultless performance will never be reached, we can usually count on support for a long way up the slope. Settling for base camp three, say, we know that we wouldn't have made it beyond camp two if we had been climbing alone.

🎜

Amateuring flowers when a new teacher passes all your tests, joining the previous stars. Here's my journal account of my first lesson with my present teacher, with whom I've now been working four years. "Where will she fit in my categories," I was asking before we met, "and where will I fit in hers?"

FEBRUARY 12, 1994—First lesson today with Judy Stone, recommended by Kim Scholes. As the week draws towards this encounter, I grow more and more anxious. What will this woman—whom I've never met— think of having taken on someone who plays the way I play?

Phyllis, noticing my increasing tension, says, "Don't you see: *she's* the one who ought to be anxious, not you." That helps a little, but I keep imaging—as the current word goes—failure: a low grade.

Come Saturday morning I manage, hurrying a little, anxiety mounting, to get to her studio in the Loop on time.

After we shake hands I tune up and she listens to me play the Brahms for a bit, walking about in front of me, studying the angle of my bow, the position of my hands.

"I see that you studied with Karl Fruh?"

"How can you tell that?"

"Well, your positions are *his* positions, and those are *his* fingerings in the Brahms; he was my teacher, you know."

I am surprised at how quickly I feel relaxed and all of her advice makes sense; I've found a good teacher again. Driving home, I feel eager to get to my daily practicing.

That's the best possible sign: if practicing feels like the thing you want to do, you've found a good teacher.

Sir Fredericke: "It were no meete matter, but an ill sight to see a man of any estimation being old, hore-headed and toothlesse, full of wrinkles, with a lute in his armes playing upon it, and singing in the middest of a company of women, although he coulde doe it reasonably well."

Then answered the Lord Julian: "Doe not barre poore olde men from this pleasure, Sir Fredericke, for in my time I have knowne men of yeares have very perfect voices and most nimble fingers for instruments, much more than some yong men." CASTIGLIONE, *The Book of the Courtier*

❦

Artur Rubenstein claimed that he did not really begin to play as he wanted until he was nearly eighty. It's not that hard to keep the chops in shape. FRANK WILSON

❦

How, Monsieur, you care not for music? You do not play the clavecin? I am sorry for you! You are indeed condemning your-self to a dull old age! NICOLAS FOUQUET, TO A MEMBER OF LOUIS XIV'S COURT

❦

It is not easy for those exhausted with age . . . to sing the strained harmonies [of the Dorian mode], but nature suggests the relaxed ones instead for persons of such an age. ARISTOTLE, *Poetics*

Chapter Six

Meditations of an Aging Pupil

SORTING THROUGH my many journal entries—some headed "cello-reach," some "cello," some "amachoice," some "AM" and some "Thumb"—I find more and more of them dwelling on the aging effect I touched on at the beginning of chapter 4. It's true that most of what I experience when playing is not much different from what it would be for any younger amateur who starts late. But hardly a day goes by without my noticing, once again, that aging does make a difference.

When we arrived in London in the fall of 1992, carrying that heavy cello, itself a full-cost passenger "carrying" its own hand luggage, including Phyllis's violin, I was having so much trouble with my left foot's fallen arch that I had to call for a wheelchair. I could not write about that in the unflaggingly cheerful tone exhibited by Lee Lockhart, in his book *With a Cello on My Back*. You can see in the following entry that my mind was even more troubled than my foot.

OCTOBER 20, 1992—Learning to "thumb" and trying to write about it is just one version of the whole problem of *taking on the world* when you know that some sort of decline is afoot. *Afoot* is the right word these days; my left foot—title of a recent fine movie—is giving me lots of trouble. Will it get worse, so that I will not be able to take any walks on Hampstead Heath? Am I moving toward a time when I not only can't run and can't carry a cello but can't walk properly, can't even beat time as I play, because of foot pain?

So I imagine again a two-line graph, one tracing my still rising ability on the cello, the other my obviously falling . . .

—*eyesight:* Unless I have a stand light, I have trouble seeing the notes, even now with my new "cello glasses";

—*hearing:* Oh, how threatening, the likelihood of undetected faulty intonation, as the higher frequencies fade away!;

—*general physical endurance, whether running, walking, or sitting:* John Holt, discussing his practice sessions on the cello, talks of "four to five hours a day"; I could no more practice four hours a day than garden for four hours;

—*patience:* I don't even have to talk about that: you can tell, just by the way I write about it, that I'm the impatient type, growing more impatient by the decade;

—*attention span/memory:* I wonder why it is that whenever I see a news account about Alzheimer's, I actually read it, and then forget what it said.

Over the six years since then, the body graph has gone on falling, and will no doubt soon smash the rising ability graph. Yet here I am, absolutely convinced that I played the cello solos and "turns" last night, in Mozart's C-major quintet, *far better than ever before.* Wouldn't it be wise just to quit while I'm still winning, sort of?

My friend Rick, age seventy-one, said the other day, "I decided about five years ago that there was no point, at sixty-six, in trying to improve any of my four languages. In fact I have a feeling that nothing I have ever been any good at will ever be any better." Once in awhile, but not often, I share his mood.

Memory decline especially spreads its influence broadly. Probably no group of young players could have the experience Phyllis and I had recently.

MAY 4, 1998—We are scheduled, according to Phyllis's calendar, to play the Schubert cello quintet this coming Sunday, a favorite, and perhaps one of the Boccherinis, with Mary and Zeke and two of their friends. So she and I practice our parts together on the wonderful Schubert (me on second cello, as usual), and even run through the famous Boccherini, with me for the first time ever doing pretty well on the colorful solo of the fourth movement. But since the Boccherini is really a bit boring I decide to go to our university library and see if there are other two-cello quintets—I've been told that there is at least a Glazunov. Lo and behold, there's a foot-high stack of them! I check them out and carry them home on my bicycle. She and I then try out bits of each of them, and find that they're either boring (the Borodin) or too difficult (the Milhaud). (Such "try-outs" are in themselves absurdly unfair to the composers, but that's another point.)

Then late Saturday we phone the Jacksons about time of arrival, but Mary begins by saying, "We're looking forward to those sextets."

"Sextets?"

So it's the Brahms *sextets*; we've spent hours working up the quintets! We quickly hang up, go to our music stands, and work through each of the not-easy sextets, Phyllis a bit more anxious than I because on first fiddle she has a lot more responsibility than the second cellist. Besides, at seventy one, her left thumb is hurting. Though we've played them before, they still need a lot of work-up.

We arrive at the Jacksons promptly at two p.m. Mary looks a bit disheveled, indeed rattled.

"Well, actually, we were expecting you at four!"

Phyllis feels shattered, guilty of two stupid scheduling goofs. We check her calendar; it says "2." She apologizes: "I guess it was because we have this concert downtown tonight at seven—my mind just sped things up."

Mary says, "Oh, it'll be okay, we could play quartets until the other two come at four."

"We *can't* play quartets!" Zeke her cellist-husband says. "There aren't any written for two cellos."

"Well, we could play trios," Mary says. "But wait just a minute; I'll phone 'em and see if they can come earlier."

She phones. Gets voice mail. Urges them to come as soon as they can.

The front doorbell rings. It is the other two players, apologizing for being slightly late for the two o'clock appointment. Mary says, "Ohmygod, I really *am* losing it; I told all of you '2' and then remembered '4.'"

After laughing awhile, and telling other stories about memory goofs, the cheerful aging six of us finally settle into opus 18; it goes okay, but Phyllis and I are not playing quite as well as we would have played had we practiced the sextets rather than quintets.

Today I will take the stack of quintets back to the library—unplayed. Today the sextets are ringing in my head, only slightly more prominently than my memory of the stack of memory goofs.

Should one complain about the nasty fact that the aging of other players affects one's playing life almost as much as one's own aging? Sooner or later you find yourself looking for some way to cut back on time spent with

Hank, whose hearing has just plain gone too far, or Louise, who has begun to lose control. Sooner or later Hank or Louise will be seeking some way to cut back on time spent with Wayne Booth, whose intonation will be even worse than it used to be.

❧

The good side is that I find many rather surprising benefits from aging—at least so far. Being older, I can experience the wonders of music in ways quite different from how those young twerps, with all their muscular flexibility and mental "openness"—not to say flabbiness and sheer ignorance—can manage. Those proud half-blind oblivious show-offs probably don't even have the word "twerp" in their impoverished vocabularies . . .

No, no, drop that attempt at ironic self-display. There's no point in playfully insulting the young, even though you do envy them. Of course you'd like to have their skin tone, their unfilled molars, their quick, comfortable thirty-second notes, their seductive vibratos . . . But let's just think a bit about what they *don't* have.

Their most obvious deprivation is of the "petite madeleine" effect. *Remembrance of Things Past*—or if you prefer the new translation, *In Search of Things Past*, or if you prefer the original, *A la recherche du temps perdu*—Proust's fabulous book, is on my mind partly because Phyllis and I read a lot of it aloud together not long ago, in French: at least one-fortieth of the more than 2,000 pages. That's not what you could call full amateuring.

As you no doubt know, Marcel, the narrator, consuming a cup of tea and a small cake called a petite madeleine, finds himself overwhelmed with the memory of the taste of another madeleine when he was very young. The joining of the two sensations sends him on a prolonged trip through the past, encountering many such overlappings of sensation and memory. The trip ends as the aging Marcel pursues the meaning of such layering of the moments, identical but not identical. To experience any sensation a second time, years later, turns both sensations into an entirely new experience, one that escapes the time-bound world in which the particular sensations occur.

Resisting the temptation to quote him here, I must dwell for a moment on that bland phrase, "identical but not identical." When I experience the "Grosse Fuge" today, more than a half century after almost memorizing it, I juxtapose, as a gift of my aging, at least three, or really five, six, or seven works, "identical but not identical": the Busch Chamber Orchestra recording I heard at Ft. Meade, anticipating my doom; the much more heavily laden version I heard in my head on that cattle car during the thirty-two hours that we wandered through France toward Belgium; the far more joyful one I heard played by the string quartet back in Paris a few months later; and on to my first struggles to play it with various friends decades later. (It is usually hard these days to talk any group, even the semipros, into attempting it, it is so aggressively resistant.)

All of these versions are with me—not greatly different in musical detail but with differing depths and qualities of emotional association. I'm not claiming that my older responses are more intense or more valuable than my first one; no mechanical register could ever compare the intensity of my emotions now with those in 1944, and no argument could prove the superiority of either one over the other. But I need no computerized text to tell me that what I lacked then and have now is a *bridging* of the intensities, a broad encounter of a third kind.

Even if that claim seems doubtful, what is certain is that I am having a new . . . but in seeking the right noun for what I'm having I meet again my old problem of the "ineffability of musical experience." Should I call what happens to the old man, as he plays the fugue with his companions, a "new experience"? That's not exactly a falsehood, but it's flat. Should I talk of "a new thrill"? Not false, but too Hollywood. "New transport"? Not false, but pretentious. "New memory"? Both flat and misleading: the experience is not just memory. "Fresh spiritual engagement"? "A love bout of the aging kind"?

Something new happens, some happening worth happening happens that could not have happened when I was young.

Often I can't even distinguish the apparent losses of aging from the apparent gains. So I must leave it to you to pursue the invitations of the following three sections. I'll be surprised if you inform me that none of them prove pertinent to the hours and years you spend as an amateur.

Why Waste Time on Jeremiads?

Since my father's death when I was six, I have never been unaware of the fragility of this fallen world. Some people say they didn't even discover their own mortality until, in their thirties or fifties, a loved one died or a near-fatal accident occurred. I remember concluding that I myself must surely die before surpassing my father's age at death: thirty five. That sense of my life's fragility was underlined by the death of my favorite grandmother when I was seven and then of my closest friend when I was fourteen. The lesson continued with the deaths in their forties of two beloved colleagues, and finally with the death of my son when he was eighteen and I was forty-eight.

Such knowledge makes optimism about your physical survival absurd, but knowing it for a lifetime makes depression about your own mortality equally absurd. It's not the certainty of your death that bothers you; it's the infringements upon your daily life that get on your nerves, the constant reminders of your fragility: the sore foot, the broken leg, the cataract. And those reminders hurt almost as much when they come to loved ones as when they hit you.

In '91, Phyllis was up on a ladder doing one of the "man's jobs" she enjoys doing, while I was napping down below; the ladder slid out from under her and she broke her knee. For many weeks both of our lives were—well, not shattered but transformed: we had suddenly both become about ten years older. She managed to continue as psychotherapist, with me ushering clients in and out of the front door and up and down the stairs. I performed all of the domestic chores that she usually does more than half of. For weeks there was no cello or violin practice, no quartet playing. I was filled with the fear that the injury would not heal. My unspoken thought was, "I'll have to live with an aging, crippled wife from here on."

Yet somehow all that quickly revived my plans for a book—not a book about amateuring, though, but a book about aging and death, with the cello far in the background: something like the reverse of the ordering in this book.

DECEMBER 15, 1991—Suddenly feel very much alive, even exhilarated, no doubt foolishly, inexplicably, first, by the notion that I might after all finish the Amnesty International lecture on time, in spite of all the tending of Phyllis, and then, suddenly, by the notion that I have all along been writing a "little" book about turning seventy. That "Thumb" stuff I've been struggling with really belongs as a very small part of a book about growing older, not a book about music playing. Why not?

Our playing was resumed long before she cast off all pain. But aging now seemed to demand fuller attention than music, not just her aging, and mine, but the aging of the world. It was that that produced *The Art of Growing Older*, my anthology of the best poems I could find about how it all feels. It is that that seems too often to dominate in depressing ways my friends' conversations these days. Even when I resist talking of our failing health, the failing world intrudes. Only if we could manage to work at conversing better would such talk qualify as amateuring.

NOVEMBER 30, 1993 [LUNCHEON CONVERSATION, FACULTY CLUB]

FJ: I think the whole world's going to hell in a handcart. The National Science Foundation has just absurdly decided . . .

BA: (who reads *The Journal of Economics*): Oh, but the world is *not* going to hell in a handcart. Things are looking pretty good, basically. If you read . . .

FJ: I don't have to read any of your conservative journals, I just happen to know . . .

PD: It's got nothing to do with left wing, right wing. I think we're just going downhill, in almost every possible way. Did you see that article this week about what's happening to classical music?

WB: (shouting them down, as is always necessary in those conversations): I think we're all just falling here into the age-old practice of those who grow old. You all must've read Castiglione on that? [It turned out that most of them had not—thus of course confirming *my* notion that true culture is dying.] Every older generation decides that all is lost. And anyway, regardless of our opinions about it, it's always been obvious to anyone who thought hard enough that all is going to be lost, ultimately, if by "all" we mean this material world.

Though I give WB the final pontifical word here, that wasn't the way things actually ended at the club. My sermon got cut off, as we moved on to discuss the orthodox Christian view that the world, along with each of us in it, is "fallen," "broken," as contrasted—"no, it really is not con-trasted!"—with the Jewish view, which echoes X, Y, and Z . . .

Now that I have the floor again, what should I say about all that? In a fallen, broken world, a world in which we can know for certain that every-thing we grasp with our senses, every "thing," every "body," will pass away, aging should surprise nobody yet surprises everybody. I have always been a bit proud of my ability to anticipate death, never foreseeing how much I would be surprised by aging. Daddy died in his prime, like Jesus Christ; he never had to face growing old, and his son didn't learn from his death that growing old was a quite different problem.

The aging cello pupil may not fear death, but he knows that he will lose one or more of his marbles before he has mastered thumb position.

MARCH 15, 1992—After wonderful quartet session yesterday, piano trios this morning on Phyllis's birthday. I always enjoy our morning sessions more than those in the evening. I make more mistakes in the evening. Why is that? The "evening effect of getting 'older'"? If I do a book about growing older while playing the cello, should it be called something like "Twilight Music," or "Tuneful Autumns"?

That time of year thou mayest in me behold
When yellow leaves, or none, or few, do hang
Upon those boughs that shake against the cold,
Bare ruined choirs where late the sweet birds sang . . .

or rather,

Bare ruined choirs, where cellist's booboos rang.

Shakespeare's sonnet (73) goes on to make the point not just with autumn and twilight but also with a dying fire, "consumed by that which it was nourished by." I am "consumed" by what nourishes me, this musical fire, in several senses—but I see no way in which it can be blamed for dousing my fires.

The journals dwell on aging increasingly as the years go by—fortunately not often with a sense of doom.

MARCH 29, 1992—Am loving cello lessons, and Phyllis says *I'm improving at an incredible rate.* I *think* she used the word "incredible," but maybe it was "unbelievably slow" or even "sluggish": I didn't have my hearing aid on.

MAY 19, 1992 [CHATTING ON PHONE WITH MY GRANDDAUGHTER, NOW SEVEN, IN VIRGINIA]
EMILY: Granpa, how old is your cello teacher?
GRANDPA: About 35 or 40.
Pause.
EMILY: What? Did you say 35 or 40?
GRANDPA: Yes.
EMILY: You mean to say your teacher is younger than *you* are?
And she giggles at the discovery that teachers don't need to be older than learners.
The good news is that my teacher yesterday *broke into applause* after I played the most fiendishly difficult exercise I've ever faced—Popper 22 on thumb position. I'm gonna write that up, for publication in the *Chronicle of Higher Position Playing* or something.

Aging as Deepening

Is it condescending for us old geezers to imply, as I'm doing here, that aging is deepening, or at least can be?

Even the proudest of us have never found it easy to describe just what deepening is, or why it's important. What is too deep for me one year may seem offensively shallow later; what seems shallow to you may seem profound to me. Still, I cannot doubt that my life with music—at least some of it—is far less shallow, in the dismissive sense, than it was at twenty. How can I defend the strong value judgment embedded in that word "shallow"? How can we deal with the ambiguous distinction between what is shallow and what is deep?

JULY 18, 1992 (WILDWOOD, UTAH)—Listened closely yesterday to Beethoven's "Eroica," consciously comparing, in my ear/mind, what he does with the theme at one spot and then another and yet another, each recurrence subtly different. Remembered earlier listening, some of it careless, inattentive, some of it totally engaged. Suddenly felt that wrestling with B's complexity and those memories was somehow "deepening" my life and that such deepening is actually a rising . . .

Yet surely "complexity" can't work as a universal standard: many extremely simple experiences are among our most valued . . . So how does one define shallowness or depth? Obviously whenever I just skim one surface after another I miss a lot. On the other hand, taking one surface experience along to another one and comparing them can also be a gain . . .

A bit later I listened to Gerry Mulligan playing a sequence of jazz variations on a melody he just assumes the listener already knows. His marvelous tricks will make no sense to anyone unfamiliar with the unplayed melody. "Shallow" listening can hear the beat and general sound, enjoy the energy, but miss the depth: the presence of more than one surface or layer. Shallow/deep; simple/complex. What does my celebration of the second half of each pair say about aging?

As I read over that now I can see that much of my listening to Mulligan does indeed depend partly on my many years. The only reason I knew the melody, named on the jacket but not played in any preliminary statement, was that it had entered my soul from adolescence on. It sang itself under Gerry's gyrations because my youth provided it, in irresistible form, allowing me now to listen as I could not have listened at eighteen, or even perhaps at thirty. Mulligan and Beethoven survive the probing of a depth-seeker.

But back to my meditations of six years ago, reminding the patient reader who needs no reminding that to meander from past to present and back again is another form of "deepening," one more gift of aging.

What seems wrong with too much pop music today, unlike the Mulligan, is not what Allan Bloom says is wrong, in *The Closing of the American Mind:* corruption of morals. Though there is no doubt a lot of that, the real problem is that too much of it offers little but surface: the soul of the listener is moved forward across surfaces too thin to allow for any but momentary value, never pausing to go deeper. The deprivation is by no means confined, as Bloom seems to believe, to popular music like rock. In everything we are offered, the goal seems to be only surface liveliness or even shock, with no hint of an invitation to depth. Even the best of classical music is most often heard as background surface: Muzak in the elevator, Vivaldi on hold-phone. And the shallower classical stuff too often seems to dominate the airways.

Is my sense of loss in our culture any different from what all who are older feel about the values of their youth? Is praise of depth no more than a disguised and feeble defense of growing older? I certainly don't want to commit the absurdity of saying that being old is better than being young. The "compensations and celebrations" of aging that my *Art of Growing Older* engages in cannot be thought of as putting us oldsters into direct competition with the young bucks. Perhaps depth and surface charms are equally valuable—two "incommensurable" values of the kind current philosophers keep urging us to acknowledge: genuine values that nevertheless in practice can clash. The last thing I want to do is to attack the blessings of youth (for those youngsters lucky enough not to be cursed by it) as I celebrate the depths that youth is denied.

Still, the rewards of depth feel undeniable.

So the villains of any book about aging and art I might write would include some of the most celebrated artists—the surf-boarders: John Cage with his passion for the ever-new; the various minimalist painters whose only recognizable skill is cutting to original "one-liners": a visual pun or piece of wit, like Duchamp's clever but destructively influential urinal.

One summer, when Phyllis and I were driving across country with our Amateur Chamber Society Directory as our itinerary guide, we stopped off at the Des Moines Art Museum and found ourselves gazing at a "Two-way Plug," by what's his name—a room-filling "copy," in some kind of rubbery blobbish plastic, of a two-way electric plug. Real fun—for a moment. But I would not even go around the corner to see it again. We had it all on first glance—at least that's what it seemed to be saying. There was no hint of any invitation to study how it was done, or how one might do another better one after practicing for a few years.

The real point is thus not just complexity—the "Two-way Plug" was intricate, on its surface—but rather the qualities revealed by repeated experience of deepening levels of complexity. What aging grants us, when it behaves generously, are deepening levels; we don't discard our first experience but build up from it.

A good illustration of how those claims apply when playing the same music over decades is a Beethoven quartet that we players have risked wearing out with many repetitions, Opus 18, No. 4, G minor. We've played it far more than the fourteen times that I've recorded in my penciled notes (when a session has gone badly, I usually don't note it). When we play it next time it's quite possible that we may lapse into an undeepening repetition: we know it cold, and that could mean *too* cold. If we come fully alive, though, it will be something different, in a genuine sense something deeper. It will be informed by that Proust effect: memories of other times, including all the times when Phyllis has complained about how difficult that last movement is for the first violin—and then played it fabulously.

Obviously even the deepest works can lose their depth, for a given perceiver or culture, after repeated probings: you get to the bottom, as it were, and the person or the culture moves onto something unworn. Beethoven could never have wanted to do "just another Mozart concerto"—though as a young learner he mimicked his predecessors shamelessly. He surely would grieve over the number of times the theme of the fourth movement of his ninth symphony gets corrupted on TV commercials these days.

AUGUST 3, 1997—What memory can do for deepening was powerfully illustrated today as we played Beethoven's piano trio (op. 1) once again with our beloved Jane Knourek. Because of arthritis, Jane has in recent years been playing much less—indeed often playing not at all. So we were much relieved when she responded favorably to our telephoned offer to stop off at her summer place again and play trios: "OK, good. I'll start practicing again." And she did. When we arrived midday, having driven about 450 miles since breakfast, she was rarin' to go.

The adagio brought me to tears as it has never done before. "You two really carried me away."

Jane answered:

"I was weeping too, it was so beautiful. And I was thinking as we played about what my best teacher, long since dead, said to me about that melody: '*Caress* the notes.' And we all just did."

Such an experience can bless only the "older." You who are young can only hope for something like it, far in the future.

❧

One of the great costs of growing older is the opposite of deepening, a kind of "shallowing": time pressures seem to increase. Any task that at thirty took thirty minutes at sixty tends to take ninety. In retirement my desk seems—and I'm sure it's illusion—much more deeply flooded with unperformed chores than it did when I was teaching full time. Time speeds up: days, months, years go by faster, with less "accomplished." So one often feels the way full-time working parents feel at 8 A.M. when the kids are refusing to get ready for school.

MARCH 2, 1994—Early A.M. was feeling overwhelmed. In-box full of corre-
spondence and manuscripts requiring response "yesterday"; a 700-page
book manuscript I'm reading for a press; Ph.D. students' dissertation
chapters; requests for speeches at this and that conference; promises,
promises. The bills have not been paid for two weeks. Have sworn that
I'll spend at least four hours a day on *Amateur*, until a draft is completed.
But I have a lesson coming up Saturday. *But* I can't expect to practice after dinner tonight (my usual time) because we're going to a performance
of *Measure for Measure*. *But* then I must . . .
   In short, there was literally no time today when I could practice.
   So what did I do?
   Well, shortly after breakfast, feeling almost immobilized, heart
actually pounding a bit, I decided to behave like a grownup after all and
settle down for an hour with the cello. Forcing my "self" to obey that decision, I felt better and better as the notes began to flow. The hour turned
into ninety minutes, only about ten of them troubled by any thoughts
about what I was neglecting. All those other matters, undeniably "more
important," including the book, were just forgotten while I worked away:
first on Popper #22, and some arpeggios in D-sharp minor (they provide
useful leaps up into "thumb"), then the 4th movement of the Beethoven
A minor, hoping that the Popper would pay off in the thumb stuff in the
gloriously demanding climax. And *glory be to the great God Thumb, it did!*
I could feel myself able to play that stuff *better than ever before—better*

than I did when playing it in London two years ago, better than I could have done eighty minutes before . . .

The result: I entered my University library study (the University is generous with us emeriti) at eleven feeling more on top of all those pressures than for days; I worked at the "Overture" for two hours, then went home and faced the cruddy in-box for awhile, thinking as I worked, "A good day; at least I got the music in."

MARCH 3, 1994—My feelings are drastically mixed, as I read yesterday's entry today, now that I've lost that feeling of triumph and face the desk again and worry about how I'll perform that Popper this coming Saturday for my new teacher. I did OK on the Beethoven last night—not nearly as good, it seems to me now, as that entry claims—but today in practice that fiendish exercise was lousy. Contemptible! Time is running out. How can I make its running feel the way it felt last night?

The Paradox of Hopeless Hope

I feel almost surrounded sometimes by young performers who are visibly hoping for top professional success, paralleling in extreme form my hope for success with the teacher. Never before has the world had as many impressively promising, ambitious, hopeful young performers. Hoping never to be caught in the amateur domain (though many of them surely must love music passionately), they practice four, six, eight hours a day, hearing from their teachers that if they keep at it, they'll reach the top.

I worry about them, but at least for them "the top" is theoretically reachable. For any of us who did not start when young, the only imaginable rung on the ladder is—well, shall we say about 3 on a scale of 1–10? An approving smile from a teacher?

What, then, can be the comfort? Well, it's just not our fault.

FEBRUARY 8, 1994—Everybody seems to be talking about this problem of learning a skill when you're "older." This morning I read in the sports page about Michael Jordan's effort to build a new career as a baseball player. He has a big media show whenever he tries out. The Vice President of the White Sox in charge of scouting says "If he were nineteen years old, he'd be a first-round draft choice. He's *not* nineteen years old." And the paper goes on about the second round of hitting-exhibit for Jordan, "who turns 31 next week. It didn't go quite as well as the first."

"It isn't for the money," said Jordan, who at least for a while in this new effort to become a baseball star can be considered a wonderful amateur: he doesn't need the money, and his fame will certainly be less than it was at his height in basketball, *and* he is committed as a lover. "It's just the idea of trying to see if I can do this. I've got a lot to prove, to my friends and family—and certainly to my [late] father, who I know is still watching me. That's a good driving force."

I was pleased to note that Jordan admitted he was nervous. Just like me. Just like most amateurs, as soon as somebody is watching, perhaps criticizing.

MARCH 20, 1995—Found myself wickedly pleased this morning to read a doctor's opinion that what has led Jordan to give up baseball is that you cannot—at thirty one!—retrain your muscles adequately to become a star in a different sport. Jordan turned out to be nothing better than a committed amateur—to baseball. His "thumb position" never got mastered.

That's how it is. The moves are not in your dendrites! But unlike a man failing to become another star in another league, and then returning to stardom in his first league, we amateurs can stay right where we are, plugging away at it—forever.

JUNE 20, 1998—What a delight to read this morning that Michael Jordan has started taking piano lessons.

APRIL 28, 1994—Saturday my new teacher Judy explained that when you're playing up in thumb position and you come to a forte solo, it's a good idea to increase the rate of your vibrato—"don't make it tense, mind, but just make it faster so you don't get a wobbly sound." Must have been told that twenty times before—but I forgot. Practiced vibrato over the weekend.

Monday I left this desk to go find a book in the library stacks, and as I was walking along in the periodical room I suddenly noticed that I had been vibrating my left arm and hand, silently practicing—just like the Rev. Harding in Trollope's *The Warden*, or just like a victim of Parkinson's disease, depending on your point of view.

Had anybody noticed? I glanced around, and there ahead was a young faculty member, by no means a close acquaintance, staring at me quizzically. I affected absolute unconcern—told him what I was really doing, recounted the story of the Warden's nervous cello practice. "You know, he not only mimes left-hand vibrato when distracted but also the bowing with his right hand." My colleague seemed amused by my account, but I suspect that he really thought he was witnessing signs of dotage.

❧

As the years move along—more and more rapidly, as is always true when aging—the good and bad are mixed. The practice and playing continued to *get better all the time:* why not? But illness and death of friends and relatives at times have seemed almost overwhelming.

MAY 5, 1997—My sister Lucille died last week, at seventy-one, after months and months of physical fading: the deepest grief for me since my mother's death in 1967 and my son's in 1969. She loved music, and her kind of generous loving brought another kind of music into uncounted lives. I'll have to resist the temptation to add to *Amateur* a long account of her life, from our singing together in childhood, on through her struggles with the piano and organ. Phyllis played at the funeral, Massenet's "Meditation" from *Thaïs;* it was the rendition of a genuine amateur.

❧

Meanwhile what about the very effort to write about all this, as the years go by—the effort to return to it now? Perhaps I'm discovering an ultimate irony here: though I've found utterly persuasive justification for the hours spent on my amateuring, I've not even mentioned any justification for the endless hours I've spent over the years writing about it. Why write draft after draft seeking adequate ways of talking about all that? Are those hours, stolen from both playing and listening, defensible?

To face that tough one, it's obviously time for an Interlude.

Learning music by reading about it is like making love by mail.
ISAAC STERN

✣

It is an impertinence to ask a man still in the game whether the game be worth the candle. He thought so once, no doubt, or he would not have begun playing; and the courteous presumption is that he persists in his opinion. . . . Whatever may be his secret guesses as to the value of the stake, your true sportsman will play the game out, and as long as he is playing his best, he makes but an indifferent philosopher. BLISS PERRY, *The Amateur Spirit* (1904)

✣

Nobody is ever patently right about music. VIRGIL THOMSON

✣

Practically everybody wants to give up their amateur standing as soon as possible. The irony is that if most writers of poetry & other dabblers would think entirely of the benefit to them & not at all of publication, the publishable merit of what they produce would be greatly & constantly increased. NORTHROP FRYE, 1946 JOURNAL ENTRY

Interlude

The Amateur Writer Quarrels with the Amateur Player

I SUPPOSE THAT most of you, if you saw my list of published books and articles and my annual royalty checks, however modest, would deny me the title of amateur writer. "You may not be a highly successful pro, but you're still a pro. You've not only written and published for most of your life, but you've actually had the chutzpah to write about *how* to write. If that isn't aspiring to the title 'professional,' what would be? Where's the love?"

Obviously I can't claim that all of my writing has been done for the love of doing it. Some bits have been produced with absolute passion, my "self" forgotten for hours or days on end. Others—this chapter would make a good example—have almost torn me apart as I've torn *them* apart and tried and tried again. My journals reveal about most projects a thick goulash of wholehearted inquiry, egotistical ambition, greed, and diverse levels of professed do-goodism.

Once the choice was made to do this book a new anxiety tore in:

NOTEBOOK, 1994 [UNDATED]—As I work on *Amateur*, feel more and more amateur*ish* as a writer. "Whatever claims to 'pro' you could make as a writer apply to territory entirely different from the land you're raiding now." Celebrating *homo ludens*, the *player plays* at the role of amateur writer, dealing with a playful cost-benefit analysis of becoming an ama-teur *player*, in order to *play up* the blessing of the gift he's been *playing with*.

How does my writing-playing relate to the playing? Doesn't it actu-ally harm it? Last night in the middle of practicing I was thinking, "How could I write about *this?*" So I was not really practicing but *thinking* about what practicing means. "Doesn't this project violate," the voice went on, "the loving-world it tries to celebrate? You know from nasty experience how easily the spirit of doing-the-thing-for-the-love-of-the-doing can be destroyed. Remember what you said to Phyllis when *The Rhetoric of Fiction* was in chaos: 'No book that is mined out of such misery can possibly be pleasant for anyone to read!' What kind of an amateur were you, then? What kind are you now?"

So today I ask, Can there be such a thing as *loving anguish*—can I claim that the anxieties I feel when struggling with the cello and writing about it are *both* just other forms of joy, playing similar chords?

Sometimes I can silence that anxious voice by remembering how many threatening hurricanes have in the past turned into reassuring breezes. Why not take comfort in the old sayings?

"You don't know how to write about a problem until you've written about it."

"I don't know what I'm saying until I see what I've said."

"Easy writing is vile hard reading."

"Trying to write on a *new* subject always takes you ten rungs down the ladder of skill."

For that matter, why not assume that *thinking* about playing, as I have to do while writing, may actually improve it? Why worry so much? In the past, whenever you've plunged amateurishly into mudholes, you've usually found that to keep on flailing about can wash the mud away.

❧

Why does the flailing about seem even rougher than with earlier books?

First, there is the problem of style levels. The tone of my early drafts is mostly rather jokey, heavily laden with comic disasters—almost as if I were trying to rival some comic columnist. Digressions of the Tristram Shandy kind and self-put-downs were multiplied, presumably aimed to interest postmodern narratologists who would love to witness my fumblings. Yet once the defense of amateuring in general took over, I began to sound too often like someone aspiring to be a pupil of St. Augustine or Whitehead, or like the moralizing Mormon missionary I once was, or like a would-be rival to Freud, probing deep motives of professionals and amateurs.

Even tougher than problems of style level has been finding a workable organization. As teacher I've always nagged students about the importance of an effective sequence: you gotta learn how to hook *and land* the prize fish. Obviously I'll want readers to have, at every step, a clear answer to the central question, "So what?" But just as obviously no kind of scholarly or chronological progression will work in this book. It contains no systematic analysis of texts—I'm not qualified to treat a Beethoven movement the way I would criticize a short story or critical argument. How much playful meandering of the Sterne and Montaigne kind can I allow? Just how much autobiography? How many technical illustrations will carry any interest?

Since my musical life provides no coherent progression from Mozart to Bach to Bartók to Haydn, to follow mere chronological journal tracings won't make sense. What will? Some sort of plot line, real or faked, is required. What can it be?

The plot line of the playing, of laboring at thumb position in your eighth decade, is unavoidably double. Considered as a struggle to *get better all the time*, it would inevitably trace, twenty years from now, a trajectory from rising to falling, from hope to failure—even if we leave death aside. The moment will finally arrive when I have not only failed to become a really good cellist but I am *getting worse and worse all the time*. Drawn as a graph, it will look like a stock-market report in 1929; viewed as a drama it will turn into tragedy.

That's the way the book project itself often feels. On the worst days the plot turns into something even more pathetic than the cello tragedy: the book itself should be scrapped, burnt, murdered. Yet sometimes, writing after a blissful quartet session the night before, the undrawable plot line rises even beyond tragicomedy to become almost a divine comedy: rising, falling, rising—though ever more slowly—to peaks never foreseen but at last coming into view. The always-poor cellist experiences unimaginable ecstasies, and though he knows that no prosaic account can capture them, he also knows that the book's aspiration is quite different. It must become a celebration of *success in dealing with failure*, an account of why failure in climbing one mountain, whether in music or prose, may be success in climbing an unforeseen neighboring peak.

Can the book itself then be an analogue of the failures and triumphs on the cello? The successful story of the failure to tell a story that is impossible to tell? If the complex story is inherently untellable, too complex in its inescapable ties to everything important about life itself, isn't the very facing of that failure a kind of success? [1]

---

1. I've dealt elsewhere with this puzzling genre—the "oldster succeeding by describing failure"—in a brief discussion of Norman Maclean's *Young Men and Fire*. I see his wonderfully successful book as the triumphant account of how an old man failed to put together a story that was inherently too manifold ever to *be* put together.

If such speculation seems too fancy, I can still claim that even in the despairing moments as writer I am an amateur in the sense of doing it for the sake of doing it, of sharing it with you for the sake of sharing it with you, whoever you are by now. Only at moments like this, after grappling with those last few paragraphs, do I think of cutting all the meditative veins, draining out all the heavier stuff, eliminating the high-flown and unprovable speculation you'll meet in the last three chapters, scrapping the potentially offensive moral and psychological judgments, and simply erasing this Interlude.

Last week my twelve-year-old granddaughter smiled slyly at me and said, "The trouble with you, Granpa, is that you're always thinking, thinking, thinking." She had read aloud and praised a draft of some early chapters. But she had bogged down as soon as she got to the "thinking" stuff.

❧

Beyond style and organization there is one problem that no other writer I know of has ever faced quite in my way. Has anyone ever before spent a lifetime teaching rhetorical studies ("better verbal communication") as an ultimate human good and then turned to celebration of non-verbal amateur pursuits like chamber music—as if words hardly count in the great scheme of things?

It was only late into the project that I began to wonder about "the wordless amateur vs. the wordy rhetorician," and then to ask whether it made sense to bring that seeming paradox into the open. How am I to deal with the conflict between my mission to improve the world of discourse and this current celebration of a practice that at heart has little to do with words?

JUNE 13, 1994—I feel at the moment absolutely confused about how what I face, here at 9 A.M., as I come to my study and settle into revising, relates to what I faced when working on earlier books. I just can't think about *how* to think about whether to bring that confusion to the surface of the book.

Somehow it does seem to belong. If I can't deal with it, how can I pretend to have faced honestly my opening question, Why do amateuring of any kind? Why, if you are passionate about the lifelong pro-amateur rhetorical project, allow amateuring of the cello kind to intrude? And why, if your main goal in life is to get as many people to join together in as many genuine ways as possible, should you celebrate a practice that by its very nature divides people into those who can and do and those who can't or won't?

Suddenly I think I see my answer: the two projects both fit under a special notion of "love," the belief that in our efforts to *communicate better*, whether in words or music, we often are, and always should be, striving to meet "the others," the "other" that is now fashionable. I've often invoked the Golden Rule in this form: *talk to and listen to others as you would wish they would talk to and listen to you.* Human love, human joining, "critical understanding" as a loving effort to understand—that has always been at the center. And it's at the center here.

Or so it now seems to me as I turn to the MS: we players are *working*, we workers are *playing*, not just to "do the music"; we are working to join one another's doings, to come together in the music. So: for the moment it seems clear that struggling to do that and then struggling to write about it are tasks beautifully harmonizable.

Harmonizable even with the "music of the spheres"? Perhaps: it all depends on how you view the "spheres." Which means that maybe I should work this morning on chapter 11.

The Melange of Problems and Motives

Abandoning coherence as the illusory goal of a professional rhetorician, I now succumb again to the autobiographical impulse: back to 1953, about a year after I had begun cello lessons. The "young" man is not thinking about the cello but about the search for a passionate center. Have I been "writing" this book ever since then?

DECEMBER, 8, 1953—Here I am almost 32 and I have no great project afoot, nothing really challenging underway to keep me up late at nights and get me up early. I am interested in what I'm doing [mainly teaching and administering]; I enjoy my reading and I enjoy writing drafts of articles . . . But that is not what I mean by a *project*. I am still exploring, still floundering around for a life's work. What I want is "the real thing" [I had been reading James's story with that title] . . . No doubt I shall be a successful teacher, a reasonably successful writer of essays. I'll publish a good book or two before I'm through. All of this is not quite the real thing, however: the passionate pursuit of something so big that it swallows the pursuer. When I write an article now, I am *usually* about as strongly motivated by the desire to publish it, for the publishing's sake, for credit, as by the desire to work through a particular problem. Of course I am hoping to stumble onto something worth losing sleep over, but I've not had it since my little critical discovery in 1949 . . .

And the naïve quester goes on at great length about the possibilities, only once noting that what he seeks is a professional role that feels as purely motivated as his cello lessons.

Thirty-nine years later the problem of career choice had long since been solved. The aspirer has replaced it with other problems relating love and music:

JULY 14, 1992—Galleys for *Older* now fought through—a nasty job, on the whole. Am struck by just how superficial my thoughts about aging are. . . . One reader has suggested that I must get in somewhere how I've coped with my son being killed at age eighteen. Can't take that suggestion this late in the game, though I do wish I had been able to find some way to write about Richard's death helpfully . . . If and when I do that book about "thumb position" should I talk about Mahler's *Kindertotenlieder* and how I can't bear to listen to it even now?

Six months later he is feeling overwhelmed with four or five different possible projects struggling to take over.

JANUARY 7, 1993, LONDON—Without too much juggling, as I enjoy here listening to Phyllis downstairs practicing Haydn's Opus 20 #2—we played it vigorously Tuesday afternoon and will play it again next week— I'm tempted to turn this entry into a page for "70" or "Thumb," my article (book?) on further thoughts about aging. Should it become just "son of" *Older?* How about making it an autobiography, or a "comforter to millions," or a "novel disguised," since these days the boundaries between fiction and non-fiction have almost disappeared? . . .

One picture of the book has it organized by themes: the cello-learning, "Thumb," just one section; then the love life; the scholarly; the "grappling with ego"; the "grappling with how to write it"; all about grappling with age. Another picture has it simply chronological, gleaning from these multiple, prolix entries of the last few months, and of earlier years, the best pictures of my turning into a septuagenarian. A septuagenarian amateur?

"A Septuagenarian on September-ing"? "From Sexagenarian to Septuagenarian"? "From Sex- to September-: A Septuagenarian Learns Thumb Position—on the Cello." That gets in the pun on September . . .

Often the prober reveals real misgivings about how a book project can kill other loves.

JANUARY 26, 1993, LONDON—A day mainly of music. Knowing that EH and JG would be here at 3 to play quartets, Phyllis and I practiced from about 9 to 11:45. . . . When the ladies came, we played vigorously at the Haydn op. 50 #6 for perhaps an hour and a half: repeating difficult sections, doing all repeats; repeating the first movement completely, and the last movement. Then we played the Beethoven #3, which went marvelously. Both of us felt that we *were playing better than ever before* . . .

Can there really be a book celebrating this sense of the ultimate payoff while aging? I think so, somewhere. But it would mean sacrifice of all the *other* books. In the night I found myself lamenting the failure to complete about six projects that lie dormant. Actually I dread subjecting myself to the discipline that finishing any one of them would require. If I cared as little for what people might say of my work as Chesterton seems to do (I'm still reading him with great pleasure) I would just finish one of them, without much discipline—that appears to have been his way—and go on to the next one.

Perhaps what I should be working on is the part of my character that wants not just to be loved by everyone but to be admired by everyone. I warm enthusiastically to Chesterton's quarrels with ego: his insistence on joy, on happiness, on affirmation. Shouldn't I, then, finish Cass Andor [a novel now abandoned, 1998]?

In less than a year he's moving much closer to a book on *all* of what he is calling "amachoices"—the neologism, now expunged, that he then felt rivaled some of the better ones among Coleridge's thousands.

OCTOBER 11, 1993—As for "Thumb," shouldn't it be called something like "Amateur"?—a project that would leave me deducting taxes not just on all my musical expenses, my lessons, etc., but all my other amateuring: concerts, plays, movies, gallery hopping—all of it contributes here, all of it can be corrupted into tax profit. Why, I might as well buy myself a Stradivarius and . . . I'd have to find an IRS agent who was himself an amateur, or even better, amateur*ish* . . . Does such speculation mean that I'm behaving like a sold-out professional? Ah, I have the solution for my soul: I'll donate all my profits to "Amnesty International" . . .

OCTOBER 14, 1993—Writing yesterday about a session in which we all seemed to become absolutely ecstatic, I suddenly realized that I am "into" the possible book on chamber music, on "learning thumb position at seventy"; speculating about which other human activities share the chamber player's intensity of what Mike Csikszentmihalyi calls "flow experience." What are the differences among total absorption in a sport contest, in an act of love making, in conducting a good class, in climbing Everest, in chamber playing and in writing about it? At 3:30 A.M. I couldn't get back to sleep thinking of all that and went to my desk hoping to write it out. I bogged down, of course, but if I do the book . . .

Seven months later he has a draft—and often feels in deeper and deeper trouble.

MAY 3, 1994 (9 A.M.)—I'm now recovered from a silly collapse of confidence of last Sunday night. I made the mistake of reading aloud to Phyllis parts of a draft of the Preface. I had chosen the worst possible moment. We were both tired. She was sorting socks from the laundry, and though I usually take my turn at that, this time I thought, absurdly, that I'd be doing my share if I "entertained" her with a touch of the book. I knew that the draft was prosaic, but I thought it clean and clear and inviting. She did not.

"Well, it's clear enough, but it feels heavy to me. Where's the wit? Where's the charm? It feels academic."

I felt that I had been hit in the groin. It's hard for me now, three days later, to reconstruct just why that blow was so devastating, but it was. The book is worthless—like all my books. No, that's not it: she hates me, she hates my work; the book is OK but she is getting even for all the energy and time I put into it and all the bad playing I've committed. No, that can't be it: she's the best critic I have, and she knows that the book is a total dud.

I went to bed sullen, silent, feeling the very core torn out of me, and I dreamed heavy, forlorn dreams, none now remembered.

At breakfast we talked about it a little. By then I had seen clearly that the preface draft did not at all do the right job: it was indeed flat, lifeless, "academic" in the wrong sense: appropriate, perhaps, to a book about Boethius on the music of the spheres but not to this book. Her brief, cold rejection had at least that much to be said for it. Still, why the hostile tone? "Well," she said, "I think it came at the wrong time of day. Then too I guess I was a bit distracted by the scene: you sitting reading to me, while I did the housework."

That afternoon when I came home from the library study, the first thing she said was, "Have you forgiven me?" To which the only honest response was, "You did nothing that requires forgiveness. Have you excused the little boy in me who takes every critical barb, however slight, as murderous?"

So yesterday, the second day after, I was back in stride—still unsure about just *how* good the book will be, but sure that it is worth doing—and that doing it is the best possible way for me to be spending my time—so long as I don't let it interfere with my deeper loves: Phyllis, the two daughters, the three grandchildren, chamber music, literature—in that order? . . .

Puzzling, the way the ego preserves its deepest faults from love to love. Criticism crushes me, whether of my playing, my writing, my beard style or my conversation. . . . How long will it be before I show any of this book again to Phyllis, or to anyone else? If the first reader said of it—as a friend recently did of a little spoof I'd attempted on current economic theory, "This is a non-starter"—would I just throw all this away?

Instead the book took over, raising that perpetual problem of amateuring that Tristram Shandy exhibits in the "madness" of various Hobby-Horse riders.

MAY 16, 1994—I fear I'm becoming a fanatical "nut" not of chamber music, exactly, but of writing about it: the book threatens to take over too much of my life, including even the practice hours, because I love the hours each day spent on it more than *almost* anything else. Today, for example, I have many other demands that should be met [he lists them]. I felt impatient when Phyllis suggested, at 6:45, that we go out for breakfast because there was no milk in the house. There was no milk in the house because yesterday I worked all day here without even thinking about buying milk. We did go out for a pleasant breakfast, and I swear that I forgot about the book for as much as five minutes at a time.

I had a hard time resisting the impulse to ask her why she has not been eager to read more of these early drafts. And here I am, at 8 o'clock, tempted to neglect those letters of recommendation and work here for the entire day. But there is no rational way of claiming that any amachoice like this justifies the sacrifice of the careers of graduate students pleading for support.

"All for love" has always been treated as it was treated by Dryden in his version of the Anthony and Cleopatra story: it's a tragic theme, because when any one value is made supreme, without the exercise of "casuistry" relating it to other values, disaster strikes.

As I look back on my vacillations, since completing *The Art of Growing Older*, I can see that they partly resulted from a justified reluctance to surrender, once again, to any total project. Knowing how I fall in love with any book that really starts coming alive, knowing that, like Pygmalion's statues, my works come alive, capture my love and take over my life, I have simply resisted crawling to this moment, when a "book" says to me, "either come live with me twenty-four hours a day or I will betray you."

MAY 22, 1994—*Amateur* is disrupting my amateur playing, taking over my life in absurd ways. Even when I am practicing or taking my lesson, I seem to be asking, "Now what about this would be pertinent to *Amateur?*" Only when actually playing quartets with others or in *some* of my duets with Phyllis do I lose this absurd violation *of* the book *by* the book. This paradox must surely be brought up front. No use pretending that I'm in any way above the de-basements. In fact, at this moment, as I seek a better word than "debasements" to end that sentence, I am stealing time from music playing, and from other amachoices that might seem obviously more important than polishing a sentence.

At the Ailey Co. ballet last night, I was steadily distracted from their fine performances by thinking about how to fit professional dancing into *Amateur*. How does the celebration of the body that these wonderful dancers are doing relate to my struggle with the body as I practice the cello? My musical love is embedded in physicality. Should I (I wondered) quote the satirical bit by Huxley, in *Point Counter Point*, contrasting the chamber players' raw physicality—their ugly bodies and the gut and hair and metal of their instruments—with the beauty of Bach's suite?

Meanwhile what had happened to dancing? Book-thoughts were backgrounding those lithe wonders. Only when they did some aggressive jazz-dancing to an insistent beat, or some gospel-dancing to gospel-music did I temporarily drop the book and join the dancing. Even those moments were brief, followed by irrelevant speculation about whether *they* were dancing for love or for money.

❧

The writing amateur, the playing amateur: they always rival one another even as they claim harmony. Since starting the book I've fallen into lapses of six months, even of two years, with three hundred pages sitting on my shelves, and in my floppy disks, and in my soul, untouched—even as I have gone on playing chamber music and writing on other (possible) books. These loves like all loves are more complicated than anything I can say about them. Like all loves they can decline, even disappear, and then—like good marriages—they come alive again. But their very rebirth revives other rivalries that will never be fully resolved.

Meanwhile, even as I write about the conflict, the harmony feels temporarily restored in the memory of our playing the Debussy piano trio last week with a new pianist. I looked over at Phyllis, as we joined in the opening passage, cello and violin in unison. It is one of the most exciting openings ever written. She was not looking at me: she didn't have to. Her face was playing the Debussy. I did not, throughout that session, corrupt it even for a moment with thoughts about *using* it for this book. As I am doing now.

THIRD
MOVEMENT

*The Love
Fulfilled*

If I don't practice for one day I know it, if I don't practice for two days the critics know it, and if I don't practice for three days every amateur I ever play with would rather be playing with someone else. ADAPTED FROM IGNACE JAN PADEREWSKI

※

In [musical] art there is perhaps no absolute bad but insincerity; there are endless shades of worse and better. DANIEL GREGORY MASON

※

The true musician would love by preference persons of beautiful disposition in the soul and harmonious beauties in the bodily form. But if there were *disharmony* he would not love this. (Italics added.) PLATO, *Republic*

※

The woods would be empty of music if only those birds sang who sing best. ANONYMOUS

Chapter Seven

Amateur Hours: Disastrous,
Not Too Bad, and Just Plain Glorious

LIKE LIFE ANYWHERE, our playing times together resist all shoving into categories. But, like life anywhere, playing times do invite one undeniable distinction: some hours are inglorious, humiliating, even detestable, some are glorious, triumphant, even heavenly. Most fall between. Our judgments of their quality may shift on reflection: what was once a painful moment of humiliation can be turned by memory into comedy; what felt like sheer triumph then, memory can turn now into embarrassment or even grief.

As memory traces our many chamber hours, preparing for this chapter, the majority of them simply fade away. Asked "How was it last night?" we would have answered "Not too bad," or "Things went pretty well." "It was worth it, but the violist was lousy and . . . " "Well, at least we managed to keep Mark from interrupting with too many jokes." Much more vivid, to no one's surprise, are the extremes: inglorious and glorious. The blessed ones will triumph here, but they should be viewed against an honest backdrop of sessions that were literally painful but that now seem either just plain funny or—surprisingly—representative of time well spent because of what they taught us. Can I actually celebrate some moments of humiliation?

My main hope is that the sheer fun of it all, including the comedy, will make you envious enough to stop reading and get working on your own amateur pursuit. If you get really hooked, you'll never find time to pick me up again. Just give or lend the book to some friend who is squandering life on . . . but there the preacher threatens to intrude again.

As in the rest of life, playing hours do not move chronologically from bad to good, even if one claims to be *getting better all the time*. If I fall on my face thumbing a run in 1968, I might not flub a note of the same run in 1998. Yet in 1998 we might have a session less rewarding than one we had with the same friends on the same composition in 1958.

Hours Inglorious and Humiliating—or Just Plain Funny

When one young friend read a draft of this chapter and asked, "Why include so much that is painful?" I retorted, "For honesty's sake." That was a poor response. The real point is to underline just how intense and important the pleasures must be, if they can far overbalance such pains. In reading the first two of these humiliations, you may well find yourself asking, "Why didn't the idiot just give it up?" But I hope the answer will be obvious: Because he wants you to see that the amateur pleasures are so marvelous that no pain could keep him from trying again.

I can't find any record of either of the following miseries. I must have felt them too humiliating even for a private file.

MID-WINTER, 1968 OR '69 [MEMORY]—A professor of physics at my university is a passionate amateur violist. I'm told that he keeps a viola in his university office; other players gather there at lunchtime to play quartets, trios, quintets—whatever they can stir up. I've never been invited, and I resent the oversight—mildly, of course, magnanimously.

One day I get a note inviting Phyllis and me to a "chamber music evening" at his house. We gladly accept, and I'm only mildly disturbed to find some non-playing auditors in attendance. The evening runs deliciously—for awhile: Phyllis and another violinist do a Bach double concerto, with a fine pianist rescuing that prolonged piano/harpsichord interlude solo that some string players feel is an act of aggression against them. We then play a Haydn quartet more than passably. Someone then says, "Wayne, how about doing the Brahms E-minor cello sonata? [Opus 38] Do you know it?" "Well, I've heard it a lot, but I'm sure it's beyond me. I've never played it." Actually I had fiddled a bit with it—that's probably why I was foolish enough to accept.

Even now, as I write about that moment of choice, I feel furious at myself for succumbing: I knew that to attempt such a sonata without hours and hours of practice was absolute folly. Yet I succumbed, perhaps because of the gemütlich setting—sort of a European-style "salon." I faced the music and, with perhaps a dozen people doomed to listen politely, began the mournful opening solo.

It was dreadful. I blush even as I write here, to think of how those guests must have suffered—to think that I hadn't the gumption, the courage, to get up from my chair after the first badly phrased, poorly intoned bars, and say, "Sorry, I've made a huge mistake. Let's get on to something else." Instead I went on flubbing, though always keeping up with the competent pianist—keeping up is never my problem—and thus never absolutely breaking down and stopping. It was just plain unmusical torture to us all, in almost every measure. (Could I now take any comfort in the thought that there may have been people in that room with so little musical experience that they didn't know how bad it all was? Not really.)

So far as I can remember, nobody, not even Phyllis, ever said a word of reproach about what had felt like an hour but was actually only about fifteen minutes. How could any if them ever find the words to describe what they had endured?

TEN YEARS EARLIER, SPRING, 1958 OR 1959—The authoritarian, German-accented director of the Earlham College student orchestra has talked many of us adult amateurs into joining students for a performance of a movement from Brandenberg concerto #4. We fail to rehearse adequately. We fail to tune carefully enough immediately before the performance. We sit down and begin, and suddenly we are an utterly sub-amateurish mess. Phyllis as always is playing courageously and without visible signs of fright (she confessed later that she had felt terrible about the sounds even she was emitting.) I feel my bow arm jiggling on the strings, producing mainly scratches. I look over at the violin section and see that others are trembling too. Some are just plain lost.

We pull together, in a sense; we stumble through to the final measures more or less on the same beats. At no point do I feel any music in my soul or anyone else's—it's nothing but embarrassment.

Today, almost four decades later, I again feel enough humiliation to make me wonder why on earth I didn't just give up on the damn cello, instead of torturing other people like that.

I did in fact give up, for decades, every invitation to play for an audience, even a small one. I don't approve of that preference; to refuse to share surely violates the whole enterprise. So, now that I'm *getting better all the*

time, I swear to accept any future invitation to listen to us. I still cannot recommend that you offer one.

❦

To share a performance with friendly music lovers is quite different from
performing before the critical eye of a professional coach or teacher, as my
example on pages 73–75 shows. Most of my "performances" in my lessons
are far worse than my practicing of the very same notes at home the night
before. I can think of no explanation except silly egotism: I want credit, and
I don't deserve it. I could fill this chapter with moments when, in the presence of teacher or coach, I simply stop playing and collapse into apologies
of the absurd kind I reported in chapter 5. There are also moments when
the arrogant professor in me takes over and resists.

JUNE 23, 1994—It is midweek at "Racine," which is the shorthand way of
referring to the "Prairie School Summer Chamber Music Institute."
About fifty of us have assembled to play quartets day and night for a full
week, with frequent coaching by the Manhattan String Quartet and
Rachmael Weinstock, the founder of the Institute. We have all been "ordered," some months ago, to prepare the Mendelssohn E minor (op. 44
#2), the Shostakovich #4 (*mostly* D minor), the Beethoven #8 (E minor),
and the Schumann F major. Phyllis and I have practiced them a lot, often with great pleasure, but increasingly aware that some parts will be
beyond even her gifts, if the tempi are anything like what the composers
desired.

Things went well yesterday. But this morning? Well, after our "average" group of strangers works for awhile on the Mendelssohn Adagio,
attempting unsuccessfully to get those deep-felt sixteenths toward the
end in sync, and with quite a lot of tension among us as our different interpretations clash, Rachmael, now 81 and admired by everyone as one
of the best coaches ever, enters the room.

I have been doing the best I can to pull the somewhat shaky group together—the 2nd violin inclined to hurry, the viola inclined to slow things
down. I am *still* trying to do that when suddenly Rachmael stops us and
says to me, "You came in too early with your sixteenth passage."

I snap back: "I did *not*."

A moment of shocked silence. Then:

"You don't say that to a coach!" he snarls, whirls about and starts for
the door.

I jump up and coax him back in with profuse apologies, though I feel certain that he had me wrong.

That afternoon when I apologized again he complimented himself on being broad-minded enough to forgive me and said, "You see, I happen to know that quartet cold!" I wanted to say, "I do too!"

At dinner I told my story to a cellist who knows Rachmael well. "Well, you know," he said, "Rachmael is desperate to be loved. Beneath his air of security, he is extremely insecure." Maybe so. But why did the little boy in me—or was it the professor?—have to be a smarty? Even though Rachmael had missed the fact that I was trying to balance between the speeder and the dragger, it was stupid of me to answer back to a teacher who has been head man for many decades.

What's worse, I'm now convinced, years later, having done a bit more work on that movement attending to a metronome, that Rachmael was absolutely right and I was wrong: I did speed up. I can laugh about that today, but the laugh is not as hearty as I'd like.

Hours of Bliss, or, at Least, Gratitude

FEBRUARY 10, 1994 —I am reading in my lounge chair, already in my pajamas at 9:30; a lovely peaceful evening. Practiced for 45 minutes after dinner. Phyllis is listening to the messages on her answering machine—mostly from her therapy clients.

She comes into the room and says, "A call here from Siegfried—their cellist has phoned in sick. Would you be willing to go over—right now?"

"Yes, I'd love to." Not a second's pause. Not a flicker of the resentment other interruptions might produce.

Later, thinking back on it, I am a bit surprised at my quick response. How could I fail to ask who else would be in the group or what they were playing? If it had been one of Bartók's, say, I'd have turned honest and said, "Sorry, I'm not up to it without a lot of practice." I didn't at first even ask myself, "Can I cover for the fact that I've not practiced much for several days?" None of that. Just "Yes, I'd love to."

Get dressed. Put cello in case, nearly forgetting the bow. At the last minute remember the mute. Locate the essential eyeglasses. Pick out hastily a few of my standard cello parts; a music stand in case they don't have enough of them; stand lights, in case the lighting is bad. Out into the twenty-below-zero night, thinking, my cello will be badly out of tune, my hands will be too cold to play well. And suddenly there I am, the three of them in front of their stands, waiting, waiting, already well warmed-up, raring to go, me still shivering.

"Wonderful of you to come. How vould you feel about late Bee-thoven?"

"Well, I just happen to have brought my late Beethoven volume . . . "

"Wonderful. How vould you feel about 127?"

"OK, wonderful." Delighted—yet on guard.

I tune up, my innards trembling: this is a bad way to begin, without warmup, my fingers tingling. I'm wishing Phyllis were here on first, or at least on second, or even on viola. Her presence always raises other people's appraisal of the Booth contribution by about 2,000 percent.

For the first ten minutes or so I do only "OK," "holding my own." Yet by the end it is all glorious. Siegfried doesn't have to shout "pianissimo!" at me even once, as he's often done in the past. Eloise says that this is the first time she's ever played the theme-and-variations movement without being crudely rushed by the cellist and violist with their ump-dee-dump-dees. "They always force us to go faster than we can manage, and you two didn't!" I had in fact fully enjoyed keeping my eyes and ears on the viola through that variation . . .

The Mozart F major goes even better. In fact it is sheer bliss—well, most of the time.

Next day: My readiness to do it, my ability to do it, after my fashion, but most of all the way we four joined made me feel, as I climbed into bed beside sleeping Phyllis at about one A.M., that all was right with the world.

Would I have gone out to play if the call had come at midnight? I think so. Does my account suppress a few minor booboos that if dwelt on would take the evening out of the class of "glorious?" Probably. It was like most of our glorious sessions: a critical listener would describe them as at best mixed. They are made glorious, at least for me, by the quality of the other players.

❧

Memory is especially rich with the hours Phyllis and I spent playing piano trios with Jane Knourek, now living far away.

OCTOBER 14, 1981—Sunday morning with Jane. Phyllis and I have *worked* hard in advance on Beethoven's sixth piano trio, then Mozart's third. B's sixth, in E-flat, is really hard for me, falls awkwardly on the strings, is not immediately ingratiating in its melodies. Yet it becomes wonderful when worked up. . . . Jane is very patient with me—how rewarding it is to play with a pianist who actually listens to and accommodates to what the strings are doing! And she plays so musically that I'm lifted into her phrasing and dynamics. One of our best sessions ever.

Ecstasies are never comparable; spiritual infinities cannot be ranked, contrary to what mathematicians claim about ranking *their* infinities. It remains true that whenever I have played wholeheartedly and without noticeable setbacks, I have the illusion—not just that I have played *better than ever before*, but that we all have: like all Beatle-lovers, bettah, bettah, bettah, bettah . . .

Dancing with Friends and Strangers

Professional players and music critics always emphasize that a group must be together for a long time before they play together with anything like perfection. Whenever a quartet loses one of the four, it takes them a while to adjust, and sometimes they just give up. These days, for example, music critics are worrying about how the style of the new first violinists in two famous quartets will jibe with the three who have played together for years.

How different that is from what we amateurs do, often playing for several hours with total strangers. An illness has forced us to call, at the last minute, for a viola replacement. Or I am at a chamber music weekend and I'm assigned to play with three people who are looking at me, and at one another, wondering, perhaps in some anxiety, just how this session will go. We begin to tune—and discover that we all have different preferences about how high the A should be. We begin to play, and discover that what's-her-name hasn't a clue about how to count beats clearly. Meanwhile they have discovered that my cello tone is less thrilling than the one produced by the cellist they played with yesterday. And then, often, it turns quickly into blissful engagement.

What I want to celebrate in that turn is not just the musical wonder but the building of new friendships unlike any others we have. The very motive that brings us into that room where we must fake intimacy with strangers can yield—sometimes after only a movement or two—true intimacy. We leave the room loving those we entered fearing.

Remember the word,
The one from the manger.
It means only this:
You can dance with a stranger.[1]

To agree to "dance" with any stranger is an act of blind trust. Depending
on the game, you offer different levels of trust. Invite me into a poker game
with strangers and I'll have my guard up. Invite me to join a tennis four-
some and the guard goes down considerably. Invite me to play a Mozart
quintet tonight with you, and I'll already be feeling friendly. The worst exploitation you might impose would be asking for too much credit for your
superior playing.

American society today seems obsessed with self-protective slogans, often justified: never trust a stranger in any situation, whether a game or not;
don't allow eye contact with strangers; be sure your chain is on the door
when you answer the doorbell; hang up when an unknown broker rings you
on the phone. Though many cultures have celebrated the freedom of dancing with strangers—reread the *Odyssey* if you doubt my word on that—we
American middle-classers at millennium-end seem increasingly to hide behind security guards and doormen whom we also increasingly mistrust.

When the Amateur Chamber Music Players were planning their first directory of names, addresses, and telephone numbers, one prospective member suggested that the association should issue membership cards, "to guard
against exploitation and fraud." A Boston journalist-violinist wrote the
founders, urging them not to worry. People who "will permit their phone
numbers to be published in this way and virtually invite strangers into their
houses" are to be trusted. "Not even a game of bridge will disclose the char-
acters of four people to one another so completely and profoundly as an
evening of string quartet playing."

How precious is any practice that preserves some remnant of the classical notion that when strangers knock on your door, you invite them in and
feed them. That's how we amateurs all work: if you love chamber music,
you must be okay. Those we are open to have in effect already survived a
succession of tacit examinations administered by their instruments and
teachers over the years. Though some wimps and even a couple of cultural
fascists have managed to squeeze through those implicit examinations,
those types are extremely rare. Call our community elitist if you prefer. But

---

1. I don't know the source of this quatrain. It was used as the central text by a visiting
preacher at an Earlham College convocation, in about 1958.

the honoring has nothing to do with money or fame. And besides—don't we all wish that all of life could be like that?

The fact remains that the range from glorious to downright inglorious is even more dramatic when dancing with strangers than it is when playing with those we already know. The strangers inevitably range from wondrous through weird to awful. At home you know more or less what to expect; in fact you have gradually weeded out the worst candidates, either because they play intolerably or because they destroy evenings by intruding their egos more destructively than you intrude yours. And you have been learning how to deal cheerfully with the idiosyncrasies of your "regulars."

Yet even at home you sometimes find yourself looking across the stands at a total stranger or two wondering, as you lift your bow, just where they will fall on your scale of tolerability, and where you will fall on theirs. When you dance with strangers you always have both hopes and fears about the new ways that may emerge.

The supply of available strangers, with the threatening range of ability, is multiplied by the Amateur Chamber Music Players directory that I have mentioned earlier. Traveling across country each summer, or when we're in Europe, we pay close attention to the ratings each listed amateur awards herself: from Pro down through A, A–, and the B's to C, the lowest except for "unlisted." I suppose we should feel ashamed at never phoning ahead to anyone who assigns himself below a B–, though we know that some modest people underrate themselves and that some genuine C's would be fun to encourage on their path to B. Can you guess why, when we're traveling in America, we usually settle on the B+ and A– strangers, but when we're in England it's the B–'s, B's, and B+'s?

❦

The music weekends and weeks we attend always produce an unpredictable variety of strangers. Often we catch clues of looming disaster. One afternoon we were assigned to play with a violist who started tuning up and, with his hands shaking, tried to tune in fourths rather than the required fifths—as if he expected to play a ukulele. You could tell from his sweating that he knew something was wrong, but as he got more and more rattled, we all felt doomed: this man would surely turn out to be the worst violist we'd ever met.

One of us—I hope it was myself—said something soothing about how everyone feels nervous at such moments. Then the first violinist tuned the instrument for him, and we started off on an easy Haydn. We hadn't gone twenty measures before we could see that he was actually a fine violist, among the better ones attending this weekend.

Before celebrating further the triumphs of stranger-transformation, honesty again requires one detailed look at near disaster.

JOURNAL, UNDATED TO PREVENT IDENTIFICATION OF THE VILLAINS—
We just attended a three-day Chamber Music Weekend. Met some wonderful players, had some fine sessions; met some pretty poor players, had some annoying sessions. Felt that we played *better than ever before;* felt that I played, too often, pretty damn badly. Was again and again transported by the playing, dwelling with Mozart and Brahms and Beethoven; was again and again distracted from the music by personality quirks and occasional disputes among fellow players. It was the best of weekends; it was—no, by no means the worst of weekends: it was an average weekend, which means "a really quite thrilling mixture."

Phyllis and I found ourselves scheduled for a session with Larry,—an ardent devotee and highly skillful violinist who often insists on too-rapid tempi—and Jim, a violist whom we met for the first time this morning. At lunch Jim, having seen the assignments for the afternoon sessions, is already groaning.

"I don't think I can stand to play again with that arrogant bastard, Larry; he spoils every session by acting as if he were a conductor or teacher instructing the stupid students. Last night he stopped us whenever he felt like it, just to lecture us on how it should go. I *hate* that. It freezes me up; I just can't go on playing when someone stops the music to criticize."

Half an hour later, everything begins with cool cordiality, but I can see that Jim is already edgy. Then, after only a few measures, Phyllis and Jim half-flub a rapid duet; it's so uneven that they *almost* don't make it together to the end of the elaborate phrase. Then they miraculously do end the phrase together, and we are going on for a couple of seconds when suddenly Larry stops playing and pounces.

LARRY: You two weren't at all together there. We should start over and...
JIM (almost shouting): I'm sorry, but I just cannot tolerate that kind of interruption. It upsets me. It really upsets me. It's rude. Phyllis and I were already back together when you started criticizing. We already knew that we hadn't done it right; we knew what it should sound like. You don't have to tell us we didn't do it right. You must think we're ignoramuses. Why do you do that? That kind of criticism upsets me so much I just can't...

LARRY (interrupts, looking pale): I didn't mean it as criticism. I just wanted to . . .

JIM (standing up): You didn't mean it as criticism? When you rudely stopped us and . . .

WAYNE (hoping to moderate): Well, ah, Larry, because you play so well you probably don't realize how your comments do often feel to others like destructive criticism . . . I know you don't mean it that way but . . .

LARRY (paler and paler): Well, I *don't* mean it as criticism; I mean it as . . .

JIM (redder and redder): How can you not call it criticism, when you tell us that we got it wrong? And why should you, on second violin, try to be in charge? It should be Phyllis, on first, who does the supervising!

LARRY (his face bloodless, his lips tight): That's the first time in my life I've ever heard the charge that the second violin is really less important than the first!

PHYLLIS: That was not what he said. He said . . .

JIM (interrupting even Phyllis): I said that the second violinist is less important, as director, and I want to make clear that if there are any more such interruptions, I'm going to leave the room.

Larry's pale face is now mottled with red spots, but he says nothing. Looking ready to attack physically, he moves forward in his chair.

What to do?

WAYNE: I wonder if I could suggest a compromise: How about stopping only when, ah, uh, maybe . . .

Nobody seems to be listening. The quarrel continues until finally Larry, still livid (but with eyes red) says something like, "All right, if you don't want to get anything *right*, let's just play it your way, any old way!" And we do start to play again, Larry utterly glum, slightly less pale but unsmiling even when anyone attempts a mollifying or jokey comment, Jim still red, looking apprehensive. The playing goes sort-of OK, but gloom, not Mozart, is in the room.

By the time we turn to Beethoven the fog has begun to lift a bit. I feel that the Beethoven (Opus 135) is a revelation: it had been quite awhile since I'd even attempted it, and this group does it quite well, though with little *brio*. To my surprise, as we stand up and begin to put our instruments away, Larry and Jim approach each other. I fear blows, but they shake hands!

WAYNE: "That handshake makes me feel even better than the one between Rabin and Arafat."

Lukewarm chuckles.

Through the rest of the weekend each man went on offering private conversational attacks on the other one. I doubt that they'll ever be friends.

❧

Closer to our usual experience is when woe turns to near bliss.

SEPTEMBER 17, 1981—Just after lunch, we assemble, four strangers, all hoping—one assumes—to make beauty together. The first violinist, Hans, is a tall, looming figure with a strong German accent: beaming smile, eager manner. Unlike some I've played with this weekend, he doesn't show off as he tunes up; instead of playing rapid spiccato arpeggios from some concerto he learned as a child, he is admirably attentive—though perhaps just a bit bossy—in getting us all into good tune. The second violinist is a heavy-eyed, plain woman in her mid-fifties; terribly nervous, fussing with her stand and her chair; has forgotten her pillow. Goes to her cabin for it, keeping us waiting; returns. Tunes nervously, excessively working the pegs again and again long after it seems to me she's in fine tune. I wish Phyllis were here.

The violist is a plump, pretty, sulky woman of about thirty-five. Is she sulking because she has predicted that we'll be beneath her? She snarls a bit about the pitch my cello has fed them. Announces that she has a bad cold. I am almost tempted to get up and leave.

More than usual shifting about of chairs and stands. Second Violin goes into a prolonged apology, in advance, for her playing. For once I resist joining that competition of apologists, saving for later my customary shattering slightly dishonest claim that "I took up the cello in my mid-thirties."

We jockey a bit over what should be played. Hans had mentioned to me, before the others came, that he'd like to play some of the "Art of Fugue," and I said I'd love to, but neither of us mentions it now: I think we both have concluded that the other two won't be up to it.

SECOND VIOLIN: I don't care what we do so long as it's not Beethoven, Mozart, or Haydn. I mean, what we come to these weekends for is to do things we don't do at home, isn't that right? I'm bored with those three anyway.

My already slim hopes vanish. What kind of musician can it be who would say a thing like that? Just how often does she play through the Beethoven quartets so well that to play them again would be boring? How many of the eighty-three Haydn quartets has she actually done justice to?

I assume that we have settled on a Haydn, but when I look at my stand I see that Hans has put out a totally unfamiliar Schubert. I panic.

"Beginning with Schubert? I'm afraid I've never played this one at all, Hans, and they are all so fiendishly hard to sight-read . . . "

"Oh, no," Hans interrupts, his German accent somehow seeming even thicker than before. "This one is very easy, very easy. And sooo beautiful. You'll find already it goes well."

So we play it, the Opus 168, D major. Actually it *does* go fairly well, with Hans's competent leading. He was right about its beauty. The other two surprise me by being better than I am, technically, and almost as good about just plain listening and keeping together. The final movement does not, like so many of Schubert's, run itself into the ground with repetitions. I love it.

All the distractions and pollutions seem washed away; the group is ageless, sexless, flawless, even though the physical appearance is mostly unchanged.

I could of course make this story more dramatic by inventing more ugly appearances at the beginning, and greater physical transformations as we move along—but I want, as always, to keep things absolutely honest. So back to the journal:

HANS (the German accent really strong now): Vane Boot and I t'ott maybe vee might do a bit of the 'Art of Foog.'
SECOND VIOLIN: Who wrote it?

Trying not to appear shocked, we explain, taking turns as we pour out praise for Bach and *The Art of the Fugue*. Second Violin still looks doubtful. Viola seems willing but again starts sulking. So I distribute the parts, which I "just happen" to have brought from home.

We do the first fugue; no serious hitches—we all know how to count, and the parts are not technically difficult. We do the second, the third. We stop for a drink of water.

SECOND VIOLIN: Let's do something else now. That just goes on with the same stuff over and over again, especially for the second violin; there's not much more that can happen later.
HANS (sounding cross): No, we'll do some more. You'll find plenty happening.

My annoyance over his dominating style fades; he has insisted rightly, when I might have wrongly caved in. We do the fourth.

SECOND VIOLIN: Now that *was* more interesting. There was more for the second violin to do. The other movements didn't really have as much for *me* to do.

WAYNE (by now perhaps also sounding a bit cross): But the second has as much to do in all the movements as any of the other parts! In this kind of counterpoint, they're all roughly equal. That's what's so wond . . .

SECOND VIOLIN: No, but this one had more for *me*.

It's hard to tell just how much she's been hearing of the intricate counterpoint gamboling: has she actually *heard* any of the incredible polyphony in the other parts?

We come to the violin and cello duet in number five. Hans insists that he and I should do it, while they listen. I insist that we should not: "It won't be fun to listen to, as played by me." We argue a bit, but I finally cave in. Then I start out abominably and after a few measures deliberately quit, remembering the fiasco when I did *not* quit after ruining the opening of the Brahms sonata.

"No, I'm not going to subject these good folks to this, Hans. Let's either go to something else or go on to another movement."

We go on.

In the middle of movement #6 Second Violin loses her place—the first time that has happened for any of us. Things do get a bit rough here as Bach moves into his rapid *Fuge aus zwei im Kontrapunkt der Quint vertauschbaren Themen*—the title and movement not quite as complex as when he gets to his upside-down and backwards gambits, but still rhythmically demanding.

SECOND VIOLIN: I'm so sorry; I was beginning to listen more carefully to the other voices and I tried to adjust when Viola slowed down too much.

Viola looks annoyed but says nothing. Hans launches into a lecture about how in playing Bach you have to listen to two things, or rather *do* two things at once: you have to listen to all the other parts, intently, yet you have to be ready to ignore one or another of them if the player gets off. The beat must be maintained at all cost, but never—don't forget—at the cost of hearing how the others are keeping the beat and surrendering to the various main themes. When *you* are given the main theme you must . . .

They both look at him as if they knew all that already.

After #7 we can see that they've both had about all they can take. "Time to quit?" They both agree. Then a surprise: as we put away the parts, Second Violin says, "Well, that was a lot more interesting and fun than I thought it was going to be."

As we take our break Viola explains, after blowing her nose again, that she is only now taking up the viola and violin again after years of neglect. She played them both as a teenager; is working really hard at it all now; feels that everything she does is just a bit behind the proper schedule of learning—it's too late.

This is the cue I've been waiting for, but I resist until after we've settled back down and played the Brahms first, which goes without hitch— rather rare, with that one—and with real feeling. When we have breathed a bit, I think it is time for my earth-shaking revelation.

"I feel a lot like Viola, always behind the true learning schedule. When I was 33 I . . . "

I make it as brief as possible. [Note that I've moved *toward* the honest "thirty-one," from "middle thirties."]

Splendid responses, especially Viola's: "Why, I think that's simply amazing. My respect for anyone who can take up a string instrument as an adult and play it the way you play it—well, it's simply wonderful. All this makes me so glad that I'm getting back into it . . . "

How can I confess, without violating the whole point of this book, that that moment felt almost as wonderful as playing the music? Why should I care that much about whether a couple of strangers enjoy my playing? For shame! What kind of amateur am I? But at least the four of us are no longer strangers.

We are not full friends yet. In fact we may never meet again. But sometimes moments like that blossom on through months and years, producing what I hope will make a proper climax to this chapter of ups and downs.

❧

THANKSGIVING WEEKEND, 1996—With none of the family coming for Thanksgiving weekend, Phyllis and I decided to try something we'd done only once before: invite two chamber players to come and play for two or three days, staying in our house.

They joyfully accepted—two fine players from Detroit whom we had enjoyed playing with on chamber weekends. They had told us that in Detroit they have trouble finding amateurs willing to play regularly: "Everyone who plays well plays semi-professionally in orchestras."

Gerda and Kay arrived midday on Thursday, left about one Saturday afternoon. Through the whole time, we played and played and played, except for eating and sleeping. At 10 A.M. Sat. Fred, "our" new pianist, arrived and we played the Schumann and Dvořák piano quintets.

So there we have *thirteen* glorious compositions (Kay counted them): one Haydn (Opus 33 #1), three Beethovens (the late B-flat, including *all* of the Grosse Fuge!), the A minor!, and Opus 59 #1, with me actually sort of revelling in the opening cello solo!); one Mendelssohn, one Hindemith, the Schubert A-minor—the two quintets—that makes only twelve: I've forgotten one already!

When have I ever had a better weekend than that? Never! But how to do justice to it? How do I describe my falling into tears as Phyllis played her viola solo in the Schumann, or my *almost* tearful response playing the same solo when my turn came? How praise highly enough the astonishing fact that the three fiddlers took turns as "leader" on first (two of them also on viola) with never a hint of tension or put down or competition? Not just the music but the congeniality was the best we've had since . . . well, maybe since never.

I was aglow for hours after they left—it's still with me.

That's what life is for, one of the great gifts: hours of love with Phyllis and former strangers and with those not-really-dead composers. It's a kind of spiritual communion unsurpassed by anything else I have known.

There's sure no passion in the human soul,
But finds its food in music.
GEORGE LILLO, "FATAL CURIOSITY"

❧

As my own playing experience increased, so did my awareness of
the elegance and subtlety of the music of those I was listening to.
FRANK WILSON

❧

A violin player hears violin music with his hands—part of his
hearing is the way his fingers corroborate the playing.   FRANCIS
SPARSHOTT

Chapter Eight

Hearing with Your Body:
How Playing Transforms Listening

EVERY AMATEUR QUEST steals time from every other. The time you spend gardening will not be spent campaigning to preserve an endangered species; the time you spend reading a novel will not be spent painting a portrait of your true love or writing a memoir.

For the music lover, the most disturbing theft that playing commits is of time stolen from listening. My celloing steals from music of all kinds, the worst losses being chamber music or jazz. Unlike amateurs in previous centuries, we all can now choose to listen at any moment to any fine composition, played better than it will ever be played by us. When George Eliot arranged for chamber music sessions, playing her piano part, she was filling a musical gap in her life; she often risked hearing badly played music as an alternative to hearing none. These days there is no such gap; time spent on worse playing turns off the switch that could at any moment *turn on* much better playing.

To confront such listening losses thus heightens the why-do-it question, underlining the ambiguities buried in the metaphor "spending time." When we spend money, the money is gone; we get something for it, but the money is gone. When we spend time on many passive entertainments, we get little in exchange but time-killing: the time is gone. But when we spend time on listening to fine music, the time does not seem so much spent as somehow redeemed, paid back; we get more than we paid for. Is not such time "spent" listening to the Juilliard Quartet or Oscar Peterson trio, to the Emerson or Dave Brubeck quartets, paid back more fully than my hacking away ever manages? Why garden, when you could visit an arboretum or flower show?

Why organize an amateur play reading when you could rent a video performance by John Gielgud or Vanessa Redgrave? Why struggle to scull better—why not just buy a motorboat? If you know that the lover you pursue is already permanently committed to a more worthy suitor, one you also love, why keep trying? Why reach for the cello bow, at the end of a hard day at the office, rather than the CD button that lets you live with the perfections of a Pablo Casals, a Janos Starker, a Jacqueline du Pré, a Rostropovich, a Yo-Yo Ma, a Julian Lloyd Webber—name your favorite? Listening, like playing, can be bliss—and it offers far fewer moments that turn into bale.

If some cruel God ordered me to choose now—"Thou must give up one or the other, either playing chamber music or listening to it!"—I would simply have to refuse the choice and let the tyrant decide. He could cut off my left thumb or forefinger and reduce me to listening. She could cleverly turn me deaf and wipe out the problem: "Go find another cello-reach!"

The fact remains that I do make a choice: a radical sacrifice is made, day after day, year after year. I no longer spend anything like an hour a day listening to professionals, and I miss it. Is the playing worth the sacrifice?

There's no easy answer beyond the loose-jointed ones I've offered already. But, to my surprise, a not-so-easy one has emerged: my effort to play has radically transformed the listening hours that I do manage to conserve.

❧

How our playing as amateurs is improved by listening to professionals is obvious. The reverse truth—that our playing-at improves our hearing-of what they play—is neither obvious nor easy to explain to anyone who has not experienced it. Somehow or other playing a melody gets it all into our synapses—or our souls—in a form that changes our hearing. As Frank Wilson puts it, "We can hear only what we've learned to hear." Hearing "has a great deal to do with motor control," and "you can and *do* hear [only] what you listen for." Wilson's scientific evidence for how playing changes hearing by actually remodeling the physiology of the brain should be convincing to any skeptic. My case, entirely anecdotal, is likely to seem weak except to those who have already experienced it.[1]

Neither Wilson nor I would expect that our cases would win in a court

---

1. The recent evidence of how keeping mentally alive actually maintains and improves the physiology of the brain is impressive. Popular accounts are appearing everywhere—in *Scientific American*, in the *New York Times*. In September 1994 the *Chicago Tribune* ran an extensive series on its front page, with headlines like, "Discoveries show circuits get rewired, new parts grow." Even the elderly can force their brains to keep on growing (September 20, 1994).

of law. How could one ever prove that non-players don't listen in the same way that players listen, and that the differences are almost all in favor of players? No claim about music I can think of could be more subjective and unverifiable. But that doesn't stop me; learning to play, or trying to learn to play, is the best step anyone can take toward deeper listening.

Two Objections

If you're a committed listener and still don't play, that claim is sure to seem extreme, if not downright offensive. An ardent listener-friend of mine recently almost snarled at me, questioning my celebration of amateuring: "The performers I've known personally, amateur or professional, are interested only in their performance; they don't really *hear* the *music*. You'll never convince me that you listen better than I do." If you have had a good deal of musicological training but don't play, you will probably want to join him. You rightly feel that you really hear all the parts of a complicated fugue or sonata movement. You follow the harmonic sequences. You note the tricks with the "circle of fifths," and you revel in the surprising key changes. What amateur can do better than that?

Second objection: the necessary concentration on technique as you learn to play can sometimes distract the player from the music, when listening. As he watches how the cellist "does it," the aspiring player may stop genuine listening: "Oh, I see now how to play that; I don't need to worry so much about my lesson on that tomorrow." Noticing that effect in myself some years ago, I finally caught on to a solution: always try to sit where you cannot see the cellist as well as you can see the others. And no matter where you sit, keep your eyes on the violist and second violinist, so that your ears will be on all four parts. Recently at a concert I caught myself, in the middle of a wonderful performance of the Benjamin Britten No. 2, wondering why the cellist of the Colorado Quartet was holding her bow in the same "Baroque" way that Yo-Yo Ma had used in playing the Bach suites a month ago. Britten had left the room, ordered out by my playing years. I had to turn my eyes to the violist to bring Britten back in.

At a coaching week recently, we attended a concert in which the Manhattan Quartet played the Beethoven C-sharp minor, the wondrous one we had all been coached on for several days. Building on my decades of living with it and my weeks of working it up, keeping my eyes mainly on the middle two players, I was transported. I can't remember any hour of listening when I have been more totally and musically absorbed. Though there were a few moments when I weakly surrendered to performance questions—

"why did Chris finger that one that way?"—I was able to keep my ears and soul on the music, actually hearing interconnections I'd never noticed before.

Meanwhile Sally, sitting on my right, was squinting at her violin part on her lap, in the dim light; it was not even the score but her first violin part. Though of course I can never know what went on in her head, I am certain that if I had listened with my heavily annotated cello part open on my lap, the concert would have been seriously damaged—not utterly destroyed but considerably downgraded. I would have heard it as if Beethoven had had the cello part as his center. Passion for performance perfection can indeed harm the music.

Intensified Listening

How do we answer such objections? Frank Wilson concludes his answer like this:

> It did not occur to me until I began my own studies [in my late thirties] that the great joy of listening to music arises in the most unexpected, delightful, and profound ways *once you have had personal experience with its creation.* As my own experience increased, so did my awareness of the elegance and subtlety of the music of those I was listening to. My own efforts at music-making may have been clumsy, but they were earnest, and rewarded me with a far less passive set of ears and eyes; I become [*sic*] more and more closely drawn into the act of creation. . . . [my italics]

Francis Sparshott puts the case even more sharply in the epigraph above: "A violin player hears violin music with his hands—part of his hearing is the way his fingers corroborate the playing." He adds a footnote: "Objection: hands don't hear, ears hear. Response: hands don't hear, but ears don't hear either. People hear."

A related argument has been almost commonplace from the earliest years of string quartet playing. As more and more composers came to think of chamber music as the highest achievement, they and their admirers often talked about it as intimate "conversation" not quite available to even the most attentive listener. As Goethe put it, almost enviously, "One hears four rational people talk among themselves." When Carl Friedrich Zelter, musician and composer, wrote to Goethe in praise of the Möser Quartet's performance of Beethoven's work, he stressed that the "essence of deep listening" is the "illusion of 'playing along.'" It lies in "*imagining* the act of creating the sounds." "Authentic appreciation," Zelter felt, "depended on the listener's capacity to imagine playing and re-enacting what was heard. . . . The illusion of participation defined true appreciation and connoisseurship." This illusion becomes reality when you have worked up a piece and then hear it played as you wish you could play it.

JANUARY 15, 1994 [LETTER TO "OUR" PIANIST, JANE KNOUREK]

Dear Jane,

If we'd known in advance that last night's trio concert (program enclosed) was to be so close to what we've been playing with you, we'd have called you and tried to persuade you to give up packing for Texas and come down to Hyde Park for it. Actually, if we'd known in advance just how marvelous the Tchaikovsky group would be, we'd have driven out to Oak Park, kidnapped you, and forced you to attend.

My main point in writing today is to report what playing with *you* has done for us in our *hearing* of their rendition of the Dvořák Dumky and the Shostakovich trio. The excitement of having worked at them several times with you paid off in a unique way. At many points I was not just out of this world but in tears — esp. in the Dvořák, but also in the slow movement of the Shost. To have struggled to realize those two wonders, with your patient help, and then finally to hear them fully realized for the first time by those more-than-professionals — that was one step higher, even, than it would have been to have heard them played for the first time *without* having had sessions with you as teacher/player.

I'm putting it clumsily, but I'm sure you know what I mean: first-time hearing is one thing; first-time hearing with the stuff of it already in your bones and muscles is quite another.

A special pleasure was the sense at every moment that *that* was what you have always been getting us to see and feel; *that* was the way you have implicitly tried to get us to play it, not by talking but by your playing. Their allegros were of course much faster than ours, but they *felt* the way your playing made it feel. And their slower movements seemed to me exactly your tempi — and emotional tone. The way you play the opening chords of what I think of as Shostakovich's elegy was exactly what Bogino was doing.

Needless to say, this was the first time I had really understood why Shost. used so many harmonics in the cello, esp. at the beginning. The cellist played them in a way that wrung my withers, and the duets with the violinist were — what? . . . heavenly? . . .

In short, you shoulda heard 'em. My only complaint, in the whole evening: they took the fast stuff in the Shost, including the Allegro with the many decrescendo diminished seconds—those discordant grunts—*too* fast: only someone like us who has played that stuff could have had a clue about just how fantastically intricate and discordant/concordant those groans are. Non-playing listeners must have missed most of it, even if unlike me they had no hearing loss.

The point of this missive, as you may have guessed, is loving gratitude: Phyllis and I both had an experience last night that we could never have had but for our "training" under Jane Knourek . . .

MARCH 6, 1994—Last night I experienced again the grand difference in listening that playing makes. The Hagen Quartet, three of them siblings from Salzburg, the second fiddle an American, all quite young, played the Beethoven C-sharp minor, perhaps his most difficult of all. We've played it many times by now, and that history I think helped a lot.[2]

The Hagen played it splendidly, though with occasional roughness, as they plunged into fortes and prestos and dynamic contrasts that Beethoven asks for and that perhaps no quartet will ever realize perfectly. My musical pleasure was at its peak; I often surrendered to that total immersion, that spiritual baptism, that the finest performances yield.

At the end, when I was almost ready to shout my bravis, the audience as a whole seemed strangely divided. One man stood up to applaud; others like me were clapping as hard as we could. Others were sitting on their hands. A voice behind me grumbled: "That's the worst performance of the C-sharp minor I've ever heard."

I whirled on the stranger. "I hope you mean that ironically!"

"Hell, no! I *know* that piece cold; I've heard it played by the Juilliard, by the Guarneri, by the Emerson, by the Quartetto Italiano, by the Amadeus, and by the Tokyo, and those greenhorns *got it all wrong!*"

"Do you play an instrument yourself?" I intended the arrogant question to crush this pedant.

"No, I don't, but you don't have to play to recognize bad intonation, poor interpretation, lack of feeling . . . "

We quarreled a bit, more or less politely, as concert hall conventions

2. Since the C-sharp minor was the center of our lives through the first six months of 1997, preparing it for the week in Racine, and since it keeps cropping up here, perhaps I should just surrender to it and change the subtitle of this book: "Why Struggle to Play Beethoven's Opus 131 in One's Eighth Decade?"

dictate. I told him, smiling ironically, that his line made me want to fight it out with our fists. Then I left him and wandered through a chatting audience that turned out to reflect our disagreement, but in milder form.

Most of the amateur players shared my superlatives. The only one who didn't was the one whose own interpretations always seem to me most questionable when we play with him. His objections were entirely like the stranger's, nit-picking comparisons of the Hagen with recordings he loves. I think he had been listening as a kind of professional *listener*, not as an amateur *player*. For us, remembered struggles had opened up listening pleasures inaccessible to listeners who are hooked on a given past interpretation.

My objection is deepened by the fact that the recordings those perfectionist listeners are trapped by have often been doctored to remove all minor blips: mechanically "perfected." Idealized listening to idealized recordings is thus quite different from our body-bound listening. We "impure" players were succumbing to a new interpretation, warmed by our knowledge of how every real performance entails some limits on perfection. We were willing to trust and admire the new reading, since it was a genuine honoring of possibilities revealed in the written notes. That the cellist's third finger had once or twice landed a hairbreadth off, instantaneously corrected, was actually part of the thrill of it.

If like us you tend to play Beethoven's prestos at a tempo he would have sneered at—more like an andante or moderato than a presto—you know how impossible it is to meet all of his demands. The better groups try to, and the best ones come close, but every amateur knows why many professional players in Beethoven's time were furious at him and why some actually quit. They were wrong, but one cannot blame them.

My point, then, is not only that the music in its impersonal purity is heard more fully and felt in the body by those who have tried to play it. It is also that listening pleasure is heightened by admiration for players performing the impossible. An analogy: I can juggle three oranges or apples. I have tried, ever since adolescence, to juggle four, and always failed. I am thrilled when I see a professional juggler managing five balls. His achievement is in my bones—sort of. My playing has transformed my "listening."

The Blissful Hangover

We can add to all this a kind of listening that I've always known but never seen discussed: the "morning-after" effect, listening in one's head, the music rising up from subconscious memory. It's true that this effect does not depend entirely on learning to play—it can come from listening intently to the same composition many times. Surely everyone has been surprised to hear this or that "silent" tune suddenly intruding on other, seemingly more pressing business. But the effect is intensified almost beyond recognition by the repetitive struggle to play the piece right. Call it the blissful *reverse* hangover?

After playing the two Brahms sextets on Friday night, I found myself on Monday, as I was in the shower thinking about Whitehead, simultaneously singing not my own cello part but a viola passage. A little later, working on an article at the computer, I suddenly "heard" all of the other five strings opening Opus 36 while I do nothing, for twenty-nine measures, but ten little pluckings and one gentle slurp. Later still, walking to campus, I suddenly realized that I was pacing to the andante of the other sextet, Opus 18.

This morning, Tuesday, reading about the usual atrocities in the morning paper, I hear intruding the lovely pattern of ritardando arpeggios at the end of that slow movement. My voice could never sing them properly; my cello had come closer. But my mind, my half-conscious, gets them right. Later the cellos are both plucking away in my head, in the marvelous pizzicato opening of the scherzo of the G Major. Sometimes, when we have worked especially hard and then experienced an especially good session, the hangover will run on for weeks.

When that happens, Brahms is not just literally in the room—a notion I'll expand in chapter 9. His achieved dream, that wonderful music, has now entered my body/soul in a way that turns me partly into Brahms. It is not only that with a conscious effort I can remember how this or that section goes: that's fairly easy and common. Almost everybody does it with the cheapest of TV commercial jingles. It is that he is now "in there," alive and well, of his own accord, as you might say, playing away even when I'm not attending to him. His will has become my will, and in a different sense, mine has become his. The "will" here is not simply some separable spirit or soul: it's in my body.

Everybody who ever pays active attention to anything knows something of what I'm talking about: fragments of memory, pleasant and unpleasant, taking over the daydreaming mind. A player's hangover runs much deeper: it is something special that happens only when you enter, as a full amateur, into the production of what is worth producing. Every amateur gardener or athlete or poet knows at least a part of what I'm hopelessly trying to describe —hopelessly because the experience is in every case subjective and unique:

my memories of Brahms, or of how it feels to plant tulip bulbs and hope for their blooming, will not be identical to yours.

❧

I am aware of a real risk of sounding arrogant here: my irrepressible conviction that too many folks out there—probably never even touching a book like this one—are wasting their lives away on leisure-time activities that produce not blissful but regretful hangovers. "Why did I spend my time on that?" "Those explosions in *Independence Day* still wake me at night!" Can it ever make sense to pass judgments on how people feel about how they've spent their time?

Well, evidence is beginning to arrive on our scene. Mihaly Csikszentmihalyi, for example, did a careful survey of how people feel about the time they spend, monitoring their feelings throughout the day, including how they feel after watching TV for a considerable stretch, in contrast to how they feel when amateuring. A large proportion reported their lowest level of spirits after passive watching.

Our minds go on reproducing and reshaping whatever we feed into them. But the reproduction is radically different depending on our degree of activity and passivity in the feeding. Too many of us spend our time simply watching other people trying to become champions. It is true that the amateuring performed by the watcher of TV sports, like the amateur listening of the concertgoer, can be well-informed, skillful, emotionally rewarding. But there really is something radically different between replaying a football game in your head "the morning after," even though you have indeed watched it with total absorption and excitement, and reliving your own active participation in a sandlot game or golf match.

As I wrote that sentence, I was surprised by an intrusion of the opening solo of the final movement of the G major, as played wonderfully by the cellist who played the first part Friday. I can predict that at odd moments far into the future, even if I don't touch the Brahms again, I'll suddenly be hit by it when totally off-guard. The blissful hangover comes not just the morning after; it can go on for a lifetime.

Four equals conversing together: this give-and-take of thought between four friends, each commenting on the common subject in his own voice and from his own character! DANIEL GREGORY MASON

❧

                                        I have said before
That the past experience revived in the meaning
Is not the experience of one life only
But of many generations—not forgetting
Something that is probably quite ineffable . . .
T. S. ELIOT, "DRY SALVAGES"

❧

Give me some music—music, moody food
Of us that trade in love.
SHAKESPEARE, *Antony & Cleopatra*

Chapter Nine

The Three Gifts

I TALK A LOT with friends—perhaps too much—about the sheer good fortune of my choosing to drop the piano and clarinet and take up the cello. But words like "fortune" and "choosing" seem less and less accurate as I have probed my journal entries and memories. "Fortune" implies plain chance, and obviously there was a lot more to it than that. "Choosing" implies deliberation, not just attention to responsibilities but a good deal of foreknowledge. To claim that "I chose rightly" implies a claim for credit for the results. "I wisely chose the right thing for the right conscious reasons."

In contrast, even though my reasons for choosing chamber music all still seem good, and though in one sense I've earned a lot by hard labor, the rewards of my amateuring are more like receiving from a friend or Phyllis an expensive gift that I have been unconsciously longing for but have not fully earned: a loving reward, an act of grace that could never be fully earned or anticipated or even hoped for. Not mere "good luck" or "wise choice," they can best be thought of as unconditional gifts.

The question of gifts from what or from whom is thus thrust upon us, and I'll face it most directly in the final chapter.[1]

❧

1. This chapter has been most immediately influenced by Lewis Hyde's *The Gift: Imagination and the Erotic Life of Property*; and C. S. Lewis's *The Four Loves*. The issues it faces relate in striking ways to those faced by Jacques Derrida in *The Gift of Death*.

When we talk about any part of life as an unearned gift, when we discover just how wrong economists are when they say there are no free lunches, when we move from cost-benefit analyses and talk about more-than-requited love, we infringe on territory usually reserved for prophets, preachers, or theologians. We don't need to drift into religious talk, however, to recognize that all amateur pursuits, not just mine, depend on unearned gifts: nobody goes it alone. The gardener depends not just on the bulb catalogue but on the tradition of gardening and botanical naming; the mountain climber is given a vast history of climbing technique and better and better equipment; the amateur movie maker, the amateur radio station operator depend on "gifts" from more recent forebears; and so on. I suspect that most avocations would yield, looked at closely, at least three unearned gifts resembling the three I dwell on now: the material instruments, the fellow players, and the composers or inventors who willed us their rich tradition.

The Instrument, and the Tradition It Springs From

In chapter 4, I stressed that the cello has often felt like a nastily resistant physical object, or like those in-your-face adolescents who imply, "I don't care about you; I'm going to do it my way." Yet more often my Becker, finished and stamped in 1964, has responded marvelously to my offers; it has given back more than I can ever give. Unlike the first two cellos that I worked against and should never have touched, it sings along with me—at least on those rare occasions when I manage to rise to its just demands.

To talk of it as a gift when in fact I had to pay for it may seem misleading. But when we ask seriously the question, "Where did it come from?" the notion of the gift begins to make sense: terms like "grace" and even "heirloom" flood in. Carl Becker did not, after all, invent his skill in cello making; he inherited most of it, from his father who in turn inherited it from the long tradition of makers. Though in one sense Carl had to earn my cello, and I had to pay for it, in fact it was largely a gift from tradition, a gift that he graciously passed along to me.[2]

2. If you have been persuaded by now to join the amateur world, you may want to know how much a good instrument will cost. My story should not discourage you: I paid $7,500 for the Becker, after selling the Urquhardt for the $3,000 I'd paid for it. Becker instruments immediately began to go up, and now cellos like mine are selling for between $50,000 and $75,000. A good bow may cost you as much as $10,000. But if you shop around you can find an adequate cello and bow for—well, let's say, for what you generally pay for the kind of car you buy. Are there better cellos to be had? Everyone says so. The prices *shout* so. But I've felt so wedded to mine that I haven't even surveyed the field. For all I know the most famous Stradivarius would have been even harder to master than my Becker.

Something like that mysterious embodiment of centuries of labor and experimentation may help explain why many players, amateur and professional, cannot resist talking sentimentally of their beloved instruments. Here's Julian Lloyd Webber on his cello:

> It has almost become a cliché for a string player to say that his relationship with his instrument is like a marriage, but in many ways it is so very true. Hours a day are spent trying to tame this temperamental creature who means so much to you.[3] The instrument is your companion at some of the most testing moments of your life—moments you have worked towards together—and it is hardly surprising that it should feel such a great rift to be parted from something you have shared so much with. When I was forced to sell my first good cello (to buy a supposedly better one), I freely admit to shedding a few tears on my way home from its new owner.

Sometimes that beloved living thing can turn inanimate or even hostile. Part of the gift is the process of entering a tradition of dealing with its promises and resistances.

MAY 9, 1994—Just back from Sleepy Hollow, where we played steadily from Thursday evening to Sunday noon. It was mostly great, but part of the time my Becker seemed to be scratching more than usual. Unlike some better players, I don't know enough about the physics of the cello, let alone my own playing, to know which of us is to blame. Does it need adjustment? Do I need new strings? Am I somehow bowing worse?

I asked another cellist, a much better player, to try it. "Seems ok; maybe needs adjustment a bit." Friday night when we played cello quintets with an even better cellist, Gunther, and heard him praising his own new cello, I asked him to try mine.

He played a few riffs. It sounded to me wonderful.

"It's a much better cello than mine," he said, "and your bow is better than my bow."

"So all the trouble is mine, not the cello's?"

"Well, it is a bit scratchy on the G-string. I'd try a different string."

Feeling like someone who has guiltily contemplated an affair with another lover, I welcomed "her" back into my arms and today will take "it" to Carl Becker, for adjustment and maybe new strings.

---

3. That doesn't quite fit my notion of the ideal spouse!

Other Flesh-and-Blood Strugglers

The way we players join, the way we blend, the way we fuse together, will always elude my verbal celebrations. "Words cannot express . . . "—how could they ever express the mystery of our "gift multiplications" as we play together, when we are at our best? The gifts of the other players to me— their very existence as produced both by tradition and by their years of practice—have been infinitely greater than anything I could ever have given in return, even if I had become a pro-amateur. The paradoxical, boundless fact is that every one in this playing community could say the same thing about the gift of the others: all of us, even the best of players, receive more than we give.

Such a statement can never make sense if we calculate in cost-benefit terms; the total is indeed far greater than the sum of the parts. Perhaps if the no-free-lunchers would do a little real amateuring on their own, and then really think about the totals, they might change their hard line.[4]

To dramatize the non-computable totals, we should look at some experience that, though it might well have ended as ingloriously as the worst we've seen so far, actually ended with a multiplication of gifts.

JANUARY 4, 1995—My companions this morning want to play the Brahms quintet in G major, Opus 111—the one with that fearful opening whomph-whomph solo demanded of the cellist. I am resisting.

WAYNE: I really can't play that part well at all. Maybe we'd better play something else.

HANNA (hostess and first violin, fine player): Oh, don't worry about it. Let's just start. . . .

Things go better than I had feared: she sets a fully relaxed tempo, and I make my way fairly well, even without having before me my own part with my pencilled tricky fingerings. As we move along, however, the sec-

---

4. An economist friend, after reading my potshots at those who proclaim "there are no free lunches," accused me of gross simplification. "We are not saying that no one gets more than he pays for; we're saying only that *someone* must pay for what *anyone* gets: the totals of pay and receive always balance, when fully understood." But that's just my point: they do not.

This dispute leads directly into the religious questions that I address in chapter 11: do we, as human beings, receive in the gifts of life more than we can ever pay for? Most who call themselves atheists will answer no. Some will go further and claim that we get less than we pay for: the scales weighing bliss against suffering tilt heavily to the right. As I tilt them the other way, I can hear a clever response: "Even as you celebrate the gifts of music, are you not ignoring the plain fact that at this very moment far fewer human beings are experiencing musical bliss than are experiencing physical misery?" I cannot stay for an answer.

ond violist has quite a lot of trouble with the rhythm of the slow movement; we find ourselves stopping too often. Then I get in a bit of trouble from rushing another important solo, and we stop again. On second try, I get it right, having belatedly figured out that the two violas are not rhythmically in unison with the cello but in radical syncopation against it; if I just pay attention to Phyllis's beat and slow down slightly, all is well.

When we stop at the end of the movement, I begin to say something to Phyllis and the other violist about my little discovery of the syncopation-battle. Hanna snaps at me contemptuously: "We've had too much talk already. Just keep it to yourself. It spoils the music to keep talking like that."

I feel myself flushing; I want to reach over and hit her—though she's too far away, and besides, I don't hit people. I've never been angry at Hanna before, and we've played with her often. To talk with Phyllis and the others not just about my booboo but about how we've made it go right seems to me part of the pleasure of the occasion. But I manage to keep quiet and play along through the last two movements, doing as well as possible but not enjoying it fully.

As we take refreshments, I try to avoid talking about it, because I'm still mad. But Hanna wants now to explain her outburst.

HANNA: I hope you understand why I can't bear those interruptions. How would you feel if in the middle of one of your public speeches somebody burst out with an interruption?

WAYNE: Well, that doesn't seem the same to me as to try to say something *musical* about the music, *between movements*, as I wanted to do.

HANNA: Well, to me it *is* the same. It's a spoiling of the full flow, and it just ruins the musical pleasure.

As we think about doing another piece, our second violist says she's too tired to carry on with quintets, so it'll have to be a quartet. Hanna suggests "the Debussy." I say that I don't feel up to it without some practice. I can see her suppressing her opinion that I mess up the ensemble less when I haven't practiced, so ask, "How about some late Beethoven?"

HANNA: Not a bad idea, unless we're too tired.

We had been playing since 10 A.M., and it was now about 3:30.

WAYNE: How about the A minor?

We agree and settle down. Miracles begin.

I play the slow, meditative opening in tune (I swear); they join me, *in tune*. We fuse, we move together. We all obediently resist saying a word. When I lose my place at one point I don't stop them but rejoin them so quickly that my slip is probably not even noticed.

We come to the fabulous, intricate, slow *"Heiliger Dankgesang eines*

Genesenen an die Gottheit" (Sacred Song of Thanks for Convalescence), with its complex fugal operations: we do it movingly, we do it right, we are carried away. Whenever we've played that with Hanna, or with anyone else before, one or another of the four has got lost, forcing us to start again, sometimes more than once. This time, no stopping.

In the final thrilling allegro, all keeps going well. Miracle of miracles, when we reach the climactic page, where the cello goes soaring up into a solo in high thumb position and then the violin joins it in unison, *I was up there*, pretty well in tune, making music in thumb position. Hanna was with me; we soared together, we ascended and descended together, and then we did it again, precisely when and as Beethoven asked us to. Well, more or less precisely.

Hanna was aglow. "That was the most rewarding performance I can ever remember doing with that. Oh, what a wonderful way to complete the day."

That was how it had felt to me. And the point here is that the final musical pleasure was actually somehow enhanced by our having quarreled and made up. Our friendship was deeper than when we began.

The "Living" Composers

The third gift is even harder to talk about intelligibly: the mysterious "body" of musical compositions flooding my life, and this book, from the beginning. As I said earlier, a free gift of some kind of music has been inherited by almost every infant since the beginning. In every culture we are born into a world of song. I now address, at the risk of seeming to insult other cultures, our distinctive Western inheritance, the huge piles of intricate compositions and the complex traditions of how they should be played. In an almost mystical way our dead composers—along with those who, like me, will soon be dead—are a living gift that in my biased view seems unique.

My proud acceptance of that gift can, I admit, produce troublesome moments.

SEPTEMBER 25, 1997 [CORFU]—The "coaching" and playing week has been going well, even as Phyllis copes with a bad cold. She goes to bed between sessions, gets up and plays for a couple of hours as if not ill, returns to bed (missing the tours of the island), then gets up and plays vigorously again in the evening. With only two full quartet groups here, we're getting more time from the coaches than we usually do.

A challenging, even embarrassing moment last night. The only other amateur cellist here is from Japan. As we chatted at dinner, he expressed his enthusiasm about chamber music.

AKIRA: It's a great inheritance you people have.

WAYNE: Well, because of what Phyllis tells me about your good playing, that inheritance is obviously yours, too. Are there many amateur chamber players in Japan?

AKIRA: Oh, thousands and thousands. In Tokyo alone we have—I would say one or two thousand.

WAYNE (consciously moving into risky territory): You know, I happen to love some Japanese music; I once fell in love with Nō drama and its music. But I wonder whether you would agree with me that this tradition you and I join when we play the Beethoven and Mozart is even more wonderful?

Long pause, with Akira looking down into his lap.

AKIRA: No, I'm afraid not. Our tradition is even more impressive.

Putting such tricky judgments aside, Akira and I went on to agree that those merely physical objects, those sheets of paper covered with black marks, vitally change what goes on in the so-called realer world. They lie there, seemingly inert—on our shelves, in our piano benches, in our car trunks as we drive to an engagement, in our suitcases as we fly from Tokyo or Chicago, solely for the sake of a week's playing. They lie, in immeasurably greater numbers, on the shelves of public libraries and private collections. And though many of them can remain silent for hours or months or even centuries, they are in fact charged with power, slyly issuing their commands: "You must come play us—come play *with* us—and when you come, you must try to do it *right*."

Some of those living orders are elementary—as if given to beginners:

No! Sorry, old man, you can't play a C-sharp there; that has to be a C; and you simply must note how in the second variation I dictate a change of key—to go on playing in two flats is just plain dumb. And you must, must, abide by my inventive dynamic markings: only then can you receive my full gift. If you play only forte when I say double forte, or if you play so loud that the viola's twist on the melody is lost, or if you don't remember that ff for me means "as loud as you can play," or if you miss my subito ppp's, you're not just dumb, you're doomed.

Somewhat subtler orders are being issued to the great conductors and players:

"Oh, yes, of course, Barenboim, I am happy with your experimenting with different interpretations, but you absolutely must not tinker with my essential structures."

"Do not overlook, Abbado, the care I have taken in subtly echoing, in the fourth movement, both the themes and the rhythms of the first. Don't overblast it."

"My subito fortes, Boulez, on the offbeat here must not be quite as loud as the ones coming up in the finale . . ."[5]

As I write, such voices are being obeyed in concert halls, over radio stations, and in recording studios. Their results are being heard by millions in recordings that are living influences on who we are.

I was in a used-record store recently, to sell some of my duplicate LPs, and I was impressed at how much trade was going on with records and tapes, classical and jazz. The proprietor paid me a dollar each for mine, and told me he could sell them for perhaps two bucks each. Here were collections of used recordings of every major composer, and even larger sections on some jazz and rock stars. It made me think again of the overwhelming mass of "the living dead." Take the B's alone, using only memory and not those shelves or any encyclopedia: Bach, Beethoven, Brahms, Berlioz, Bartók, Borodin, Boccherini, Bruckner, Berg, Busoni, Britten, Bridge, Bennett— and on outward from the classical to other classics like "Bird," Bix Beiderbecke, Basie, Brubeck, and the Beatles.

Add just the Sch's or M's and you have a library so full that it might well produce the "awesome fear" that Edmund Burke and Kant and others discussed under the idea of the sublime. "Beauty" is lamentably too bland a term for this huge "body," partly because so much of it is deliberately not beautiful. Like so many moments offered in Beethoven's later work and by living composers today, whether classical or pop, vast parts of our pile are aggressively ugly, angry, threatening, in some moments even despairing— yet they often turn it all into the sublime.

In one obvious respect, the life revived by the recordings comes closer to

5. I find it revealing that in contrast to all the postmodernist deconstruction of texts and radically revised performances of classical drama, sometimes seeming to reject the very notion of authorial intention, classical music continues to be performed—usually—with full respect for the composers' intentions, elusive or not. While Shakespeare is frequently performed and criticized in ways that the Bard would never recognize, Beethoven's notes—because of the very nature of notes—continue to issue their rigorous demands: "Play me, and not some twisted version of me." This doesn't mean, of course, that performers don't at times exhibit atrocious denials of what the score asks for. But they never go as far as a recent production of *Hamlet* that gives Fortinbras' final speech to Horatio!

meeting the composers' demands than anything we do in our sessions. The dead, deaf Beethoven, hearing himself resurrected by the Juilliard, would be astonished, even thrilled, though he'd probably complain about some details. Hearing himself half-resurrected by us, he would no doubt leap from his coffin and leave the room. Yet for us, our grapplings with those dead scores outclass even the best of the recordings: as we play or listen to other amateurs play, the resurrection is almost always amazing.

❧

What are resurrected are fortunately not those who lived real lives while composing. Reading honest biographies of those we worship I often feel my admiration declining. Who would choose to live day by day with the "real" Wagner, Beethoven, Benjamin Britten, or Tchaikovsky? Yet as we resurrect them they have sloughed off their money-grubbing, fame-driven, exploitative, often totally miserable selves and become disinterested, generous-spirited, exhilarated, loving friends. The pedestrian, often suffering person, back then, mandated to step out of the mire and into the composing mode, shakes off the irrelevancies, and emerges as the one we live with now.

As I think about that paradox—the contrast between the Beethoven I long to live with daily and the Beethoven I meet in biographies—suddenly the image arises of my worn, marked-up, falling-apart volume of the late Beethovens, and along with it the A-minor quartet comes flooding in again, uninvited, the differently vital movements competing in memory. Memory settles again on that molto adagio we played with Hanna, Beethoven's holy song of thanks to God for his recovered health. Thinking of that fugue—really that series of fugues—I want to go downstairs right now, as I recover from an illness much less threatening than Beethoven's, and play my part, hearing the other parts in my head. The real Beethoven suffered from the illness and recovered. The Beethoven I live with now went to his desk and willed me a miracle.

The sheer wondrous power of that living, writhing loveliness—the corpse-corpus, the ink-smeared sheets, many of them yellowing and crumbling, lying there in effect longing to be played! How can such a collection of physical objects, dead as a doornail, be said to be a loving, animate creature—a gift to me and Phyllis and our friends?

Since my efforts to describe this gift land me in so much sheer ineffability, perhaps I should just scrap this section, following Wittgenstein's endlessly quoted sentence: "What we cannot speak about we must pass over in silence." If that were true of all loves it most certainly would be especially true of this one. Neither this strange "body" nor its powerful soul can be fully expressed except in performance.

JULY 20, 1993—Last night went to a chamber music "festival" in Park City [it was a tiny Utah mining town when I was a kid living fifty miles away; now, as everyone knows, it's a burgeoning ski resort and "cultural center"]. We were a bit skeptical about whether that tourist trap would offer a good performance, and the skepticism grew when we learned that the performers were a "pick-up" group of unfamous players hired to come to Utah and make the festival.

The central selection was Brahms's G-minor piano quartet, Opus 25, the one that Schoenberg orchestrated splendidly, hoping it would come to be honored as Brahms's "fifth symphony." We found ourselves in a "chamber"—that is, a small church—listening to four people who had known one another for only a week or so and who were visibly nervous as they began.

Within a few moments that "chamber" seemed electrified. How to put it? It "came alive"? We were all "transformed"? It was not just that the music was sounding as I'd never heard it sound before—it was that you could feel the players themselves feeling caught up as if by surprise. Giving their first public performance of this work, after only limited time for rehearsal, they were in effect discovering/recovering Brahms as they played.

I was especially impressed by the young woman cellist, Gayle Smith, so I followed her after the recital to offer thanks. Her face was flushed with excitement, and she burst out, "Brahms was really in the room, wasn't he?"

Grief, and the Living Dead

If you are tempted to say that such talk is at best only metaphorical and a bit naive as it turns printed notes into persons, think one more time about what we mean by "being alive" and "being dead." If being alive means, as it should, producing actual effects in the living world, in the world of physical creatures, then—to repeat—Beethoven and Bach, Mozart and Brahms, Stravinsky and Shostakovich are effecting more literal changes, mental and physical, and thus are more alive, in that practical sense, than when they lived. As Wallace Stevens says of the great poets, they are "not the dead lying in the earth, but the dead still living." In "those huge imaginations . . . what is remote becomes near, and what is dead lives with an intensity beyond any experience of life."

This vital power of the living record is dramatized for me when I encounter in my journal a song my five-year-old son Richard had just made up. He ran into the room, obviously excited, and said, "Daddy, I just made up a song." And he sang it—and here it is, alive now because I transcribed it in that journal, where it has lain for about four decades, in one sense inert but demanding to be brought to life:

"Did you notice," he said, "that the notes go down when the words do? It's a song about American and English soldiers going down through the earth to fight the Chinese." (This was 1956.)

So here today, as I sing from my transcript of his song, Richard, killed by a car thirteen years later, Richard the living composer, has changed my world, however slightly: he has brought me to tears once again with his song, just as Brahms did with the G-minor piano quartet. They are not tears of simple grief: his little creative act has turned the grief into a living act of commemoration. As I've been claiming about Beethoven and the others, the continuing effect of his composition means that Richard is now alive.

I would never want to say that this kind of living replaces or outranks the flesh-and-blood boy we lost; it could not have occurred without being brought to life by my rereading the journal entry, and I had to be living in the other sense to do that. Yet it is a fact, not mystical conjecture, that the song itself, lying there inert in the journal pages, long forgotten, waiting to be sung again, has a life, a healing power, of its own.

And spiritual healing is one of the things music is about—a claim that is rather different from the pragmatic defense of amateur painting that I reported Churchill offering in the Overture.

SEPTEMBER 9, 1994 ["SLEEPY HOLLOW"]—Last night after we'd played Haydn quite remarkably, Alan Garber suggested that we do the Shostakovich number 8, perhaps the gloomiest, most despairing composition I know. For much of it, the cello and viola mournfully dwell on unmoving low notes, and all four players dwell again and again on a mournful four-note phrase that the tortured, torn composer saw as an abbreviated spelling of his own name.

Its "beauties" are thus of a highly threatening, even potentially destructive kind. I can imagine some depressed listener being led to almost suicidal thoughts when attending to it fully, and that's a danger not to be ignored. There was indeed a radical shift to a subdued, solemn mood when we were finished with it, the opposite of the effect from the Haydn.

I have no way of knowing whether the other players felt spiritually harmed by the gloom, the sheer grief of it, but the effect on me was less actual gloom than quiet tearful elevation: how paradoxically marvelous to share in a full creative expression of just how terrible life has been for so many in our time!

❦

The gift of sad music, then, if it's good music, need not make you sad; like the best of the blues, such music imitates sadness as a kind of affirmation. The composer or performer simply cannot be feeling hopelessly depressed when he manages to create music that expresses hopeless depression. The capacity to write and play and sing such music is already a transcendence of the mood that it in a sense pretends to succumb to.

FEBRUARY 27, 1995—Last night the Chicago Symphony and chorus, under Solti, performed Shostakovich's "Babi Yar" symphony—#13, Opus 113. Again the miseries could be called the center—yet the effect on me could not be called misery. To feel elevated through sharing a created version of misery and despair—that is indeed a risky and paradoxical experience.

What gift could be worth more than the invitation to live an inexpressible grief and at the same time somehow to come out on the other side, partially healed, living with the long-since dead griever, and thus more able to face everyday living?

FOURTH
MOVEMENT

Rising Dissonance,
Resolved to Heavenly
Harmony

It was a satisfying life [in those days] in a way people today do not understand. There was a joinery of lives all worked together, smooth in places, or lumpy, but joined. The work and the living you did was the same things, not separated out like today.   BILLY PRETTY, IN *The Shipping News*, BY ANNIE PROULX

❧

The great frustration of my career is that nobody really wants me to do my own work. Basically, *The Godfather* made me violate a lot of the hopes I had for myself at that age.   FRANCIS FORD COPPOLA

❧

Kid, the fun is over. There are guys in New York looking at these figures, saying "This is the kind of money you can make in the movie business?"   ONE MOVIE EXECUTIVE TO ANOTHER, ABOUT THE PROFITS OF *The Exorcist*

❧

For money has a power above
The stars and fate, to manage love.
SAMUEL BUTLER, *Hudibras*

❧

I run, I run to the whistle of money.   THEODORE ROETHKE

Chapter Ten

"Making It," Selling Out, and the Future of Amateuring

THAT CONCLUSION OF chapter 9, with its claim about "transcendence" of "everyday living," raises a host of questions about amateuring. Just what after all is the "everyday life" I escape as I pick up my bow? Why are we all so eager to transcend it, often with mere passive escape? What is life for, and how do we choose among the varieties of transcending?

Such broad questions raise innumerable temptations that I must now resist—perhaps thereby earning your gratitude. Readers of different drafts have flooded me with justified complaints about my neglecting to make enough of this or that first-cousin to my celloing. One reader fumed about my neglect of Plato's pursuit of the ideal soul's harmony, with his aggressive advocacy of an education based on gymnastics and music—music in a much broader definition than we've relied on here. Another philosopher lamented my silence about Aristotle's pursuit of *eudaimonia* (real happiness), in his *Nicomachean Ethics*, and the joys of pure contemplation pursued even further in his *Metaphysics*. A Jewish friend was shocked by my neglect of Maimonides' claims that loving human actions can be an actual imitation of God—"a bit elitist, but so is your amateuring." A broad-ranging specialist in Romanticism said, point-blank: "You just cannot do that book without a chapter on the history of speculations about love, from Shakespeare to . . . well, actually to the present!" I'm sure that if I had shown the manuscript to any Arabist, she would have condemned my neglect of Avicenna's wonderful speculations about what "pure" living amounts to.

And the flood is not just of philosophical issues and historical tracings. Psychological, sociological, and political questions compete for the foreground as soon as we seriously celebrate love-driven leisure and probe the conflict among diverse loving motives.

To spend the rest of my life pursuing all such questions implicit in the phrase "for the love of it" would surely be a splendid way to go—a glorious kind of pro-amateuring. I'm tempted. I could fill my remaining days with raids on my university's library, absorbing or perhaps refining or refuting claims made in the 32 books on "recreation" and "re-creation," the 119 books on "leisure," the 150 books on "play," and the thousands of books on various religious, political, metaphysical, and scientific loves—not to mention the innumerable sociological analyses of leisure and of working for the love of the work: of becoming professional for the love of the profession. My own shelves are laden with inviting (threatening?) unread books on all of these subjects.

But the truth is, to do a satisfactory scholarly book even on a small slice of all that would require the author to begin almost as early in life as this aspiring cellist should have begun his exercises.

❧

To some musical amateurs the most important of these questions is likely to be of the religious kind I reserve for chapter 11. But for those who care about our society's future, the more pressing challenge comes from those who pursue forms of pleasure that violate the loving pursuits at our center here. Seductive pleasures are to be found everywhere—no doubt in increasing numbers year by year. So why not pursue this or that rival excitement, especially the excitement of vigorous competition in a society in which competing often becomes a religious, pleasure-filled passion?

For me the most revealing defense of competing as the best answer to that question was offered by Norman Podhoretz, way back in the sixties, with his book *Making It*. His argument is still curiously up-to-date (though the book is out of print); it's all about Podhoretz's exciting discovery of the rewards for any writer who embraces "making it" rather than simply plugging away for the love of the writing. For him it was sheer bliss to cast aside his parents' pious nurturing: they had taught him to deplore the pursuit of money, fame, and power. Discovering the joys of that pursuit—especially of fame—became the center of his life. He regrets that it took him so long to discover that the greatest rewards in life come when one deliberately fights to get ahead of others and to join those at "the top."

That fight necessarily leads him to downgrade or even ignore such old-fashioned matters as truth, beauty, integrity, or high literary quality. Of course he never argues that those motives should be totally discarded, but they are definitely pushed down the scale, topped by winning. His book, he says, is an echo of Norman Mailer's "bid for literary distinction, fame, and money all in one package."

Podhoretz offers no serious probing of the borderlines implicit in such a conversion to the new religion of "making it." I assume—at least I hope—that he would be shocked, then and now, at the cruel excesses committed by many sellouts who would claim to belong to his cult. Certainly he would never defend those fellow devotees who commit murder for cash or for winning in politics. His relatively moderate case is that the drive for genuine literary excellence can be easily harmonized with commercial motives that were misguidedly attacked by his culture when he was young. And he reveals at every point that winning yields more pleasure than pursuing excellence.

His book is still worth reading for its open—and sometimes even honest—revelation of the many motives besides wealth that can deflect an author from writing something for the sake of getting it said. But at every point I detect the sellout in him demanding admiration for having discovered the truth: winning is the ultimate happiness. It's as if he were saying: "I have sold out, I admit it; I am no longer primarily pursuing goals I was taught to respect. So now I must find a way to describe my selling out as somehow not just exciting but honorable—knowing that my book will appeal to other sellouts. I'm hoping that to praise the pursuit of money and fame will yield not just money and fame but honor for telling the nasty truth."

His most illuminating account is of a sumptuous conference he attended on Paradise Island, meeting a collection of stars and fat cats. Suddenly he discovered just how much his previous ethical and aesthetic scruples had denied him. His account of surrendering to the rat race is so joyful that I'm tempted to quote it at much greater length than the following:

[I]t gave me a taste I would never forget of what it was like to be a general among generals. Not everyone in the group may have been what Mailer calls major league so far as intrinsic achievement was concerned, but major league most of them certainly were in terms of the kind of fame that in America was directly convertible into wealth. I looked upon those who possessed such fame, and I liked what I saw; I measured myself against them, and I did not fall short. . . . I left Paradise Island with those words [from Odets, "The best of everything is good enough for me"] ringing in my head. Think poor? I had been thinking poor, I could now see, all my life. Even when I thought I had stopped doing so— when, for example, I had triumphantly silenced the voice of depression-Brooklyn . . . I had still been taking it for granted that the best of everything was not for the likes of me, that thinking rich and even thinking famous were dangerous habits of mind, and sinful ones as well. . . [What I learned was that] not to expect was a way of not demanding *what was now there to be had*, and that not demanding was the surest way of not getting. I left Paradise Island resolving to demand.

So: he liked what he saw; he did not fall short. He left resolving to demand fame (and whatever power and money could lead to it). He did face some doubts down the line, even some depression, not wanting or daring to shout, like Bellow's Henderson the Rain King, "I want! I want! I want!" But the message is basically unqualified: making it has become more important than anything else.

How can I resist sermonizing against someone who sermonizes like that? Why should I trust anything else Podhoretz ever says, once he has boasted that his goal as a writer is to make it, at whatever cost? Without knowing much about the man who later turned the fine magazine *Commentary* further and further to the right—whether in the service of truth or fame we'll never know—I can't help wondering how he's been spending his leisure time, since he "made it" by writing about making it.[1]

✿

At least since the publication of Mandeville's *The Fable of the Bees* in the eighteenth century, we've been offered innumerable arguments along Podhoretz's line. Author after author has claimed that even though putting personal triumph at the center often harms others, no society could flourish without implanting the desire to win, crushing other competitors. As

---

1. Podhoretz does do some distinguishing, earlier in his book, among the various kinds and degrees of corruption. For example, he says that money is "rightly suspect as a destroyer of other unquantifiable values, not to mention the unlovely traits of character which have so often been brought to the fore through its pursuit, acquisition, and possession. Fame, on the other hand, does no one any direct harm," and desire for "social position," properly defined, is a great liberator.

A brief counter to Podhoretz's naiveté about making it is provided by James Atlas in "The Art of Failing." He traces the terrible effect on himself when, possessed by the Podhoretz dream, failure struck. But he also tells the story of one man who first "made it," then failed, then succeeded again and finally transcended the whole rat race. To put making it at the center of life now seems to him not just destructive but ridiculous. "Are you still important?" he jokingly asks his highly successful hero at the end. "Dean laughed. 'Not to me.'"

James Boswell's acquaintance put it, praising his own work as engineer: "I sell here, Sir, what all the world desires to have—POWER." Mandeville's slogan equating "private vices" and "public benefits" reached a peak not long ago with the clearer version, "Greed is good."

The flood of such arguments has naturally produced a flood of anxious defenses of diverse virtues that ought to be immune to selling out. And that flood has always been accompanied with pathetic lamentations claiming that it's too late: all is lost. The world once honored the virtues but it no longer does. The apocalypse is at hand. As the famous hymn "Abide with me," by H. F. Lyte, puts it, "Earth's joys grow dim, its glories pass away; / Change and decay in all around I see." As Raymond Williams demonstrated in *The Country and the City*, it is almost impossible to find a time, at least in Western culture, when prominent authors were not sounding like Gertrude Himmelfarb, John Ellis, William Bennett, and other lamenters in our time: the values we once lived by—fifty years ago, five hundred years ago, two thousand years ago, or four thousand and four years B.C.E.—are now betrayed.

The jeremiads, whether thoughtful or careless, conservative, radical, or liberal, do seem to be increasing dramatically. I myself sometimes feel, after reading the morning paper or the latest issue of a left-wing or right-wing journal, that we amateurs, whatever love we pursue, are sliding down a hopelessly slippery slope. Though available leisure time itself may or may not be increasing, amateuring time seems obviously betrayed everywhere, in the name of one or another form of making it. Machiavelli, now usually read as a celebrator of winning at all costs, is *said* to have said, after tracing earlier authors' laments about the decline of genuine values, "The difference is that this time the fatal decline is real." Is it real, this time?

Well, how could anyone ever prove that the willingness to sacrifice some worthy love for the pleasure of getting ahead is worse today than it was in the misery-laden London portrayed by Dickens in *Little Dorrit* and Trollope in *The Way We Live Now*, or the Athens of Shakespeare's *Timon of Athens*, or the Florence of Machiavelli's *Prince*, or the world of Dante's *Inferno*? The corruption of loving time for the sake of one or another form of ego-stroking victory is probably older than the Neanderthals. The fall of Adam and Eve can best be explained as the succumbing to the temptation to "rise" at any cost. Their sin was immediately echoed by Cain's murder of Abel: Why do you and I, brother, offer sacrifices to God? Why, naturally, to get ahead! And—CRASH!

Why did neither of them suggest instead playing a game of marbles, or singing a hymn together?

❧

It would be foolish to seek a decisive answer to the question of whether we are really declining. What is clear without statistical proof is that, as Connie O'Connor argued in her polemical *The Leisure Wasters*, too many of us too much of the time are spending our hours rather than redeeming them. Even if we had evidence that 90 percent of all Americans were amateuring joyfully, we could still say that too many are either making themselves miserable by struggling to win or surrendering to mere entertainment. And we would not have escaped the problem of how to wake up those twenty-five million—or however many will make up 10 percent by the time this book is published.

It is depressingly easy to find more or less reliable stories about our contemporaries whose true loves get destroyed by this or that rival: those who harm themselves and others by pursuing victory at the expense of the loving pursuit itself. I'll begin with a few of those, then turn to equally unprovable anecdotes celebrating those who practice daily some full amateuring pursuit. The rest of this chapter could thus be summarized either as "Which kind of person portrayed here would you prefer to be?" or as "What on earth can we do to fight off the various temptations and deflections and reconvert the sellouts?"

❧

How "Making It" Defeats the Amateur

MUSIC, FOR THE LOVE OF IT. When the rock star Kurt Cobain committed suicide on April 8, 1994, he left a note that included this sad lament:

> I haven't felt excitement in listening to as well as creating music . . . for too many years now. I feel guilty beyond words about these things. For example, when we're backstage, and the lights go out, and the manic roar of the crowd begins, it doesn't affect me the way it did for, say, Freddie Mercury, who seemed to have loved and relished the adoration of the crowd.

I can only guess at what led Cobain to lose the love, but it is clear that for a long time he had been making his music out of motives that he could not respect. His profession had become not making music for music but making music for money and fame, and he was sensitive enough to see the emptiness of that. No longer an "amateur" about anything, Cobain felt that his time was up.

The director of the general education program at a famous music school told me not long ago that many students there cannot be induced to care for anything but getting to the top. "It is not only that they refuse to spend time on serious reading of Plato or Shakespeare. They ignore everything about music except for whatever narrow line they've chosen to excel in. For example, very few of those who aspire to be string soloists ever engage in chamber playing. That's not the most likely road to fame."

1960, PARIS [MEMORY]:—The newspapers reported that the night before the finals in an international violin competition, someone broke into the center and cut the four strings of one of the main French hopefuls. The cutter, never caught, obviously hoped that next day the enemy, playing on new strings perpetually stretching out of tune, would be also out of the running. First things first.

MAY 30, 1997—My twelve year old friend seemed deeply anxious last night, and when I asked him why, he said, "I'm bothered by the question, 'Why is Mary on first chair in our orchestra's cello section and I'm not?'"

Am I wrong in thinking that more kids feel that way more of the time than used to be true? I must admit that that's exactly how I felt in high school when Phil Jensen was put on first chair as clarinetist and I was put down as second. But my nephews and nieces and grandchildren seem to be engaged in more competition in a week, musical and non-musical, than I would have experienced, at their age, in a year. And such actual competition is turned to deadly competition in the experience of "virtual" killing battles that some of them spend a lot of time on, in their computer games: triumph in life comes from getting most points for the most killings.

PAINTING, FOR THE LOVE OF IT. Most critics of the arts are understandably quite cautious about direct attacks on selling out. The attacker always risks sounding as I sometimes may do here: hypocritically above the battle. One fine exception is Robert Hughes's account of the life of Andy Warhol as a star-studded, self-conscious, self-celebrated, self-exploiting sellout. The Warhol whom Hughes and very few other critics have portrayed honestly seems to be saying to himself daily, "I know I'm violating genuine artistic standards—but do I not deserve full credit for exhibiting the supreme virtue: honest contempt for traditional standards?" Hughes summarizes the Warhol effect like this:

> Warhol was the first American artist to whose career publicity was truly intrinsic. . . . By today's standards, the art world [in the forties and fifties] was virginally naive about the mass media. . . [Publicity] was regarded as

extrinsic to the work—something to view with suspicion, at best an accident, at worst a gratuitous distraction. . . . To be one's own PR outfit
was, in the eyes of the New York artists of the Forties or Fifties, nearly
unthinkable—hence the contempt they felt for Salvador Dali. But in the
1960s . . . the art world gradually shed its idealist premises and its sense
of outsidership and began to turn into the Art Business.

Nothing could be flatter or more perfunctory, or have less to do
with . . . "pure peinture" than Warhol's recent prints. Their most dis-
cernible quality is their transparent cynicism and their Franklin Mint
approach to subject matter . . . [Warhol's] work never ceases to prove its
merits in the only place where merit really shows, the market. . . . [We
have entered] the age of supply-side aesthetics.

That critique was published in 1993. I then learned, in 1998, that Warhol's
exploitative silkscreen portrait of Marilyn Monroe recently sold for 17.3
million bucks, four times his previous record. How sad that Warhol could
not be alive to savor his own payoff! How really sad to think about the
"loves" expressed by those bargaining patrons, who could have been spending their bargaining time learning how to paint better than Warhol.

"SPORTING," FOR THE LOVE OF IT

FEBRUARY 21 1994—Last night, surfing for evidence about amateuring, I
saw some former Olympic champions talking about how deadly the
competition has become, at the top: how competitors steal one another's
shoes; how they spread vile, upsetting rumors about the dangers of the
rink or ski slope or weather; how they study opponents' psychological
weaknesses and do their best to heighten the anxieties.

1997, FALL—I received a letter today from a friend who spends his daily
amateur hour probing the sports pages:

> I'm most troubled by the way so many athletes, professional and amateur, seem
> to have lost the fun of it. They cheat, they deliberately injure their rivals, they
> turn to drugs to help them win. They "build up" the body beyond endurance, or
> they fast into anorexia. We read everywhere of pathetic gymnasts like Christy
> Henrich, who dieted herself into anorexia until, at age 22 and down to 60
> pounds, she died—officially pursuing an "amateur" career, but so determined
> to win that she in effect killed herself for it.[2]

2. As I reread that passage in the spring of 1998, after having read some serious studies of
the "spiritual" motives of some anorexics, I think my friend is overconfident about probing
the sufferers' minds.

Hers is a gruesomely extreme case; not many have died pursuing amateur careers; far more have died in professional boxing, football or soccer. The teen-age girl-gymnasts seem the most pathetic evidence of fake-amateur corruption—of how the desire to win with the body can destroy both body and soul. The evidence is strong that too many coaches of amateur athletes, like the coaches of professionals, care more about winning than about the welfare of those they coach.

It's not that they want their students to die. Like the "better" masters in the time of slavery, the coaches have strong motives to keep their charges healthy. But in sports and arts that require either extra muscle (like shot-putting), or minimal weight (like gymnastics and ballet or jockeying), the temptations to give advice that proves destructive are these days strong. If my income depends on getting youngsters on the Olympic team, why shouldn't I insist that they work at not weighing more than ninety-four pounds?

(Can you explain to me, by the way, why the top tennis players at Wimbledon are still called amateurs?)

Thinking of his lament, as I spend at least one or two minutes a day on the sports pages, I notice that many pros are saying, "We're not doing it for the fun of it any more." Mike Royko once reported that Ryne Sandberg had resigned from the Cubs, giving up millions, simply "because the fun is gone." (Was that his real reason? We'll never know.) Columnists fall all over themselves with the accusation "It's all for the money, or for the fame that yields money." Then they dwell on the countercases, because as exceptions they are more newsworthy: man bites dog. Then they themselves continue to sell out news-truth for news-cash.

Is selling out in sports worse than ever before? Who knows? Before despairing, we should remind ourselves, as Anne Weiss and other writers on the Olympics insist, that the destructive de-amateurizing of sports is as old as the invention of the discus. The original Greek amateurs were not paid in cash, but they were fiercely and often cruelly competitive, seeking the fantastic awards granted winners. In one game, the pancratium, David Chester reports, though they were not allowed to bite or gouge, they could strangle, and several were killed. Similarly, if we claim that a medieval jousting knight aimed to kill his opponent for the love of it, it's a bit hard to determine "love of what."

SCHOLARSHIP AND OTHER PURSUITS OF TRUTH, FOR THE LOVE OF IT.
At almost every university I visit these days I hear the claim that inquiry for the love of inquiry is dead: it's all a quest for fame and money and political power. "The notion of pursuing truth wherever it leads is so old-fashioned

as to be laughable." "The very term 'truth' has no meaning anymore." Our courtrooms are full of academic "experts" highly paid for "scientific" testimony about truths that are too often demonstrably skewed or even reversed for cash. The tobacco-company trials are the most prominent example, but there are many others.

Again we must remember that even if the laments are justified, this is by no means totally new. Cheating "scholars" of many varieties have always been found in every culture; we can be sure that many a medieval alchemist, affecting deep scholarship, was as dishonest as the Canon in Chaucer's "Canon's Yeoman's Tale." Are any scholars today more dishonest than T. J. Wise, who duped our ancestors by producing fake first editions of the great poets, and was not exposed until just before he died in the 1930s? Are our scientists more dishonest than the perpetrators of the Piltdown man hoax, finally uncovered in 1912?

Still, I've never until lately heard complaints like this one from a colleague, an editor: "It's got so bad that I find myself suspecting every article submitted to our journal: Does this author care about anything other than getting published? More and more of the articles seem to be filled with made-up citations, and the bibliographies are compiled by punching the computer keys." Evidence is mounting that more students are plagiarizing these days than ever before—using Internet sites like "www.cheater.com."

Academic scholars are not, however, the only official proclaimers of truth who sell out to other pleasures and rewards. Laments about the decline of the public intellectual can be found everywhere. The world used to be full of Edmund Wilsons and Hannah Arendts; now we have superficial journalists, TV commentators, and national columnists who are being paid exorbitant speaking fees by the very institutions that they are expected to criticize objectively. TV talk shows like *The McLaughlin Group* and *Crossfire* hire stars who sometimes show by the very looks on their faces that they detest the meaningless shouting; they know that as soon as the green light goes on, their IQ drops thirty points. Editors of books, magazines, and newspapers reveal, sometimes even openly, a willingness to corrupt their product in the service of cash: just trace the decline in quality of your favorite magazine over the past decade, or the ratio of serious books to trash at Simon and Schuster.[3] Take a look at the choices made by editors of the Murdoch me-

3. You should perhaps discount that nasty slap, since it is offered in the forlorn hope of getting revenge against Simon and Schuster for how they mistreated *The Art of Growing Older*, first by eliminating their quality line, Poseidon Press, and firing my splendid editor, and then by selling out (I choose the phrase advisedly) to Paramount, which sold out to Viacom, which, according to the morning paper, is selling out to the British publisher Pearson P.L.C. I can't help wondering if there is a single editor there—wherever "there" is by now—who is motivated primarily by the love of lovable books.

dia, including the suppression, for example, of news about China that might hurt the boss's income.

Truth in journalism or the publishing industry? What is that?

PHILANTHROPY, GIVING FOR THE LOVE OF IT. America has always had one of the most favorable records in charitable giving. And for all anyone really knows, incidental giving—the kind that makes no serious dent in the pocketbook—may be as plentiful as ever; national studies claiming decline can't possibly reflect how much is given privately. The media are full of reports of huge gifts by the nation's wealthiest.

Full volunteer service, however, the move toward the full volunteer-amateur, is another matter. Several studies, reliable or not, have claimed that volunteer public service has recently fallen sharply, even while the most wealthy, like Bill Gates, get headlines for huge gifts. People are either too busy with professional demands, the reports claim, or, as Steven Forbes complains, they are too worried about losing their ranking among the Fortune 500.

The defining question the amateur must ask any philanthropist is not just "Do you give some money, here and there?" but "Do you spend at least an hour a day practicing volunteer service, practicing philanthropy, practicing the arts of giving effectively, because you enjoy getting better at it?" Giving effectively is after all an art in itself. Amateur*ish*, comfortable, more or less blind giving of the kind I too often exhibit, without practice, is usually time (and often money) wasted, and it can often backfire. What's more, many philanthropists can be shown to give with full knowledge that the gift will increase their profits. And too many of our wealthy pleasure-hunters are worse than that: they are now fleeing the country, giving up their citizenship, in order to avoid taxes.

❧

Well, that's perhaps more than enough of threatening speculation. But it would be easy to add examples from other areas traditionally claimed as territory for loving, disinterested commitment: public service, including political leadership; civil service, official and voluntary; medicine and nursing care; law; even spying for the CIA—for the good of the nation. (After Aldrich Ames was exposed as a CIA sellout, the director expressed the fear that nobody spies any more out of sheer patriotic motives.) While in most branches of our lives there are traditions honoring devotees who performed because they loved the performance, in most there are now rumors that the love of it, the sheer joy of it, is being lost.

Would it be foolish to waste more time worrying about all that—for example, about how few doctors can now claim that they still care more about the Hippocratic oath than about doubling their income?

Assuming that the answer is yes, I now shift gears and move forward.

Hope Springs Eternal

MUSIC. Surely the best answer to all the negative data is the abundance of players playing for the love of it right now as I write. How could any cynic respond to the evidence provided in the listing, in the little journal *Music for the Love of It*, of at least 130 "Adult Amateur Summer Music Workshops of North America," for the summer of 1997? One hundred and thirty amateur musical gatherings all over the country! Not to mention untold numbers of weeks and weekends around the rest of the world: in England, Germany, Japan, Italy; in Prague; on Corfu. The listings include not just chamber music but Bach and Mozart festivals, a dulcimer symposium, an Annual Early Brass Festival, a Band Camp for Adults, Jazz Improvisation, Instrument Building, Recorder and Early Music, and the Western Wind Workshops in Ensemble Singing. Add to those the thousands of groups not even listed as summer festivals: the jazz combos, gospel choirs, madrigal societies, bell ringing clubs, bagpipe bands . . .

I wonder if any other amateur choice can rival that rich supply? On the other hand, the cynical voice intrudes, as it too often does: What percentage of our actual population is engaged in those marvelous occasions? What is the ratio of players to bored listeners, or of actual amateur painters to the number who go to spectacular museum exhibits, spending thirty seconds per painting? What is the ratio between real golfers and those who watch the championships on TV, or between genuine dancers—ballet or folk or ballroom—and those who are dragged to performances by their spouses and are bored because they don't really understand what goes on, as any amateur would? If you read through the annual *New York Times* listing of Summer Festivals in the "Arts and Leisure" section, you find hardly any invitations to do anything other than watch or listen to other people performing.

There's nothing really wrong in that, obviously; at least they are not selling out. But it does worry this touter of the joys of amateuring.

PAINTING. Well, there are so many amateur painters around, and their stuff is generally so awful, that they almost tempt me to cancel this book. The main trouble is that, unlike the sounds my cello sends into the air, what they produce endures; it floods our scene whether we want to see it or not, most of it not nearly as good as Winston Churchill's oils.

But there I go again, surrendering to bias when what I intended to do was to cheer the hordes onward. I do hope that more amateurs who exhibit their clever visual concepts would, like our painter-friend Natalie Lerner, practice hard enough at the amateuring to produce works worth looking at.

SPORTS. Once we turn our attention away from the media's emphasis on championships and salaries, we find a sporting world full of athletes who have no real hope of earning either money or fame—but who just love the game. For all anyone could ever prove, there may be more genuine amateur athletes in the world today than bored professionals or sellouts, and proportionately more than there were in 1900 or 400 B.C.E. There are indeed many who resemble the pro-amateur fiddlers I've celebrated: pros who seem really to love what they're doing. Contrary to my negative anecdotes, when we probe deeper we turn up a world full of athletes who have no real hope of earning a thirty-million-a-year salary but who go on playing the game for the love of it.

As I write I hear behind my house the voices of four boys in their early teens shooting a basketball into an improvised hoop—a wicker basket nailed to a telephone pole. They are there almost every afternoon and on Saturdays and Sundays. It's no doubt true that many of them some of the time are bugged with the certainly futile hope of becoming another Michael Jordan. But some others will surely go on playing after all hope for pro fame is lost. I'm sure that they often feel the true amateur spirit, playing for the sheer fun of it.

Consider my friend's account of his son-in-law's amateuring:

> Jerry ran in the LA marathon. The winner did it in 2 hours 13 minutes. Jerry did it in 3 hours 57 minutes. There were over 14,000 in the marathon, and Jerry was 3,349. He gets great satisfaction out of this. I just plain fail to see how anyone could enjoy this.

Obviously Jerry and many thousands of those 14,000 see the point of it without the slightest hint of a dream of winning. You can't even accuse most of them of utilitarian motives like doing it for their health. Running the marathon is for most people not the road to health; in fact many have died in the course. I like to think that for most runners it's just the road to . . . well, to more running: to whatever it feels like as you do it. We can assume that most of them do hope to *get better at it all the time*, or perhaps to match Oprah Winfrey's famous but average pace of 1994. But most of them know that they have no more hope of coming out a winner than I have of becoming a cellist in the Chicago Symphony.

JUNE 12, 1994, NEWS ITEM:—Michael Jordan happened upon a sand lot basketball game and joined in. He played and played, and said afterward that he couldn't remember a time in years when he'd had that much fun playing basketball! He does usually look, when winning with the Bulls, as if he's having fun. But in his own view, it's a far different kind of fun from what he felt playing with those kids.[4]

SCHOLARSHIP. Again my personal encounters quarrel against the lamentations. Most of the scholars I know well have never deliberately violated truth for the sake of money or fame; at least I've never detected their doing it. That doesn't mean that they have not experienced moments when the worst side of professionalizing poisoned their true loves. But I can think of far more signs of genuine amateuring and pro-amateuring here than in most other areas of American life. All the scientists I know attack furiously the notion of cheating on scientific results, and they all argue that the numerous publicized episodes of dishonesty are unrepresentative. I believe them. The scattered stories of misdeeds hit the headlines. My friends' decades of devoted inquiry—how could a reporter turn that into news?

Equally impressive to me is that a large number of my teaching friends claim that they teach for the love of teaching. That does not mean that everything they do in their job is done for love, but they would not change jobs if offered a larger salary doing something else. Most of them could easily have made more in other professions. I know several who have turned down higher offers from other universities, because they love the teaching life at the University of Chicago. And I know even more at liberal arts colleges, community colleges, high schools, and elementary schools, who might echo one friend who said, "I'd rather die than quit teaching."

No one will ever know the actual ratios between those who are devoted and those who would prefer another job if it paid as well. Again my face-

---

4. Rumor has it—I refuse to spend the time necessary to check it—that Jordan's later contracts have forbidden his playing in amateur groups. If that's true, we move back from hope to lamentation. But why not, for joyful emphasis, repeat the rumor I reported on page 114: in June 1998 Jordan started taking piano lessons!

to-face encounters make me suspicious of the fully negative picture. In recent years I've conducted summer seminars with high-school teachers from the Chicago Public Schools, and I've asked them why they went into teaching and why they keep on teaching in conditions that are often highly discouraging—to put it mildly. Hard as it is to detect genuine motives behind overt claims, I would swear that at least half of those beleaguered souls are telling the truth when they say that they chose teaching and stay with it because—as some literally put it—they believe in saving children. A smaller percentage have explicitly spoken my formula: they do it for the love of it—at least on the good days. They are pro-amateurs.

Unfortunately when we turn to the behavior of non-academic public intellectuals—journalists and essayists and TV commentators—the rumors and my experience jibe a bit too well. I cannot find much evidence for hope, unless some kind of popular outrage manages to be effectively expressed. I'm sure, though, that there must be thousands of honest journalists out there who love writing and speaking and who resist lying—or at least stretching things a bit—for the love of gold.

If you happen to be one of them, please tell me about it.

PHILANTHROPY. Though no philanthropist I know of has ever called herself an amateur at that game, surprising evidence is emerging that at least some of the wealthy, and what are called the "really extremely wealthy," are actually practicing their philanthropic skills in order to *get better at it all the time*. As I said above, just giving money here and there is not amateuring; only learning how to do it better qualifies. And now many are doing just that. Alex Kuczynski reports an astonishing new trend. Many of the nouveau riche see themselves as needing professional help, training themselves in how to give money for the love of the giving, "and some are willing to spend up to $20,000" to learn how.

> A growing number of foundations and other organizations have begun holding workshops, field trips and even therapy sessions to teach the wealthy and—in the words of one provider of such services, the really extremely wealthy—the finer points of giving. These include not only . . . how to evaluate organizations . . . but also a lot of intellectual soul-searching about what values the givers are hoping to spread. [In the $20,000 course in Practical Philanthropy run by the Rockefeller Foundation] students read Aristotle, learn to analyze financial statements, travel abroad . . . to view third world poverty close up and practice meditation.

That news in the morning paper excites me. I hope—perhaps naively— that the teachers themselves in such programs are practicing genuine philanthropy, for the love of it.

❧

I am of course tempted, pursuing this sampling of amateurish speculation, to add many another field. The most tempting is one that in an earlier draft received many pages: "Creative writing—for the love of it." On the negative side, one could easily argue that all is lost, citing laments by novelists about how the publishing world no longer allows them to write what they want to write, rejecting it or doctoring it to ensure commercial appeal; one could then answer those laments with evidence that the number of people writing poems and reading them to one another is expanding at a fantastic rate. Almost all poets are inescapably amateurs, in my definition: with little hope of other rewards, they write for the love of writing—and of sharing it with others. No poet writes hoping to have a best seller that will gain a movie contract. Yet thousands—millions?—of poets, many amateur*ish* but almost all genuine amateurs, are at this moment sharing their poems with one another! Amateur reading groups, conducting what are called "slams" because they slam their beloved poems back and forth at one another, are multiplying at a great rate.

So on we could go, forever. But instead of adding more depressing or cheering gossip, I must turn finally to two other lines of speculation: What are the causes of the bad news (regardless of just how bad we interpret it to be) and what can anyone offer as cures—measures that might nourish amateuring?

Causes

I run into scores of guesses about what really tempts so many people into avoiding or escaping or betraying amateuring. None of the guesses can ever be resolved with a full statistical study. Perhaps most prominent is the age-old hypothesis that all of us human beings are from birth essentially, "originally" wicked, inheriting Cain's inability to keep the soul aimed at the right targets, naturally more driven to winning than loving, inescapably temptable into the non-amateur pleasures of knocking down or at least triumphing over others. Some evolutionists stress this line, while others insist that altruism is also in our genes. I have found no study claiming that amateuring is in our genes, though since play, fun, laughter, and humor are genetically universal, amateuring is a plausible candidate.

More often these days I meet explanations like the one in this letter from the friend I quoted earlier—moving again toward the "we're losing it all" line:

> You asked, What's different now? Well, it's that there is more money at the top and less effective inculcating of basic or implacable or unchallengeable standards at the roots—that is, at the beginnings, in early childhood.[5] Our children, by no means "naturally" or "originally" wicked, are not educated, by parents and church and community, into the belief that there are some things one simply does not do, no matter how great the reward, and certain other things one really *ought* to do, regardless of cost or consequences. Instead they are being educated to believe, as they watch the behavior of characters in the media and observe how various celebrities run their lives, that the goal of life is to get it all, at whatever cost. The most popular TV show, "Seinfeld," teaches—or so I read— that the lead characters needn't be "likable or admirable. . . They are willing to sell out for . . . money or sex." Cheat skillfully enough in business and you can win the world. Play your cards, as well as your chords, right, and you can become more than a millionaire, even in music—and in sports more than a billionaire.

In short, he seems to be saying that education outside the classroom as well as inside is for too many kids entirely about Podhoretz's "making it."

Some complainers simplify this causal lament: "The cause, the curse, is consumer capitalism." As we learn in First Timothy 6:10: "The love of money is the root of all evil." Others extend the money charge to "the commercialized media." Some combine capitalism and the media with the curse word "technology." And of course many stress the sheer increase in the availability of passive entertainments—so passive as hardly to deserve the name of recreation or pastime. I've even heard sociologists claim that our problem is that we have no class system with a permanently "liberated" aristocracy: in traditional societies, like England's, where status came not with money but with birth, many aristocrats were freed of any temptation to gain status, and they were thus freed to become amateurs or dilettantes who could commission Beethoven and Mozart to do compositions they themselves would help perform. Whenever Phyllis and I play one of the "King

---

5. For an excellent brief autobiographical account of how money now corrupts life in our culture, see James Atlas, "The Whistle of Money." Atlas touches ambiguously on the way in which the newly wealthy, "bound and gagged by money," make at least halfhearted raids into amateur territory.

of Prussia" quartets by Mozart, I find myself envying that king, who could both commission a work and then have the fun of playing it.

Where do I come out on this overwhelming list of causes? Well, as I always do on the question of causes: no human condition can result from a single cause. I see more social and economic forces pushing us out of the domain of amateuring than ever invite us in. But for the purposes of this book, the single most important cause is that you, and you, and you, and sometimes even the self-touting author-cellist, choose, when the chips are down, the wrong time-killer. We either sell out, to win, or collapse onto the couch, in defeat. Nobody will ever pin down finally the answer to why so many of us in this time do it so much of the time, with our time.

Cures

Are there any institutional moves that might help to shift our motives and practices or teach us how to resist the invitations to sell out?

The suggestions I've met are as diverse as the causes, ranging from religious conversion, through political revolution, to annihilation of TV and all Web sites. While I would of course like to see major reforms in many directions, political and economic and technological, and I'll go on doing what little I can to support them, I have no confidence in any one of them. No institutional change will make much difference unless we can transform the prevailing picture of what makes a successful life. All of us want to succeed, in some sense of the word; all of us pursue some form of happiness or pleasure. But unless we construct a culture in which true happiness is seen as something far beyond getting ahead—Podhoretz's "making it"—amateuring is doomed.

Some institutional measures might indeed have a powerful influence on that cultural reconstructing. The Rockefeller Foundation's program for would-be philanthropists, teaching the rich how to become real amateurs, probably works, at least on some of the more serious signers-on. Another program that might serve as a model is sponsored by Chamber Music America, the national organization of professional chamber groups; it provides, with the support of the National Endowment for the Arts, "rural residencies" for professionals who love music more than fame. The grants deflect players from the big-city professional scene to small towns where they can pursue, and teach others to pursue, music for the love of it. By now such groups are located in nine states. The players postpone their struggle for fame—at least for a time—by nurturing music. The DaPonte String Quartet, for example, has moved to rural Maine, accepting a grant that provides each of the four only $9,000 a year plus lodging. There they do their professional practicing daily, but they also play with amateur local groups, perform for groups in rest homes, give lessons for absurdly low fees (actually in one case violin lessons were "sold" for twenty pounds of shrimp). One of them gave up a tenure-track job at a university for this "decidedly less certain career path."

Now these are all people who, when trained in the conservatories, knew that the highest professional success almost always comes from sticking to the competition scene and aspiring to orchestral positions or solo performances. They were most often advised not to concentrate on chamber music, and especially never to disappear from the front lines into the boonies.

Robert Mann, founder of the Juilliard Quartet, told me once that the greatest gift of his career was its contradiction of what his advisers had told him to expect when he was choosing, in the forties, what kind of performance to pursue. They warned him strongly against chamber music, because "you'll never make as good a living at it." He defied them, for the love of it, and the choice paid off—in all the right ways (as also, of course, in the Podhoretz way). Like him, the DaPonte four have chosen string quartet playing, much of it totally off the professional circuit, presumably for the love of the playing.

Though the cure they represent may seem extremely slight, it is not slight for the kids they are teaching, in that small town in Maine, or for the elderly in the rest home where they perform regularly—without pay. When faced with the "Why do it?" question I've dwelt on—why drag yourself and your family away from the rat race—one of them answered, "Because the music comes first."

Their story almost tempts me to drop the cello and become an amateur supporter of some similar institutional program. Doing so would serve as a cure, not of course for the national picture but for those few individuals who would get touched by the program. Like those who volunteer for Recording for the Blind because they love literature, or those who run soup kitchens because they love feeding the hungry, they're serving and spreading amateuring as they go.

❧

Is it foolish to dream of some cultural revolution that would spread that spirit—an explosion of amateuring, as people become increasingly fed up with alternating between overpressed or even detested labor and merely passive fun? Probably. We can be certain that the world will never be totally "saved." My main hope is that you and I will do what we can, especially with our progeny, to ensure that they implant some genuine love, and some detestation of selling out, into their bones.

From Harmony, from Heav'nly Harmony
   This Universal Frame began:
   From Harmony to Harmony
Through all the Compass of the Notes it ran,
The Diapason closing full in Man.
JOHN DRYDEN, "A SONG FOR ST. CECILIA'S DAY"

❧

Every work of art has "two faces," one directed towards eternity
and the other towards its own time. We can perceive the infinite
in music only by searching for this quality in ourselves. As human
beings we do not possess infinite qualities, but as musicians we
can create an illusion of infinity.   DANIEL BARENBOIM

❧

Music for the music lover is religion and nothing less.
BERNARD HOLLAND

❧

Music is one of the greatest gifts that God has given us: it is divine and therefore Satan is its enemy. For with its aid many dire
temptations are overcome; the devil does not stay where music is.
MARTIN LUTHER

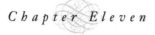

Chapter Eleven

The Music of the
Spheres—But What Spheres?

IT HAS BEEN CLEAR since the Overture that thinking about amateuring, rather than just reveling in it, raises not just the social and political issues of chapter 10 but philosophical and religious issues that we might well wish to dodge. Why not just play, and then play some more? Most amateurs in fact do not attempt any defense beyond the "sheer love of it." What better reason do you need?

But to ignore these issues is to plunge us back into the amorphous floods of leisure-squandering that my judgment-laden celebration has questioned from the beginning. A defense of sheer fun, for those who are overworked or depressed, would by no means be worthless: it might pull at least a few of them out of the doleful dumps. But a defense of real amateuring requires the defender to push the "why" question into the deepest of all waters: "Why live at all?" "Why spend your life this way rather than that?"

"What does your kind of time-spending yield that others do not?" "Why, for that matter, should music, and especially chamber music, rank so high for you among all the other possibilities?" "Are you not at heart finally downgrading all pursuits except music?" "Have you not turned your choice into a kind of religion, music into a kind of god?"

If this book were in praise of gardening, similar questions would have to be faced, but with attention not on how human music echoes any divine music of the spheres but on how the gardener's manipulation of nature relates to Nature's riches: it was, after all, the "spheres" that granted us human beings seeds that grow. If the book put painting or sculpting or stargazing at the center, the questions would again be faced, but with attention on how the results we create echo the creation of infinite beauties by the "spheres." Name your most beloved cello-reach, start thinking about it, and you will find yourself pursuing analogues for the three gifts of chapter 9, and echoes of the speculation about music that I turn to here.

❧

We join now a long tradition of always inadequate thinking about how music relates to the divine, from Pythagoras and Plato through Boethius to a fair number of current musicologists. My journals and notebooks and abandoned book projects, including two novels, are full of shallow attempts to explain the truth and power and depth of music—shallow because I've never settled into prolonged professional scholarship about it.

In 1969 I found myself, after about four months of grieving over the death of my son, exploring the power of music to heal. Music had somehow been providing more solace than even the best poetry and fiction, and I soon began a hopeless attempt at a book about life, aging, death, and "musical time." I speculated daily about time past, time present, and time future, often probing T. S. Eliot's *Four Quartets* for assistance. That led to attempts at Proust-like playing with time and memory. If the overly intimate, Tristram-Shandy-like tone of the following excerpts from that non-book bothers you, please forgive the sufferer who was trying, sometimes successfully, to regain his lost affirmation of life.

NOV. 3, 1969 [MANUSCRIPT, LONDON]—If you think, reader, that I am worried about you and your criticism, out there in the future somewhere, we ought to get things straight: I shall be very much upset if you fail to understand or enjoy what I have to say, *through some fault of mine—* some stone unturned, some section left out. On the other hand, those misunderstandings that are your fault, oh friend, I can do nothing about, and to be worried about them would be as pointless as to worry about anything else, *in the future.*

But how can I worry about your response and yet not call it worry about the future, a form of the futurism that plagues the world? Well, to worry about whether I have done everything possible to make the book accessible (yes, admittedly, in some future time) is precisely the same as working as hard as I can on it, *in the present.* To work to please you, my ideal reader, is thus precisely to work to please myself—not in that old self-aggrandizing way boasted of by so many modern novelists, but in a perfectly reasonable, unanswerable sense that *as* I care for you, revising and revising in the effort to draw you into my orbit, we may well become at one "level" (oh, the delights that are to be discovered in this Platonic atmosphere!) identical!

Yesterday Phyllis and I sat in the Queen Elizabeth Hall listening to the Amadeus Quartet playing Beethoven's C-sharp minor. Leaving the rest of the audience aside for a moment, there were three of us there: *Beethoven* (only the aggressive, puzzling, tradition-shattering C-sharp minor part of the "late" Beethoven—him only, true enough, but surely you're not going to argue that *that* part is somehow less important, to you, to me, or to Beethoven, than the embittered quarrelsome man whose body died in 1827); second, *the quartet* members counting as one, because they were *almost* totally in synch *in* their performance—that is, the C-sharp minor part of them was identical (Yes, yes, I know that there's a problem here about each not *playing* an identical part; but presumably, being the players they are, they *heard* the other parts, as I did); and third, Phyllis and me, also counting only as one whenever we really listened (occasionally I became divided, like the others, and no doubt Phyllis did too: there was a moment when I noticed that the young lad sitting in front of me *smelled* like my son, just as Phyllis had pointed out at intermission, and my mind, or part of it, wandered away from the music—but generally I (we) was (were) completely *with* the music for the whole time: no world, no time, no players, no Booth other than the C-sharp minor—simultimeously (to coin a) present in the souls of—well, I can't even say all three of us: we were now one.

Now then: there that "one" was, but where was "there"? The C-sharp minor part of each of us was fusing in a mysterious way—not mysterious because rare (similar fusions are taking place at this very moment all over the world) but because it contrasts so sharply with what many people think of as "reality." A part of each of the "three"—let's say a small part, in order not to upset the would-be realists too much from the beginning—becomes identical.

There is Beethoven, one hundred and forty-three years ago (he wrote the C-sharp minor in his final year; it was published posthumously) writing away at that marvelous theme and variations in the fourth movement, *doing the best he can* to weld together the most astonishingly contrasting elements. Here is the four-players doing the best it can to make the revolutionary welding accessible. And here we am, doing the best we can to turn our "self" totally into it: all of us impersonally slogging away (these tears about my son's death? ignore them, irrelevant) to turn ourselves into that deathless quartet. And partially succeeding. Though our emotions and associations are no doubt radically contrasting, our lives in the melodies and harmonies merge.

And here am "I" today, carrying Beethoven around in my head all day—especially that fifth variation—you know, the one with the little breathless chords, everyone pulsating together, no separate melodic voice, just that pulsation (quite different from the heart's a-thump-a; entirely different from my heart's ectopic beat . . .)

And the grieving "young" man suddenly cannot resist giving not just a visual illustration of the pulsations but a long paragraph on the petty chores of his day, claiming that all the while the music from the night before was ringing in his head. It's hardly surprising that he never manages to make clear the full meaning of the "merging" of all those musical selves. He would certainly put all that differently today, now that we are flooded with speculation about the "virtual" selves created and fused or morphed or destroyed on the Internet. Wasn't he a bit ahead of—as well as out of—his time?

Finally he gets back to life and death and time:

> Meanwhile, sitting in the wings, there is another candidate: a twenty-one-year-old music lover in 1942, a Wayne Booth who in so many ways was not with it, not at all with it, but who now wants to make his claim to be one of us, or, rather, one with us, *to have been* with it and therefore *to be*, now. I've been thinking—and even saying to Phyllis—that that young man is as dead as Richard, no deader, but as dead. I sometimes even mourn his loss—all that naive vitality—though of course I don't have time or room for that lately. Yet here he is, in effect claiming to be alive right along with the three of us other "aspects of Beethoven."

DECEMBER 30, 1942 [CHICAGO]—*Monday I spent several hours before our quartet singing engagement in the best possible way: listening to Beethoven quartets. First I went to Marshall Fields and took the Opus 131, C-sharp minor into a listening booth. I have known this quartet for two years now, but decided that day to make a rather thorough "study" of it.*

Reading that, I can't help thinking of how the rest of the world was spending that Monday of 1942—the ironies piled on ironies: young men fighting all over the world, some few of them heroically, and the young missionary cheating Marshall Fields and the Mormon Church and the

United States Army by occupying that listening booth, with no intention whatever of buying a record or converting anyone or getting drafted. You see, I am not trying to praise that young man, just join him.

1942—By the time I had listened to each movement through twice, then played the whole thing consecutively, I was so engrossed in the work that I could hardly break away, though I knew I had listened longer than any non-buyer should.

Longer? Can he be telling the truth? Three times through? That would be at least two hours, maybe longer. What were the salesmen doing, permitting such destruction of the records?

1942 [SAME DAY]—*. . . there is no music anywhere to compare with string quartets, and of string quartets none can compare to the last four or five by Beethoven. In these quartets I notice more than anywhere else the necessity of effort for enjoyment of art. The C-sharp minor did not particularly impress me when I first heard it, but I kept going back to it, partly because there were parts in it which did attract me on first hearing (the scherzo, for example). The climax— so far—was Monday; I walked from Marshall Field's much happier than I had felt for weeks. . . .*
    But that was not all. I proceeded to another music store and listened to the Opus 132, first shaking off the impulse to get the 131 again. . . .

And that fortunate freeloader sits down and analyzes the A minor, LP side by LP side, and even writes out the melody of the final movement . . .
    Now you may want to exclude that lonely young man from our glorious harmonious fusion, here in 1969, because of his flat (when it is not inflated or just plain clumsy) style. Irrelevant. (You may exclude yourself because you've never *listened* to the C-sharp minor; another problem entirely. Stop reading, this instant, and go listen to it five times straight!) Anyhow, I think he makes my case.
    There's no point in mourning the loss of that lonely listener, the "body" part of him now as dead as yesterday's kipper. The Beethoven part of him is right here, right now, in me as I write. If he ("I") had died that day, as he left the second shop, after what I calculate as up to four-and-a-half hours of stolen listening time, it wouldn't affect the present judgment one jot—except that I wouldn't be here to tell you about it, and that does matter to "me," though only slightly, as I write. The point is that he, my young confused hypocritical music-loving self, didn't have

to wait for my present blessing on his struggling soul for the validation of his life. He had it then, in the music; he thus has it still, and for all time—if you'll trust that phrase.

❧

Since fumbling with all that three decades ago, I have gone on speculating about just how music relates to ambiguous terms like "depth," "complexity," "repetition," "wisdom," "truth," "death," and "time." You can see why diverse versions of traditional religious questions have been clamoring for entry. The one question shared by *all* religions is not "Is there an intervening god I can appeal to?" For many, like the Buddhists, that god was never born, and for many others he has died. The central question is rather "Just what in life is really valuable, and to what do I owe my gratitude for it?" The very word "life" here encompasses the whole of time and space, the very existence of being rather than non-being: traditionally called "God's creation." And a central issue in that question is the age-old conflict between what is old and what is new, what has died or will die, and what has not died or will not.

Over recent centuries, Western culture has been increasingly invaded by the notion that true human value lies only in what is new or unique—or for many, what practical moves are useful in increasing novelty. As movement after movement has destroyed faith in various "realities" (truth, substances, essences, gods, even the possibility of reliable discourse), the quest for individual, original, creative novelty has taken over.

When novelty takes over, all claims about permanent truths finally disappear, because they are about something not novel, not original, not freshly created. Genuine truth, for both believers and unbelievers, is just plain old, or rather old and new. For unbelievers it is old in the sense of fading or worn out. For those of us who cling to one or another religious notion (even while admitting that no one of them ever fully covers concepts like God or the Divine), any one truth is old in the sense of being permanently, eternally valid, even though perhaps just recently discovered or recovered or pursued. It is simultaneously past and present, and it will be alive in the future. If, in contrast to belief in anything like that, the ultimate value of life is finding some way to "make it new," then either we must discard all religion or develop new, fragile religions of novelty and creativity,[1] which is what many poets and philosophers have done since the Romantic period.

1. Or the "orgiastic irresponsibility" that Derrida subtly attacks in *The Gift of Death*.

This religious problem—are any truths eternal?—one that simply transcends all debates about specific pictures of God, lurks behind all discussions of art, and especially of modern art. Should the experience of art (or truth or beauty) be a movement from one novelty to another, or should it at its best be a deepening repetition of the best encounters, the chief novelty residing in the deepening itself?

MAY 10, 1997—The very notion of amateur practice presupposes repetition, sometimes threatening boredom. I happen to be practicing daily again on the fabulous C-sharp minor, partly because I love it but more immediately because it has been assigned to us for our week-long coaching time in Racine. Practicing it as musically as possible, I am forced, because of its difficulties, to go over the same phrases again and again. That can become, as the lovers of novelty insist, a path to miserable desiccation.

How many times can one play the opening of the scherzo, struggling with technique, without becoming bored? Considered superficially, it is one of the most repetitive movements ever written, before the advent of Philip Glass; I've heard players say that they just can't stand doing so many repetitions. Why should Beethoven risk boredom by offering five repetitions that cannot even by professionals be made to sound much different each time? One cliché I've heard forty times from teachers and coaches is, "Never play a repeated passage the same way." Playing this scherzo, that rule is impossible to live up to, even for professionals. How many times can I practice that speedy opening cello solo, sol-mi-do-mi, louder and louder, without getting bored and turning on a CD?

Well, the contrast between boredom and deepening depends entirely on how one does the practicing. If I study the score between practice sessions, if I put on a record and listen a bit and then go back and play, if I begin thinking about how this part relates to that part, if I allow myself to speculate about just why Beethoven insists on this wild, jokey, often ugly, almost crazy romp, and why he asks us to play it one time as loud as possible and the next time as soft as possible, the weirdly revolutionary movement sinks in ever more deeply.

So here I was, reveling in Beethoven's originality, as I tried, paradoxically, to celebrate the opposite: a repeated deepening experience with the "same" artwork. And what I now discover is that the novelty Beethoven himself was proud of was not novelty in the sense of never having been "there" before. What Beethoven does is like what Bach thinks of himself as doing: he discovers one more part of the "mind of God." Or—to use less orthodox language—he pursues the range of possibilities for creating/discovering the music already implicit in the "spheres": the totality of what is now or will ever be responsive to our explorations.[2] The possibilities for harmony and rhythm and dynamics have always been somehow there, waiting for Beethoven to discover them. Whatever could not possibly be done with music—the limit of possibility—is also part of God's nature. "God could not make a stone so large He couldn't lift it." Beethoven could not write a composition that used frequencies only dogs could hear or discords that did not employ the vibrations God's nature established. Even Beethoven could never have created a world in which octaves and the other sixteen-plus overtones and the circle of fifths did not exist; even Schoenberg could not compose a passage in which notes were sounded without natural vibrations, or in which notes were both sounded and not sounded at the same time. Even those today who compose in quarter-tones or little more than atonal glissandos are limited by the inherent range of possibilities, impossibilities, powers, and limitations of "the universe," or what earlier thinkers in this vein liked to call the "cosmos."[3]

After Beethoven had "discovered" his creations, they waited for us all to come along and discover them again. Living into the Romantic period, Beethoven not surprisingly stressed novelty. "Art demands of us that we not stand still," he wrote, discussing why each of his quartets was great "in its own way." But when he died, shortly after completing the C-sharp minor quartet, and before it was performed, let alone published, he left us a legacy that complicates any notion of standing still. As we "stand still" in repetitions of his work, we do not stand still in the sense of becoming merely repetitive: we can learn that repetition of what some see as old can be far more meaningful than probing for what appears strikingly new.

❧

My use of "the spheres" as grounds for caution about embracing novelty places me in tension with much contemporary theory about art. My doubts about the novelty hunters can be best illustrated by an encounter I had with

2. For a fine article on Bach's inventions/discoveries, see Rosen.

3. I find it hard to resist adding a quarrel with those cosmologists who take the big bang as occurring ex nihilo: nothing was "there" before. Can they really believe that the physical laws producing, allowing, a big bang (or whatever the origin really was: it's still debated hotly) did not in some sense precede or encompass the actual, physical bang, as they encompass us at this very moment? Some current physicists are facing such questions honestly, recognizing that they have stumbled into theological territory. See my next book, maybe.

John Cage, way back in 1967. Here is what I wrote in the Minneapolis airport, waiting for a flight, just after a contentious, hour-long cab ride with
Cage. Our conversation carries further the speculation about deepening
that I played with in chapter 6.

APRIL 19, 1967—. . . stimulated at this conference [at Carleton College]
    by encounters with John Cage (avant garde musician—will he be known
    in 25 years?), Harold Bloom (scholar of romanticism, Yale), Germaine
    Brée (Proust, et al). My talk last night was warmly received by most, but
    it angered Cage because I attacked the superficiality and carelessness of
    Marshall MacLuhan. He refused to attend the reception afterwards be-
    cause I would be there—the man who had betrayed MacLuhan. On the
    panel this morning there was only a slight reconciliation. Then we were
    planted together in the airport limo and had some real talk. He con-
    fessed his anger, and gave his main reason: MacLuhan has really spoken
    for him, John Cage.
    JC: He articulates what I and my generation are attempting to do. When
        you read a man who not only summarizes your past effort but stimu-
        lates you to new ideas for creating new works, of course you are grate-
        ful. And *you* seemed to reduce him to something laughable. [I admit
        as I write here an hour later—but I didn't admit to him as we rode
        along—that though MacLuhan *is* laughable in his extremer moments,
        I should not have seemed to *dismiss* him with laughter.] I thought
        what you said was really unforgivable; I was ashamed to be applauded
        by the same audience that applauded you. And all of your dreadfully
        old stuff about reason! Do you really believe in reason?
    WB: Oh, yes. And I can't understand why it should bother you that I
        should. You believe in it too, in my definition. Besides, if you are, as you
        claim, really open to all experience, if you're really willing to accept
        what is unusual or outlandish, I should think that the more outlandish
        my defense of outlandish reason, the better you'd like it. Why not just
        incorporate it into your music, as you claim to incorporate noise?
    Cage remains silent.
    WB (boldly pushing on): Are you never tempted to compose works again
        in traditional forms?
    JC: Yes, of course, but I think it is my responsibility to resist such temp-
        tations. My responsibility is to go on pushing myself into what is new.
    WB: But why is it faulty to use the traditional forms?
    JC: Because they're old, that's why. Old, old. Only what is new is worth
        doing or saying.

wb: Do you mean that? Do you really mean that? If I listen to a string quartet now that I heard when I was thirty, surely the most important part of my experience—assuming that I really listened at thirty—will be identical. There will be additions as my life has changed, and subtractions too, probably. But why should I try for a novel listening?

jc: *Only* what is novel in the listening is worth doing. The rest is dead.

We finally came to the question of whether the value in our experience of a work of art lies, as he insists, in what is unique, individual, in each individual response, or rather in what we share with other viewers, and with the past.

jc: You and I do not see the same work or hear the same work—thank god we don't.

wb: But there are many similarities. We cannot avoid them and there is no reason why we should.

jc: If there are, they are accidental, coincidental. We're going to see more and more new forms in the world, new explorations. And each of us will experience them differently.

wb: Right, to a degree. But all of the new forms will depend in part on traditional forms, as the Beatles, for example, are developing new versions of traditional effects—their works are highly linear, sequential, full of climaxes.

jc: Oh, I don't agree at all. The Beatles are not at all traditional—they do not use climaxes but rather a simple, repetitive, A-A-A form—no changes in dynamics, no changes in harmony. It is like folk song.

wb: Aha! So within each piece they repudiate the novelty you praise?

jc: No, you've misunderstood me. They're doing something new as they repudiate traditional forms.

wb: But there are climaxes—the whole thing is carefully controlled, as it is finally released—I'm not talking about the process of composition. Especially in the lyrics.

jc: Yes, but the lyrics are almost deliberately obscured. I just can't hear them. . . . Do you know "The Yellow Submarine"?

wb: Yes, I love it.

jc: Me too. But is it in any way traditional?

I then gave a brief formal analysis, perhaps a bit pontifical: the metaphor of the "yellow submarine"—the bright island of friendship and cheer, moving into the unknown—a MacLuhanesque outburst of bouncy exhilaration that reinforces, or is reinforced by, the bounce of the music . . . And so on.

He thought for a minute or so.

JC: I see here how the same thing can be explained in radically different vocabularies. I would never have thought of using such terms . . . [He's being polite, I think. He really views my formal analysis as absurd.]

WB: But you pushed me into those terms—I don't believe that my words are the experience, any more than yours would be. What's more, I am convinced that you and I must have very similar experiences of the work itself—an experience of the very same notes producing our bouncy exhilaration.

He did not accept the phrase, or reject it—but insisted again that the valuable part of our experience would be what was unique in it. I used further examples of shared experiences: string quartet playing, sex . . . He denied them all.

JC (as we approached the terminal): No, I'm sorry, Booth, but you've got it all wrong; all aesthetic value lies in novelty. What is not novel—I repeat—is just plain dead.

We parted amicably, JC still convinced that I was living in the nineteenth century, which in a sense I am; and WB convinced that Cage is headed for hell in a handcart. The search for novelty or uniqueness as a supreme value can lead only to dead ends, even though novelty, when we stumble upon it in looking for other values, can make those values more appealing to us for a time—and more likely to sell on the current scene.

❧

Here then are three separate experiences: the talk with Cage, the recounting in the airport, and this re-encounter here, three decades later.[4] I haven't the slightest doubt that the original was more valuable—at least it was considerably more intense—than my account of it in the airport, even though its literal details are permanently lost. The rich particularity of that ride gets partially lost, and no doubt doctored somewhat, even when recorded only an hour later. But—and here comes something quite wonderful that I wish I could discuss in a Platonic dialogue with the late Cage: my experience in putting the two encounters together is entirely new, and it is both fun and valuable to me as it goes on. I wouldn't want to be doing anything else on

4. Though I have not altered the airport account, my many drafts could be said to multiply the three into scores. The many different versions of "the Cage experience"—it was, for example, to be included in that 1969 book—can feel overwhelming as they deepen and mystify that brief encounter. Thanks to Adam Kissel for suggesting the Platonic addition.

this tempestuously rainy Chicago morning. Suddenly Cage comes back to life:

JC: So you're finally admitting that I win. It *is* the novelty, the new patterning emerging from what are not really repetitions but new versions, that makes the experience count.

WB: Well, in a sense, yes. In my *body* with its particular history, each recounting is new, just as each rehearing of the Beatles, now in the late nineties, reveals loves and doubts that I didn't have when we talked. The novelty does count, I'll give you that. But don't you see—committed surface-surfer that you are—that whatever genuine new depth I discover through those novelties has been there all along? No truth, no beauty is ever really new, *in the universe*, though it may be new for me and you and our kind. If you would just settle down, wherever you are now, and *read* Plato's *Phaedrus* or *Timaeus* . . .

He begins to walk away, looking disgusted. I follow him, almost shouting:

WB: Hey, don't go away; I'm sorry I mentioned Plato. We may actually be coming to some kind of understanding here. I admit that in returning to these experiences, insofar as the return is alive, I'm in one sense making them new. But I think I still have you by the short concepts, if you go on insisting that *only* what is uniquely new is worth bothering about. Because even this new experience is a very old one: it is precisely the experience I had before in putting together my various experiences of the C-sharp minor. In each case the accounts are pale reflections of the moments with the music, and the accounts are greatly different—

Cage disappears into the great empyrean, where all will become clear to him . . .

❧

Doomed forever to fall short of clarity, I must try one more time, hoping that repetition will again prove its deepening powers. Music, and the repetition of music, by going deeper and deeper, arouses thoughts and feelings that for me can only be called religious, or at least spiritual—though both terms are sadly corrupted on our current scene. Some self-professed atheists, music-lovers with whom I have discussed the connections of musical and celestial harmonies, flatly reject any religious connection at all: "The beauty is just plain *musical*. Why muddy it up with that sentimental religious jargon that so many people around the world use to justify inhuman behavior?"

As I reject their rejection, I join (though with many uneasy reservations) a tradition of talking about music that far predates the invention of what I've called chamber music; it even predates Plato. From the ancient philosophers until two or three centuries ago, innumerable writers have claimed that music was not just what musicians play but the very foundation of all things: the universe was itself playing music at every moment, the "music of the spheres," and the resulting "heavenly Harmony," though in a sense silent, was itself responsible not just for actual beautiful sounds but for everything good, true, or beautiful in the world. It was in our bodies as we do gymnastics or have sex; it was/is the spheres as they create and enfold us.

That harmony was not ever something invented anew in any fresh musical moment: it was discovered and joined, or at least aspired to, not only by musicians but by all creatures whenever they lived in harmony with the creation. Its proportions, its intricate frequency patterns were traced by mathematically-minded philosophers, narrated by poets in their myths, and imitated in actual melodies and harmonies. Joining with it was for many what made our lives worth living. In short, our very innards vibrated to the same tune the musicians played, which in turn echoed the inner patterns of the cosmos—or if you prefer, the patterns provided by the very nature of God.

I must move cautiously here; the line between inquiry in such matters and superstitious babble is never clear. We recently played with a violinist who insisted that we tune not to 440-per-second on the A but to 376, because "that is the frequency of the spheres." Besides, she insisted, "it is the frequency within your body; and when you play up to 440, out of harmony with your cells, you're likely to induce cancer." That's obviously wild guessing. But what is certain—and what we know hardly anything about—is that physical connections underlie our very capacity to "vibrate" in excited response to musical vibrations.

In speculating about that we are moving toward the speculations of a fair number of modern physicists who, since the development of quantum physics and its so-far irresolvable anomalies, have thought hard and long about how our existence connects with the cosmos.[5] So many versions of

5. For a good anthology revealing where we stand as scientists and theologians debate the relation of science and religion (with music in the wings), see Mark Richardson and Wesley Wildman, *Religion and Science*.

the "anthropic cosmological principle" have touched on religion that Timothy Ferris, in his fine summary of current cosmological theory, finds himself having to spend a great deal of time trying to fight off those scientists
who are speculating about religious connections, and resisting his own sense
of how much his thinking overlaps with theology. Like so many others, he
denies God while reviving another version of him.

Perhaps the most famous traditional story joining music and the spheres
is the Orpheus myth. As the early sixteenth-century poet Robert Henryson
puts it, Orpheus descended from a variety of muses (some of them skillful
amateur musicians), but it was two of them, Calliope and Urania, who
poured into him his magical musical powers. Henryson's rich poem "Orpheus and Eurydice" begins with the story of how Jupiter begat on Memory
the nine muses. The last one was Urania, "Celestial Harmony," "rejoicing
men with melody and sound." The fourth was Calliope, "maistresse" of all
"musick." The god Phoebus then crowned Calliope as his queen and together they gat Orpheus—the most famous musician of all time. No wonder, Henryson goes on to say, that Orpheus was born fair and wise, gentle
and full of liberality, with a god as father, an aunt who was Celestial Harmony, and a mother who was

> A goddess, fyndar of all armonye:
> quhen he wes borne scho set him on hir kne,
> and gart him souk of hir two paupis quhyte
> The sueit lecour of all musik perfyte.

That is to say, Urania offered him her two white music-filled paps, so that
he imbibed from her the sweet liquor of all the perfect music he was later
to perform. How could any world resist obeying his music, as he charmed
the beasts and trees and even the lords of the underworld to do as he
willed.[6]

❧

Such speculation forces us to address the mysterious harmony between us
as animal creatures and the domain of musical possibilities that awaited our

6. I thank John Hollander for his guidance through this wonderful neglected tradition of
viewing the cosmos as music. Hollander's *The Untuning of the Sky* is a splendid celebration that
also traces the countertradition of condemning music as trivial, as mere distraction, even as
devilish corruption of the soul. For more about music and the cosmos, see Anthony Storr's
Music and the Mind.

discovery from the beginnings of non-time. We somehow harmonize, at our best, with harmonies we did not make.

The range of physical and mental realities with which music has been claimed to harmonize is astonishing. The "spheres" people claim to join are not just the planets and stars in their orbits; they range from our deepest thoughts to current speculation about how quanta interrelate and how our bodies are at every moment radiated with diverse rays from "out there" and about how various physical structures echo or create our aesthetic responses.

Whether we think the religious impulse behind such speculations wild or sane, the sheer amount of human speculation about how music ties us to this or that center is, while not decisive proof of any one connection, impressive evidence that music *connects* us with more than music.

Here is a small selection to add to Henryson's re-creation of Orpheus:

Dust as we are, the immortal spirit grows
Like harmony in music; there is a dark
Inscrutable workmanship that reconciles
Discordant elements, makes them cling together
In one society.
WORDSWORTH, *Prelude,* "INTRODUCTION"

Since I am coming to that holy room,
    Where, with thy quire of Saints for evermore,
I shall be made thy Music; as I come
    I tune the instrument here at the door,
    And what I must do then, think here before.
JOHN DONNE, "HYMN TO GOD IN MY SICKNESS"

While I lay bathéd in my native blood,
And yielded nought save harsh, and hellish soundes:
And save from Heaven, I had no hope of good,
Thou pittiedst (Dread Soveraigne) my woundes,
Repari'dst my ruine, and with Ivorie key,
Didst tune my stringes, that slackt or broken lay.
Now since I breathéd by thy Royall hand,
And found my concord, by so smooth a touch,
I give the world abroade to understand,
Ne're was the musick of old Orpheus such,
As that I make, by meane(s) (Deare Lord) of thee,
From discord drawne, to sweetest unitie.
HENRY PEACHAM, *Minerva Brittana*

Sure there is music even in the beauty, and the silent note which Cupid strikes, far sweeter than the sound of an instrument. For there is a music wherever there is a harmony, order or proportion; and thus far we may maintain the music of the spheres; for those well ordered motions, and regular paces, though they give no sound unto the ear, yet to the understanding they strike a note most full of harmony.   SIR THOMAS BROWNE, *Religio Medici*

Music, the greatest good that mortals know,
And all of heav'n we have below.
JOSEPH ADDISON, "SONG FOR ST. CECILIA'S DAY AT OXFORD"

Two and a half millennia ago, Pythagoras proclaimed his teachings on the harmony of the spheres. To my mind, this doctrine is not just the fanciful product of a highly-strung imagination, but a true revelation granted to a sublime spirit. I firmly believe that some primordial phenomenon of nature was unveiled, in sound, to this great mentor of men, and that he, in actual fact, perceived the harmony of the spheres—though not with his physical ear. . . . [W]e should have no doubts as to the ability of so highly inspired a man to hear with his inner ear the harmony of the spheres and to experience it as an adventure of the soul.
BRUNO WALTER, *Of Music and Music-Making*

I dreamed I was clutching at the face of a rock, but it would not hold. Gravel gave way. I grasped for a shrub, but it pulled loose, and in cold terror I fell into the abyss. Suddenly I realized that my fall was relative; there was no bottom and no end. A feeling of pleasure overcame me. I realized that what I embody, the principle of life, cannot be destroyed. It is written into the cosmic code, the order of the universe. As I continued to fall in the dark void, embraced by the vault of the heavens, I sang to the beauty of the stars and made my peace with the darkness.
HEINZ PAGELS, FAMOUS PHYSICIST AND AMATEUR OF MOUNTAIN-CLIMBING

DR. ROALD HOFFMAN, . . . a Nobel-Prize-winning chemist, . . . regards beauty as a key element of science. "I do not know a single curmudgeonly chemist who would not respond positively to this lovely creation," he wrote (about a new ring-shaped molecule). "Perhaps some day this ferric wheel will find a use. . . . I do not really care. For me, this molecule provides a spiritual high akin to hearing a Haydn piano trio I like."

❧

Fortunately one does not have to pursue such speculations to agree that we amateurs do enter a world of wondrous mystery where we receive free gifts—connections, harmonies—that touch upon all other wonders. The gifts are free in many senses, as I argued in chapter 9. We enter that world unpaid and with no thought or hope of payment. The more I love the music as we play it, the more my companions are led to love—and vice versa; the more the music gets loved, the more love it has left to offer.

To celebrate doing things for the love of the doing does not mean that all other doings are contemptible. We would all perish tomorrow if nobody today worried about consequences. What's more, the path of the amateur is obviously only one of many temporary escapes from quotidian pressures and corruptions. Personal love, friendships, having children and grand-children, working to relieve suffering and injustice here and now, pursuing a religious calling, prayer and meditation (when they are not just for show or just a plea for some payoff)—these can all transcend the "anxiety of the horizontal." Stepping aside from the consequentialist path that too often ends in nothingness, they can thus redeem the world.

Whatever other path we choose, whatever our successes and failures, the good news is that re-creations are available to most of us. Though millions of sufferers in every age still must struggle from day to day merely to survive, with little freedom to choose anything other than survival techniques or an occasional mournful song, the history of cultures shows that the lives of all but the literally starving can be at least partly redeemed by the song of the amateur. The song sung by the hungry peasant, like the song lived by every other amateur, by every gardener or painter or poet or dancer or star-gazer who is dwelling in the practice itself—that song should not be thought of as mere argument that life is worthwhile: the loving act sings the very gift of life itself.

Meanwhile, how glorious it feels, on a sunny Sunday morning or on a blizzardy winter evening, to welcome friends with their instruments and settle into a "payoff" that costs no one, not even Orpheus, a penny.

Glossary

allegro molto vivace—ma non troppo: As fast as you can take it, but, damn it, slow down a bit for the cellist

cantabile: Singing, lilting

circle of fifths: See Slonimsky for a two-page explanation

con fuoco: With fire, maybe a bit of anger or ugliness

con brio: Fiery; spirited

da capo: Back to the beginning—good advice for the whole book

do: Pronounced "dough"; see *fundamental*

dolce: Sweet, gentle, loveable

dominant: See *sol*

dynamics: Variations between loud and soft; too often ignored by us amateurs

dying fall: Any sad fading away as the latest notes descend; especially prominent in minor mode, with minor thirds or minor seconds

embouchure: The developed lip for producing a good sound on a wind instrument

fundamental: The note (sometimes called "do," sometimes "the tonic," sometimes "home tone") that most tunes, until the serialists, suggest from the beginning as home base, and then return to at the end. The term is absolutely untouched by some postmodernist claims that there is no such thing as a fundamental.

giocoso: Jocose, humorous. See *scherzando*. Proper spirit for reading much of this book

gusto: Right, you guessed it

Heiliger Dankgesang eines Genesenen an die Gottheit: A song of thanksgiving, addressed to God, by one who has survived an illness

humoring: Adjusting pitch; has nothing to do with humor

la: Pronounced "law," by most Americans; second note of a minor third

lusinghiero: Seductive, flattering, coaxing: proper instructions for chapter 2

major mode: The scale you rely on when you sing something like the opening of "The Star-Spangled Banner"

mi: Pronounced "mee"; sing "can" in "Oh-oh, say can you see, by the dawn's early light . . ."

minor mode: Sing to yourself almost any sad song you know.

minor second: Half step; sing "Oh, dear!" sadly, with the second word lower but as close to the first as feels comfortable

minor third: Half-step above a major second; three half-steps above "do"; imagine yourself singing an insult to an enemy: "Nyah, nyah"

morendo: Dying, with a dying fall: rival title for chapter 6

opera: Plural of opus. How it ever came to mean "opera" I'll never know.

opus: Opus

religioso: "You figure it out"; rival title for chapter 11

ritardando: Just drop the last four letters and slow down; proper instructions for reading the whole book

scherzando: Jesting, playful, watch out for ironies

sixteenth: The torture chamber for amateur cellists; in England known as semi-quaver: a note one-fourth as long as an ordinary beat, or one-sixteenth as long as a full measure of four beats. If the tempo is allegro, the quarter notes are going at about 150 per minute, which means that if you're thrown a passage with sixteenths, you have to play 600 notes per minute or 10 notes per second. You'll hear famous pros achieving them clearly. You'll never hear me.

sol: Pronounced "so"; the fifth tone of a diatonic scale. The "dominant"

strings: Both the strings on the instruments and the players in any string section

subito pianissimo: Suddenly, startlingly, extremely quiet

thirty-second: See *sixteenth* and multiply by two

timbre: The quality of sound produced

tonic: See *do* and *fundamental*

tremolo: With shaky trepidation, anxiety, real or faked; rival title for whole book

turn: Sort of a quick trill, without enough time to get it right.

Well-tempered clavier: The untempered keyboard, used until the eighteenth century, would play in tune only on a small number of scales. By tempering—adjusting so that the intervals between all twelve notes in an octave are equal—organists and pianists were enabled to play roughly in tune in any key. Sold on tempering, Bach did forty-eight fabulous preludes and fugues to illustrate the new freedom of scale-choice that the "tempered" scale had produced. But the change introduced special problems for us string players when we play with those keyboardists: we have to adjust constantly to their "crude" intonation. In some keys we can't even play double stops with a finger at strict right angles to the strings—a G-sharp and a D-sharp, say, in the key of E major—since the fifths on the piano, unlike our open strings, are not *strictly* in tune.

Everything clear?

Bibliography

In addition to works mentioned in my text, the following list includes a selection from the thousands of potentially relevant books. Any philosopher,
sociologist, historian, psychologist, musicologist, or theologian glancing
through my list will find grounds for protest of the kind I reported at the beginning of chapter 10: "Why has this ignorant amateur mentioned so few serious studies of chamber music by professionals, or histories of how violon-
cellos are made?" "Why has he not mentioned Georg Simmel's immensely
important discussions of leisure?" "What, not a word about Thorstein Veb-
len's *Theory of the Leisure Class* or the journal *Leisure Studies*?" "Where is
Schopenhauer on doing something for love of the doing?" Why no grappling with Nietzsche's celebration of active power over mere "democratic,
passive adaptation"? "Where are Japan, India, China, Africa?" (Well, as for
Japan, have a look at Olszewska!)

I can only assure such complainers that I have indeed read everything
anyone in any language has ever written that relates in even the remotest
way to my subject(s). I invite you to come browse in my library, once you
have figured out why Cage, Cobain, and Cohen appear in this book together
for the first time in history.

Adams, Noah. *Piano Lessons: Music, Love, and True Adventures*. New York:
    Delacorte Press, 1996.
Alperson, Philip. *What Is Music? An Introduction to the Philosophy of Music*.
    University Park: Pennsylvania State University Press, 1987.

Amateur Chamber Music Players Newsletter (1123 Broadway, Room 304, New York, N.Y. 10010. The November 1986 issue has a good bibliography, "Books about Chamber Music.")

"The Amateur Scientist." *Scientific American.* (415 Madison Ave., New York, N.Y. 10017. Regular monthly column, currently edited by Shawn Carlson. The column "Mathematical Recreations" also often engages with amateuring.)

Anderson, Nels. *Man's Work and Leisure.* Leiden: E. J. Brill, 1974.

Angier, Natalie. "An Amateur of Biology Returns to His Easel." *New York Times*, April 28, 1998, B11–12. (About Gary Larson, the cartoonist/biologist/novelist.)

Aristotle. *Ethics.* Esp. book 7.11 and book 8 (friendship).

———. *Metaphysics.* (Everything under *eudaimonia*—happiness—relates to themes addressed here.)

———. *Politics.* Most of book 8.

Atlas, James. "The Art of Failing." *New Yorker*, May 25, 1998, 67–73. (Pursues the problem of how to escape the culture of "making it.")

———. "The Whistle of Money: Watching the Era of Success Pass You By." *New Yorker*, Feb. 2, 1998, 34–37. (Without mentioning Podhoretz, portrays the harm that the ideal of "making it" does to our culture.)

Aulich, Bruno, and Ernst Heimeran. *The Well-tempered String Quartet: A Book of Counsel and Entertainment for All Lovers of Music in the Home.* Trans. D. Millar Craig. Sevenoaks, England: Novello, 1951. (Orig. *Das stillvergnügte Streichquartett*, Munich, 1936.)

Barenboim, Daniel. *A Life in Music.* New York: Charles Scribner's Sons, 1992.

Barrett, Cyril. "Leisure in Western Painting." In Winnifrith and Barrett, 69–80.

Barzun, Jacques. *Pleasures of Music: An Anthology of Writing about Music and Musicians from Cellini to Bernard Shaw.* Chicago: University of Chicago Press, 1951. (Fascinating quotations, some of which I've used in epigraphs.)

Benjamin, Walter. "The Work of Art in the Age of Mechanical Reproduction." *Illuminations.* New York: Schocken Books, 1969. (Orig. 1936.)

Berlin, Isaiah. *The Sense of Reality: Studies in Ideas and Their History.* Ed. Henry Hardy. New York: Farrar, Straus and Giroux, 1997. (One of many philosophers wrestling with the "incommensurability" of values that I refer to often and rely on always.)

Bernstein, Leonard. *The Joy of Music.* New York: Simon and Schuster, 1959.

Bierwirth, Arthur. *The Wonderful World of Amateur Music: The Other Side of the Performing Arts.* Hicksville, N.Y.: Exposition Press, 1976.

Biskind, Peter. *Easy Riders, Raging Bulls: How the Sex-Drugs-and-Rock-'n'-Roll Generation Saved Hollywood.* New York: Simon and Schuster, 1998. (If you choose to look at this fascinating book, be sure to place quotation marks around that word "saved," or make it "saved/damned.")

Blum, David, ed. *The Art of Quartet Playing: The Guarneri Quartet in Conversation with David Blum.* New York: Alfred Knopf, 1986.

Bonds, Mark Evan. *Wordless Rhetoric: Musical Form and the Metaphor of the Oration.* Cambridge: Harvard University Press, 1991.

Boswell, James. *The Life of Johnson.* London, 1791. (My selections can be found in almost every dictionary of famous quotations.)

Botstein, Leon. "The Patrons and Publics of the Quartets: Music, Culture, and Society in Beethoven's Vienna." In Winter and Martin, pp. 77–110.

Bowen, Catherine Drinker. *Friends and Fiddlers.* Boston: Little, Brown, 1935. (The best account I've read of the glories—and disasters—of amateur chamber playing.)

Bromhead, John. "Harold Abrahams: Athlete, Author, and Amateur." In Winnifrith and Barrett, 99–108.

Burnett, Whit. "The Everlasting Quartet." *Atlantic Monthly* 186, 6 (Dec. 1950): 43–47.

Cage, John. *The Charles Eliot Norton Lectures, 1988–89.* Cambridge: Harvard University Press, 1990.

Campbell, Karen. "Playing for the Fun of It." *Christian Science Monitor* (March 21, 1997), 10:1. (About William Selden's experience with the directory of Amateur Chamber Music Players.)

Carse, James P. *Finite and Infinite Games: A Vision of Life as Play and Possibility.* New York: Ballantine Books, 1986. (A pretentious, abstract, often misleading but stimulating plea for us to rise above the "finite" and engage in "infinite" playing. Carse seems not to realize that music— barely mentioned—is the best path to his notion of the infinite.)

Chamber Music [Journal]. (Chamber Music America, 305 Seventh Ave., New York, N.Y., 10001.)

Cheater Web site: www.Cheater.com (Though "Cheater" provides term papers for use by plagiarists, its denials of wrongdoing almost make its organizers sound like honorable amateurs, doing the cheating for the love of it.)

Chester, David. *The Olympic Games Handbook: An Authentic History of Both the Ancient and Modern Olympic Games.* New York: Scribners, 1971.

Chesterton, G. K. *Generally Speaking.* London: Methuen, 1928.

Christensen, James. *Chamber Music: Notes for Players.* Plantation, Fla.: Distinctive Publication Corp., 1992.

Clayre, Alasdair. *Work and Play: Ideas and Experience of Work and Leisure.* New York: Harper and Row, 1974.

Churchill, Winston, *Painting as a Pastime.* London: Odham, 1948.

Cobain, Kurt. Suicide note. Quoted by Greg Kot in *Chicago Tribune,* April 17, 1994, section 13, p. 7.

Cobbett, Walter Wilson. *Cyclopedic Survey of Chamber Music,* 2d ed., with supplementary material edited by Colin Mason. London: Oxford University Press, 1963.

Cohen, Ted. "Objects of Appreciation: Early Reflections on Television, with Further Remarks on Baseball." In *Philosophy and Art,* ed. Daniel O. Dahlstrom, vol. 23 of *Studies in Philosophy and the History of Philosophy.* Washington, D.C.: Catholic University of America Press, 1991.

———. "Sports and Art: Beginning Questions." In *Human Agency: Language, Duty, and Value,* ed. Jonathan Dancy et al. Stanford: Stanford University Press, 1988.

Collins, John. *The Two Forgers: A Biography of Harry Buxton Forman and Thomas James Wise.* New Castle, Del. Oak Knoll Books, 1992.

Cooke, Charles. *Playing the Piano for Pleasure.* New York: Simon and Schuster, 1941.

Cooke, Deryck. *The Language of Music.* London: Oxford University Press, 1959.

Cowling, Elizabeth. *The Cello.* New York: Charles Scribner's Sons, 1975.

Crowson. Quoted by Paul Griffiths in an obituary. *New York Times,* September 29, 1998, A24.

Csikszentmihalyi, Mihaly. *Beyond Boredom and Anxiety.* San Francisco: Jossey-Bass, 1975.

———. *Finding Flow: The Psychology of Engagement with Everyday Life.* New York: Basic Books, 1997.

Dale, Steve. "Ralf Gothoni's Remarkable Journey." *Chicago Tribune,* July 25, 1994, Tempo section, 1–2.

Dare, Byron, George Welton, and William Coe. *Concepts of Leisure in Western Thought: A Critical and Historical Analysis.* Dubuque, Ia.: Kendall/Hunt, 1987. (Extensive bibliography. See esp. part 1: "Leisure as Essence: The Athenian Ideal," by Dare.)

DaPonte Quartet. See Weber, Bruce.

Daube, J. F. *The Musical Dilettante: A Treatise on Composition.* Ed. and Trans. Susan P. Snook-Luther. Cambridge: Cambridge University

Press, 1992. (Orig. 1773. See esp. Snook-Luther's introduction, explaining how the word "dilettante" covered, for the upper classes in the Enlightenment, many of the points that I claim for amateuring here.)

Derrida, Jacques. *The Gift of Death*. Trans. David Wills. Chicago: University of Chicago Press, 1995.

Denney, Reuel. *The Astonished Muse*. Chicago: University of Chicago Press, 1957.

Dewey, John. *Art as Experience*. New York: G. P. Putnam and Sons, 1954.

Dix, William S. *The Amateur Spirit in Scholarship*. Cleveland: Western Reserve University Press, 1942.

Drew, Robert S. "Embracing the Role of Amateur: How Karaoke Bar Patrons Become Regular Performers." *Journal of Contemporary Ethnography* 25, 4 (Jan. 1997): 449–68.

Driver, Christopher P., ed. *Music for Love: An Anthology of Amateur Music-Making*. London: Weidenfeld and Nicholson, 1994. (A splendid collection of ninety-three celebrations of musical amateuring, by Chaucer, Casanova, Jane Austen, George Eliot, Thomas Hardy, James Joyce—and on down to the nineties. Some of them might well serve as summaries for this book.)

Dumazedier, Joffre. *Toward a Society of Leisure*. Trans. Stewart E. McClure; foreword by David Riesman. New York: Free Press, 1967.

Durant, Henry. *The Problem of Leisure*. London: G. Routledge and Sons, 1938.

Durkheim, Emile. *The Elementary Forms of the Religious Life*. Trans. Joseph Ward Swain. New York: Free Press, 1965.

———. *Professional Ethics and Civic Morals*. Trans. Cornelia Brookfield. Glencoe: Free Press, 1958.

Eliot, George. See Gray, Beryl.

Ellis, John M. *Literature Lost: Social Agendas and the Corruption of the Humanities*. New Haven: Yale University Press, 1997. (An overdone but informative polemic.)

Epstein, Harold. See Yang, Linda.

Espy, Richard. *The Politics of the Olympic Games*. Berkeley: University of California Press, 1979. ("The modern olympic games symbolize the struggle between man's ideals and the reality within which he must live.")

Ferris, Timothy. "Seeing in the Dark: Why Are Amateur Stargazers . . ." *New Yorker*, August 10, 1998, 54–61.

———. *The Whole Shebang: A State-of-the-Universe(s) Report*. New York: Simon and Schuster, 1997.

Fink, Lois Marie, ed. "From Amateur to Professional: American Women and Careers in the Arts." *Women's Studies: An Interdisciplinary Journal* 14, 4 (1988).

Finnegan, Ruth. *The Hidden Musicians.* Cambridge: Cambridge University Press, 1989.

Gardner, Martin. "A Quarter-Century of Recreational Mathematics." *Scientific American* 279, 2 (August 1998): 68–75.

Goethe. See Zelter.

Gothoni, Ralf. See Dale, Steve.

Gray, Beryl. *George Eliot and Music.* New York: St. Martin's Press, 1989.

Greenbie, Marjorie L. *The Arts of Leisure.* New York: McGraw Hill, 1935.

Guarneri Quartet. See Blum, David.

Haynes, Harold. *Chamber Music Repertoire for Amateur Players: A Guide to Choosing Works Matching Players' Abilities.* Cambridge: H. Haynes, 1994.

Herter Norton, M.D. *The Art of String Quartet Playing: Practice, Technique, and Interpretation.* Preface by Isaac Stern. New York: Simon and Schuster, 1962.

Heschel, Abraham J. "The Vocation of the Cantor." In his *The Insecurity of Freedom: Essays on Human Existence,* 245–46. New York: Farrar, Strauss and Giroux, 1966.

Himmelfarb, Gertrude. *The De-Moralization of Society: From Victorian Virtues to Modern Values.* Philadelphia: Coronet Books, 1995. New York: Random House, 1996.

Hindemith, Paul. *Elementary Training for Musicians.* London: Schott, 1946.

Hoffmann, Roald. Quoted in *New York Times,* July 15, 1997, B13.

Hollander, John. *The Untuning of the Sky: Ideas of Music in English Poetry, 1500–1700.* New York: Norton, 1970. (Orig. Princeton, 1961.)

Holland, Bernard. "Listening Is Either/Or; Or Is It?" *New York Times,* Feb. 2, 1997, H31.

Holst, Imogen. *An ABC of Music.* New York: Oxford University Press, 1963.

Holt, John. *Never Too Late: My Musical Life Story.* New York: Delacorte Press, 1978.

Holton, Robin. "The Point of Amateur Painting." *The Artist* (Tenterton, England) 108 (March 1993): 9.

Horna, Jarmila. *The Study of Leisure: An Introduction.* New York: Oxford University Press, 1994. (Includes a fine, extensive bibliography.)

Hughes, Robert. "Andy Warhol." In *The New York Review of Books: Selected Essays from the First 30 Years*, 211–24. New York: NYREV, 1993.

Huizinga, Johan. *Homo Ludens: A Study of the Play-Element in Culture*. Trans. R. F. C. Hull. Boston: Beacon Press, 1955. (Orig. 1944.)

Hyde, Lewis. *The Gift: Imagination and the Erotic Life of Property*. New York: Vintage Books, 1983.

James, Jamie. *The Music of the Spheres: Music, Science, and the Natural Order of the Universe*. New York: Grove Press, 1993.

James, William. "Sport or Business." *The Harvard Graduates' Magazine* (December 1903).

Jarvis, Stephen. *The Bizarre Leisure Book, From the Alan Whicker Appreciation Society to Zen Archery: A Fun, A-Z Guide to 150 Off-beat Leisure Pursuits*. London: Robson, 1994.

Johnson, Samuel. See Boswell, James.

Jordan, Michael. *For the Love of the Game: My Story*. New York: Random House, 1998. (The quotations about and by Jordan are from *Chicago Tribune Magazine*, June 1, 1994, 17; and Feb. 8, 1994, Sec. 4, pp. 1, 4.)

Keller, Hans. *The Great Haydn Quartets: Their Interpretation*. London: J. M. Dent and Sons, 1986.

Kerr, Walter. "The Decline of Pleasure." In Murphy, 154–75.

Kuczynsi, Alex. "The Very Rich Pay to Learn How to Give Money Away." *New York Times*, May 3, 1998, Y-1, 28. (How dabblers in charity can become amateurs.)

Lambert, Craig. *Mind over Water: Lessons on Life from the Art of Rowing*. Boston: Houghton Mifflin, 1998.

Larrissy, Edward. "Leisure and Civilization in English Literature." In Winnifrith and Barrett, 27–38.

Leppert, Richard D. *Arcadia at Versailles: Noble Amateur Musicians and Their Musettes and Hurdy-gurdies at the French Court (c. 1660–1789)*. Amsterdam: Swets and Zeitlinger, 1978.

Lewis, C. S. *The Four Loves*. New York: Harvest Books, 1971. (Orig. Glasgow: Collins, 1960.)

Lindsay, Joyce and Maurice. *The Music Quotation Book: A Literary Fanfare*. London: WBC Bookbinders, 1988. (Source of some epigraphs.)

Lloyd Webber, Julian. *Travels with My Cello*. London: Pavilion Books, 1984.

Lockhart, Lee Macdonald. *With a Cello on My Back*. Sutter Creek, Calif.: Essiccs Co., 1984.

MacAloon, John J. *This Great Symbol: Pierre de Coubertin and the Origins of the Modern Olympic Games*. Chicago: University of Chicago Press, 1981.

Mackley, Carter, "Dangerous Play," *Sunstone* (Dec. 1996): 13.

Maclean, Norman. *A River Runs Through It.* Chicago: University of Chicago Press, 1976. (Implicitly a celebration of amateur fly-casting.)

———. *Young Men and Fire.* Chicago: University of Chicago Press, 1992.

Mandeville, Bernard. *The Fable of the Bees: or Private Vices, Public Benefits.* London, 1724. (Orig. 1714.)

Maimonides (1135–1204). *The Guide of the Perplexed.* Trans. Shlomo Pines. Chicago: University of Chicago Press, 1963. (Esp. pt. 1, chap. 54; pt. 3, chaps. 51, 54.)

Marsh, Leonard. *At Home with Music: The Recollections and Reflections of an Unabashed Amateur.* Vancouver: Versatile Pub. Co., 1972.

Martineau, Harriet. *Health, Husbandry, and Handicraft.* London: Bradbury and Evans, 1861.

Mason, Daniel Gregory. *Artistic Ideals.* New York: Norton, 1927. (Chapters 3, "Workmanship," and 6, "Fellowship," are most pertinent to amateuring, though aimed at would-be professionals.)

———. *The Quartets of Beethoven.* New York: Oxford, 1947.

Mathieu, W. A. *The Listening Book.* Boston: Shambhala, 1991.

———. *The Musical Life: Reflections on What It Is and How to Live It.* Boston: Shambhala, 1994.

Meyer, Leonard. *Explaining Music: Essays and Explorations.* Chicago: University of Chicago Press, 1978.

———. *Music, the Arts, and Ideas: Patterns and Predictions in Twentieth-Century Culture.* Chicago: University of Chicago Press, 1967.

Miller, Lucy. "From All Walks: Amateurs in America." *American Music Teacher* 46, 5 (April-May, 1997): 26.

Montaigne. *Essays.* Trans. Donald M. Frame. Stanford: Stanford University Press, 1967.

Murphy, James F., ed. *Concepts of Leisure: Philosophical Implications.* Englewood Cliffs, N.J.: Prentice-Hall, 1974. (Sixteen essays grappling with the questions of my chapters 9, 10, and 11. See esp. Kerr.)

Music for the Love of It. (Journal published six times a year: 67 Parkside Drive, Berkeley, Calif. 94705.)

Neumeyer, Martin. *Leisure and Recreation: A Study of Leisure and Recreation in Their Sociological Aspects.* New York: A. S. Barnes, 1936.

Nietzsche, Friedrich. *The Dawn of Day.* New York: Gordon Press Publishers, 1974.

O'Connor, Connie. *The Leisure Wasters.* New York: A. S. Barnes, 1966.

Olszewska, Anna, and K. Roberts, eds. *Leisure and Life-style: A Comparative Analysis of Free Time*. London: Sage Publications, 1989. (Essays on the fate of leisure in nine contrasting nations.)

Osler, Sir William. "The Medical Library in Post-Graduate Work." *British Medical Journal* (October, 1909): 925–98. (Includes a fiery claim of the importance, for every doctor, of "hobby-horse riding.")

Pack, Arthur N. *The Challenge of Leisure*. New York: Macmillan, 1934. (Esp. 150–70.)

Pagels, Heinz. *The Cosmic Code: Quantum Physics as the Language of Nature*. New York: Simon and Schuster, 1982.

Parhamovich, Elaine. "Recollections of a Beginning Violinist." *Music for the Love of It* (October 1996): 6.

Perry, Bliss. *The Amateur Spirit*. Boston: Houghton, Mifflin and Co., 1904.

Pieper, Josef. *Leisure, the Basis of Culture*. Trans. Alexander Dru, with intro. by T. S. Eliot. New York: Pantheon, 1964. (Orig. 1952.)

Piltdown Hoax. See Walsh.

Plato. *The Complete Works*, any edition. (Can you think of any dialogue by Plato that is not pertinent to something I have said?)

Podhoretz, Norman. *Making It*. New York: Random House, 1967.

Rahner, Hugo, S. J. *Man at Play*. New York: Herder and Herder, 1967. (Play as related to religion; celebrates, with qualification, the *eutrapelia* praised by Aquinas.)

Richardson, Mark, and Wesley Wildman, eds. *Religion and Science: History, Method, Dialogue*. New York: Routledge, 1996.

Ridley, Aaron. *Music, Value, and the Passions*. Ithaca: Cornell University Press, 1995. (A persuasive argument that musical effect is tied closely to our highest human values, and in turn to our physical lives: voice, motion, etc.)

Robinson, Bernard W. *An Amateur in Music*. Newbury, England: Countryside Books, 1985.

Rosen, Charles. *The Frontiers of Meaning: Three Informal Lectures on Music*. New York: Hill and Wang, 1994.

———. "The Great Inventor [Bach]." *New York Review of Books*, October 9, 1997, 51–55.

Ruskin, John. "Work." In *The Crown of Wild Olive: Three Lectures on Work, Traffic, and War*. London, 1866. (Delivered before the Working Men's Institute, at Camberwell.)

Russell, Bertrand. "Lecture Three: The Role of Individuality." In *Authority and the Individual*. New York: Simon and Schuster, 1949.

Salzman, Mark. *Lost in Place: Growing Up Absurd in Suburbia*. New York: Vintage Books, 1996.

———. *The Soloist*. New York: Random House, 1994.

Sand, George. "*Lettres d'un Voyageur*, no. IV," in *Revue des Deux Mondes* (June 1835): 698–736. (Quoted by Barzun.)

Schopenhauer, Arthur. *The World as Will and Representation*. Trans. E. F. J. Payne. 2 vols. New York: Dover Publications, 1969. (Esp. vol. 1, and p. 262.)

Schweitzer, Albert. *J. S. Bach*. Trans. Ernest Newman. London: A. and C. Black, 1911. (Orig. 1905.)

Seinfeld. See *Chicago Tribune*, May 15, 1998, Tempo section.

Sheed, Wilfrid. "Why Sports Matter." *Wilson Quarterly* 19, 1 (Winter 1995): 11–25. (One of four relevant essays appearing under the title "Endangered Pastimes: The Future of Sports.")

Sherman, Russell. *Piano Pieces*. New York: North Point Press, 1997.

Shattuck, Roger. *Forbidden Knowledge: From Prometheus to Pornography*. New York: St. Martin's, 1996.

Simonnot, Philippe. *Homo Sportivus: Sport, capitalisme et religion*. Paris: Gallimard, 1988. (See esp. chapter 3, "L'érotique d'entreprise"; and chapter 7, "Amateurs et dévots.")

Slonimsky, Nicolas. *Lectionary of Music: An Entertaining Reference and Reader's Companion*. New York: McGraw-Hill, 1989. (Source of some epigraphs.)

Sparshott, Francis. "Aesthetics of Music: Limits and Grounds." In Alperson, 33–100.

Spencer, Donald S. *The Carter Implosion: Jimmy Carter and the Amateur Style of Diplomacy*. New York: Praeger, 1988.

Spielman, Helen. "From the Heart: Professional Amateur." *Music for the Love of It* (Dec. 1997): 4–5. (One of many short articles Spielman has contributed to various journals dealing with amateurs. Similar pieces by her and others appear in the periodical *Amateur Chamber Music Players Newsletter*.)

"Status: What We Look Up To Now." *New York Times Magazine*, November 15, 1988. (Displays how what I think of as "Podhoretzism" has triumphed, in thirty-five areas of current life, from politics and painting down through Hollywood and dining to gambling. See especially articles by Andrew Sullivan, Alan Wolfe, and R. W. Apple, Jr.)

Stebbins, Robert A. *Amateurs: On the Margin between Work and Leisure*. Beverly Hills: Sage Publications, 1979.

———. *The Barbershop Singer: Inside the Social World of a Musical Hobby.* Toronto: University of Toronto Press, 1996.

Stern, Richard. "Assessment of an Amateur." *Teeth, Dying, and Other Matters.* London: MacGibbon and Kee, 1964.

Strad, The. (London: Orpheus. Monthly "for professionals and amateurs of all stringed instruments." Founded 1890.)

Storr, Anthony. *Music and the Mind.* London: HarperCollins, 1992.

Sullivan, Andrew. *See* Status

Sullivan, J. W. N. *Beethoven: His Spiritual Development.* New York: Alfred Knopf, 1972.

Super, Donald Edwin. *Avocational Interest Patterns: A Study in the Psychology of Avocations.* Stanford: Stanford University Press, 1940.

Talmage, T. De Witt. *Sports That Kill.* New York: Harper, 1875.

Targan, Barry. "Harry Belten and the Mendelssohn Violin Concerto." Iowa City: University of Iowa Press, 1975.

Thaxter, Celia. *An Island Garden.* Boston: Houghton Mifflin Co., 1895. (Includes paintings by Childe Hassam.)

Ungar, Andrew. "Baba Yaga at the Workshops." *Music for the Love of It* (June 1997): 1, 7.

Walter, Bruno. *Of Music and Music-Making.* Trans. Paul Hamburger. New York: Norton, 1961. Original, 1957. (Esp. 11.)

Walsh, John Evangelist. *Unraveling Piltdown: The Science Fraud of the Century and Its Solution.* New York: Random House, 1996.

Weber, Bruce. "Love Story of a String Quartet and a County in Maine." *New York Times,* May 13, 1996, B2.

Weiss, Ann E. "Amateurism: Ideal or Evil?" In her *Money Games: The Business of Sports.* Boston: Houghton Mifflin, 1993.

Williams, Bernard. *Morality: An Introduction to Ethics.* Cambridge: Cambridge University Press, 1972. Paperback: Canto, 1993. (Splendid refutation of utter utilitarianism.)

Williams, Raymond. *The Country and the City.* London: Chatto and Windus, 1973.

Wilson, Frank R. *Tone Deaf and All Thumbs?* New York: Viking Penguin, 1986. (A guide to taking up the piano in one's "later years.")

Winnifrith, Tom. "Funeral Games in Homer and Virgil." In Winnifrith and Barrett, 14–26.

———. *The Philosophy of Leisure.* London: MacMillan, 1989.

Winnifrith, Tom, and Cyril Barrett, eds. *Leisure in Art and Literature.* London: MacMillan Academic and Professional, 1992.

Winter, Robert, and Robert Martin, eds. *The Beethoven Quartet Companion*. Berkeley: University of Calfornia Press, 1994.

Wise, T. J. See Collins, John.

Yang, Linda. "Harold Epstein Dies at 94: Renowned Gardening [Amateur] Expert," *New York Times*, July 11, 1997, A 20–21.

Zelter, Carl Friedrich. Quoted by Botstein, p. 79, from *Briefwechsel Zwischen Goethe und Zelter*, ed. Max Hecker.

Index

Computer games, 21; "virtues" taught by, 179

Conductors. *See* Barenboim, Daniel; Botstein, Leon; Busch, [Adolf]; Solti, Sir George; Stokowski, Leopold

Conferences of amateur chamber players, 184. *See also* Prairie School; Sleepy Hollow

Congress, 64

Connoisseurs, 8, 57, 189

Conversation, 55; as amateuring, 32; performing music together as, 152; about religion, 5; about playing, 2, 5. *See also* Friendship

Cooke, Charles, 69

Coppola, Francis Ford, 172

Corruption: produced by emphasis on improving or "betterment," 58; by pursuit of money, 59–61; speculation about, 55, 174–83. *See also* Deflections

Cosmology, 205–6. *See also* God; Religion

Cost-benefit analysis, as opposed to amateuring, 6, 8, 13, 32, 58–59, 117, 160, 162, 162n, 194, 209. *See also* Futurism

Creative writing, 188. *See also* Poetry

Crowson, Lamar, 62

Csikszentmihalyi, Mihaly, 124, 157, 163

Dalby, Max, 47

Dancing, 21, 126, 209; as metaphor for musical playing, 84, 91, 96; with strangers, 137–46

Dante Alighieri, *Inferno*, 177

DaPonte Quartet, 190–91

Death, 51, 105–6, 115, 119, 122, 159, 194, 196–98; and music, 22–25, 32–35; and life, meaning of, probed, 164–70

Debussy, Claude, 97; quartet, G minor, Op. 10, 127, 163; piano trio, 127

Deepening: contrasted with boredom, 198–99; through performing, 153; through repetition, 104–5, 109–12, 194–98

Deflections from love of it, 33; by graduate study, 38; by professional aspiration, 39. *See also* Corruption; Making it; Money; Fame; Power

DeLuca, Kay, 145–46

Derrida, Jacques, *The Gift of Death*, 159, 198n

Dickens, Charles, 36; *Little Dorrit*, 177

Difficulties with playing, 69; distractions from playing, 2; inescapable imperfection, 37; physical problems, 7; technical impossibilities, 9–10; unforeseen, 53. *See also* Anxieties; Disasters

Disasters, 119; performing, unmitigated, 132–35; threatened but transcended, 139–40, 142–45, 162–64

Donne, John, "Hymn to God in My Sickness," 207

Drinker, Henry, 41–42

Dryden, John, "Song for St. Cecilia's Day," 192

Duchamp, Marcel, 110

Dvořák, Antonin, 9; quartet, A-flat minor, Op. 105, 37; piano quintet, A major, Op. 81, 145; piano trio, "Dumky," E minor, Op. 90, 153

Earlham College, 53, 60, 138

Education, 21–35 passim, 87–99 passim, 173; in music, decline of, 178–79; flaws in, as destroyer of amateuring, 189

Ego: intrusions by, 134, 145; struggles with, 123–25; as threat to amateuring, 5, 40, 41; triumphs over, 146. *See also* Anxieties

Eliot, George, 52, 93, 149

Eliot, T. S., 158; *Four Quartets*, 194

Elitism, danger of in amateuring, 157, 162n, 193

Emerson Quartet, 149, 154

Emotion in music. *See* Bliss; Spiritual; Tears

Envy, 40, 41. *See also* Ego

Études (exercise books), 12, 89

Evaluation, quarrels about, 154–55

Failures, 5, 11–12, 21, 45, 119; mind-body problem as producing, 82–84; reasons for, physical, 70–72, 106; reasons for, psychological, 72–76; resistance of cello as cause, 76–82; success in dealing with, 119. *See also* Disasters

Fall, the, 54, 107, 188

Fame, 51; joy in pursuing, 174–76; pursuit